Boswell's
Children

Boswell's Children

The Art of the Biographer

edited by R.B. Fleming

Dundurn Press
Toronto & Oxford
1992

Editing: Judith Turnbull
Design and Production: GSN
Cover design: Andy Tong

The publisher wishes to acknowledge the generous assistance and ongoing support of **The Canada Council, The Book Publishing Industry Development Program** of the **Department of Communications, The Ontario Arts Council,** and **The Ontario Publishing Centre** of the **Ministry of Culture and Communications.**

Care has been taken to trace the ownership of copyright material used in the text (including the illustrations). The author and publisher welcome any information enabling them to rectify any reference or credit in subsequent editions.

J. Kirk Howard, Publisher

Canadian Cataloguing in Publication Data
Main entry under title:
Boswell's children

Papers from a conference on biography and history, held at the Centre of Canadian Studies, Edinburgh University, May 2–4, 1991.
Includes bibliographical references.
ISBN 1-55002-177-X

1. Canada – Biography – History and criticism – Congresses.
2. Biography as a literary form – Congresses. 3. Biography – 20th century – Congresses. I. Fleming, Rae Bruce, 1944– .

CT21.B67 1992   809'.93592'0071   C92-095302-6

Dundurn Press Limited
2181 Queen Street East
Suite 301
Toronto, Canada
M4E 1E5

Dundurn Distribution Limited
73 Lime Walk
Headington, Oxford
England
OX3 7AD

Contents

List of Illustrations

Foreword:
Biography and History

Ged Martin

Historians use biography. Indeed, many historians are themselves biographers, and it is almost a rite of passage that the second or third book in a professional career should study the life of a figure from the past. Reading lists supplied to undergraduates often indicate that the key study for a period or a problem is biographical. Too easily we assume that since biography and history both deal with things past, they must be identical forms.

This assumption merits scrutiny, for there are fundamental differences of approach. Analogies are often misleading, but there is something to be said for seeing the historian as a weaver. To write history is to construct a fabric using strands of varied textures and colours. The craft of biography, on the other hand, requires the spinning of a single thread, with an emphasis upon a single human experience, perhaps at the expense of the subject's interaction with the weave of other lives. The more traditional "Life and Times" approach did plait the coloured thread of the favoured individual into a wider fabric, but always ensured a background of plain broadcloth.

In practical terms, this dichotomy between the individual and context, the solo and the team, has earned many a diligent undergraduate the comment from an instructor "Your essay overstresses the role of ..." How, the undergraduate may be tempted to reply, is it possible to offer a moderated assessment of the role of an individual whose biography has been recommended as the key text for the assignment?

Yet the problem inherent in the art of biography goes deeper. L.M. Montgomery was aghast when a friend suggested that he might attempt to write her life (the very phrase is revealing). "Biography is a *screaming farce*," she protested. "No man or woman was ever truly depicted. Biographies, even the best, are one- or at most two-sided – and every human being has half a dozen different sides." Maud Montgomery in fact left extensive materials for her biographers, and one contradictory element in her alarm was outrage at having "some of *my* soul moods depicted," but her protest raises another biographical issue for the historian.[1]

Take a simple example, that of a historian who, in weaving a piece on mid-nineteenth-century Canada, encounters John A. Macdonald. The historian turns to a biography of Macdonald for insights that may explain his responses to certain issues and events. *Pace* L.M. Montgomery, the biography may seductively portray one or two aspects of Macdonald's character and stress some of the imperatives that drove him – perhaps emphasizing aspirations of nation-building that chime with the author's own patriotism or with the perceived needs of a later generation. However satisfactory this portrayal, it would still neglect the four of five other traits of personality Maud Montgomery attributes to every human being, maybe even burying them altogether. Of what use, then, is such a biographical tool for the historian? It is certainly of limited value as a predictor of Macdonald's behaviour at any one time. The scholar seeking to understand Macdonald's actions in a single episode in 1873, for example, would find an overall picture distilled from a whole life spanning 1815 to 1891 of little value.

We may take the process of doubt one alarming stage further. What if the biography offers a beguilingly believable but actually misleading picture of its subject? In the case of John A. Macdonald, this speculation prompts uneasy reconsideration of the two-volume study by Donald Creighton, the more so as it is reasonable to assert that in 1990 the *Dictionary of Canadian Biography* provided an alternative starting-point for Sir John A.'s life in the form of a magnificent twenty-page essay by J.K. Johnson and P.B. Waite.[2] Their bibliographical note describes Creighton's work as "unforgettable, splendid, but flawed," and reproves him for making "daring assumptions" not merely about Macdonald but also "in his reading of characters in apposition." Yet Johnson and Waite still view Creighton's study as "probably the greatest Canadian biography yet published in English." There would seem to be some internal inconsistency in this assessment, one that offers its own clue to the nature of biography. Three decades after the publication of J.M.S. Careless's *Brown of the Globe*,[3] an equally massive study of Macdonald's rival, Creighton retains the country's biographical crown because of the sheer grandeur of his portrait of Macdonald.

"I had only previously written novels where I was free to invent," confessed Mary Rose Callaghan when she discussed her approach to writing a life of Katharine O'Shea, who became the wife of Charles Stewart Parnell. She quickly discovered that the methodology was not so very different: "You don't *create* characters in fiction, you find them. It was the same for a biography."[4] No doubt there are biographers who would blanch at this admission, but the argument raises yet another fundamental question for the historian: do we have the sources from which a character may evolve? Historians of nineteenth-century Canada may not possess all the material they might wish for, but in the general picture by and large, if one thread has disappeared, another will likely serve equally well. The biographer, in contrast, may simply face a blank, and – worse still – that blank may be at its blankest through precisely the phases where information would be most valuable.

Biography draws upon a good deal of amateur psychology and even bogus heredity. We assume that people grow by accretion, that they are shaped by their early experiences and later on are influenced by episodes in which they become participants or witnesses. These assumptions are hard to substantiate from the record. Since few individuals display signs of greatness in their early childhood, little evidence survives from what are conventionally called the "formative" years. However small, that evidence tends to have an enormous superstructure of interpretation loaded upon it. This is even true of royal children, who were of interest as future monarchs. The young George III was upbraided by his mother with the admonition "George, be a king!" The story may be pure legend, since it was not published until the year the king died, in his eighties. The story became a popular key to the explanation of the American War of Independence: urged by a domineering mother to assert his royal prerogative, the weak George became the interfering monster so roundly abused in the Declaration of Independence. Of course, many other factors led to the independence of the United States, and most British political decisions, mistakes or otherwise, were the responsibility of ministers and not of the sovereign.

More recent speculation has suggested that Princess Augusta may simply have been telling her son to improve his table manners.[5] A similar tale gives an equally vivid and equally unhelpful glimpse of the young Victoria. When she had reached the age of ten, the news was gently broken to her in a history lesson that she would one day be queen. "I will be good," she is reported to have said. Since history lessons for children consisted largely of tales of good and bad rulers, with the bad ones often coming to a nasty end, the young Victoria would have been decidedly odd had she declared her intention to engage in wicked activities, which in any case she was too young to appreciate. Building a whole interpretation of the sanctimonious miseries of the Victorian age upon one statement by a shocked little girl (the most attractive part of the story was that Victoria burst into tears as the implications of her fate hit her) is to erect a sky-scraper upon a tissue.[6]

If we know little about royal children, we probably know less about those who were not marked out for greatness from birth. Generations of biographers of Charles Stewart Parnell have quoted the comment of his nurse: "Master Charley is born to rule." The implication is that the qualities that later led him to be hailed – first in Toronto – as the "uncrowned king of Ireland" were discernible even in the nursery. Yet few have emphasized that the record also shows that Nurse Twopenny was very fond of her charge, and few have troubled to interpret her remark as the description, not of a masterful, but of a highly strung child. Similarly, a story supplied to an early biographer in 1880 by Parnell's mother – that her son had once glued his toy soldiers to the floor in order to ensure that they did not fall in battle against his sister's army – was later used by an Ulster Unionist to imply that even as a child Parnell could not be trusted to play by the rules.[7]

At the age of nineteen, Parnell entered Cambridge. An unspectacular undergraduate career ended four years later when he was expelled after becoming involved in a fight. Parnell's biographers have speculated up and down the range of probabilities in attempting to measure the relation-ship of this experience to his later career as an implacable leader of nation-alist Ireland. The truth is that we do not know and cannot know just how his expulsion affected his development. There are indications that the adult Parnell himself told the story of the ignominious end to his student career, but this in itself does not reveal whether his abrupt departure from an elite English university really moulded him or whether he found it a conven-ient episode to explain away the fact that he had trodden such an alien path in the first place.[8] It is not surprising that Parnell's two most recent biographers have him in the House of Commons by chapter two.

A more specific example can be traced in the surviving remnant of an exchange of letters between the British colonial secretary, the Duke of Newcas-tle, and the outgoing governor general of Canada, Sir Edmund Head, early in 1861. From Newcastle's point of view, the biographical assumption is reason-ably plausible. The previous year, the duke had accompanied the young Prince of Wales on the first official royal visit to British North America, a tour that had been marred by pertinacious demonstrations of unwanted sectarian loyalty by Orangemen. Dukes, of course, were much too august to settle scores, but Newcastle was evidently anxious to assemble a dossier on the misdeeds of King Billy's followers. Apparently it was suggested to him that the Orange Order had been a cause of commotion in New Brunswick during the late 1840s, and for further information, he turned to Head, who had been lieutenant-governor of the province at the time. Head could not remember. He consulted Lady Head. She had a vague memory of an Orange riot and recalled a murder in Saint John that was linked to the Order. There had been some bloodshed at Woodstock around the time of their arrival in the province, but the passage of a mere thirteen years had left the bank of recollection remarkably bare. "It is singular that such important events should have faded so entirely from my memory,"[9] Head told Newcastle in 1861. Nevertheless, backed by every indication of legitimacy of the craft, the biographer might assume that Edmund Head was indeed influenced or shaped by the turbulent behaviour of the Orange Order in his province. In how many other cases has biography built a milestone from the forgotten pebbles of a distant experience?

Thus, by concentrating on the individual experience, the biographer may, on the one hand, play up an episode that left the subject largely unscathed and thereby, on the other, underemphasize the extent to which people are shaped not so much by what happened in their own lives as by their collective inheritance of ideas and myths through family and community. Here there may be a particular challenge for historical biography in Canada, simply because so many prominent people throughout the country's history were born abroad. The *Dictionary of Canadian Biography*, one of the country's greatest scholarly projects, naturally enough emphasizes the Canadian career in each entry, but this may sometimes be to the detriment of a full understanding of where, in every sense, the subject was coming from.

Considerations of this kind prompted the decision to mount a conference on biography and history – "Biography and History: A Canadian/Irish Colloquium" – in Edinburgh in May 1991. The date seemed appropriate: 1991 was the centenary year of the deaths of both Macdonald and Parnell. Their similarities and equally their differences pointed up some of the issues surrounding biography. John A. Macdonald had been a central figure in Canadian public life for over three decades, dying at the age of seventy-six. Even stripped of his Creightonian grandeur, Macdonald could be seen as a builder and creator, able to play a key role in shaping new structures of government and the outlines of a state. Parnell had dominated Irish politics for half that time, and his demise came at the untimely age of forty-five. A Protestant and a landowner, he asserted his sway over a mass movement of Catholics and tenants in an old, established society. Here, then, seemed an opportunity to bring together scholars interested in Canada and in Ireland for comparative discussion of the role of the individual and the problems of reconstruction, with emphasis on issues and problems of biography. The conference lived up to these aims. Notably, Parnell and Macdonald attracted only two commentators. Have we passed from the era of heroic biography into an era more interested in the archaeology of humbler lives?

However, more crucial in the administrative unfolding of the conference was the issue of whether it could take place at all. Edinburgh University has the only fully established centre of Canadian studies in any British university, but it is a very small unit. Even Exeter University's Institute for Cornish Studies is larger. With just two members of academic staff, the Edinburgh centre attempts not merely to impersonate a whole department, but additionally to run a program of events intended to make Edinburgh a meeting place for academics interested in Canada on both sides of the Atlantic. In the academic year 1990–91, the centre found itself in the pleasantly alarming position of coping with an influx of students into its undergraduate courses. This was in part a university-wide phenomenon, one that constrained the supporting contributions from the centre's many active supporters in other departments, but Canadian Studies emerged from the start-of-the-year crush with the highest student-to-staff ratio in Edinburgh University's Faculty of Social Sciences. By midway through the year, it was touch-and-go whether the conference would take place at all.

Into a very large breach stepped Dr. Rae Fleming, who arrived as a visiting fellow planning to see through to press his own biography of the railway entrepreneur Sir William Mackenzie. In writing the life of Mackenzie, a biographer had to contend with the virtual absence of private papers that might have thrown light upon his motivation and personal drive. In fact, what proved to be an obstacle in the specific biography had become an asset shaping Fleming's wider response to the issues involved. In the event, *The Railway King of Canada* would be haunted not so much by Mackenzie's obsessional campaigns to lay steel from one end of Canada to the other as by the fleeting spirit of Biddy Young, Kirkfield's publican whose legend had first established a folkloric link between writer and subject.[10] It was Rae Fleming who took charge of organizing the Biography and History Conference in Edinburgh in May 1991, and to him should go the credit for its success and for the volume that now emerges from it.

Ged Martin
Edinburgh
April 1992

Notes

1 Mollie Gillen, *The Wheel of Things* (Halifax: Formac/Goodread Biographies, 1983), 77. I owe this quotation to Ann Barry.

2 Donald Creighton, *John A. Macdonald: The Young Politician* (Toronto: Macmillan, 1952), and *John A. Macdonald: The Old Chieftain* (Toronto: Macmillan, 1955); and *Dictionary of Canadian Biography*, vol. 12, *1891–1900*, edited by Francess G. Halpenny (Toronto: University of Toronto Press, 1990), 591–612. P.B. Waite further discusses Creighton's approach in an important published lecture, *Reefs Unsuspected: Historians and Biography in Canada, Australia and Elsewhere* (Sydney: Macquarie University, 1983).

3 J.M.S Careless, *Brown of the Globe*, vol. 1, *The Voice of Upper Canada, 1818–1859* (Toronto: Macmillan, 1959), and *Brown of the Globe*, vol. 2, *Statesman of Confederation, 1860–1880* (Toronto: Macmillan, 1963).

4 Mary Rose O'Callaghan, "Katharine O'Shea and C.S. Parnell," in D. McCartney, ed., *Parnell: The Politics of Power* (Dublin: Wolfhound Press, 1991).

5 John Brooke, *George III* (London: Constable & Company, 1974), 611–12.

6 Elizabeth Longford, *Victoria R.I.* (London: Pan Books, 1966), 38–39.

7 For "Master Charley," see F.S.L. Lyons, *Charles Stewart Parnell* (London: Collins, 1978), 27–28; and Paul Bew, *C.S. Parnell* (Dublin: Gill and Macmillan, 1980), 6. For the toy soldiers, compare T. Sherlock, *The Life of Charles Stewart Parnell M.P., with some account of his ancestry* (Dublin: T.D. Sullivan, 1880), 31, and St. John Ervine, *Parnell* (Harmondsworth: Penguin, 1944), 44.

8 Ged Martin, "Parnell at Cambridge: The Education of an Irish nationalist," *Irish Historical Studies* 19 (1973): 72–82.

9 National Archives of Canada, Newcastle Papers, microfilm reel A-308, Head to Newcastle, private, 2 February 1861.

10 R.B. Fleming, *The Railway King of Canada* (Vancouver: University of British Columbia Press, 1991).

Acknowledgments

In a collaborative work, there are even more people than usual to thank. First of all, I want to mention Dundurn Press editor Judith Turnbull, whose helpful advice was always offered in a friendly manner, and also Kirk Howard, publisher of Dundurn Press, whose keen interest in Ontario and Canadian history earns him the accolades that have come his way. The contributors to this volume were a delight to work with and must be thanked for their cooperation. Also deserving praise are the various archives, libraries, historical societies, photograph repositories, and individuals for making available the photographs and cartoons that illustrate the text. I want to thank Will Hoyle, Lindsay, Ontario, for his skilful reproductions of slides and old photographs.

Several people generously donated time to read and comment on essays: Anna Childers, Elwood Jones, Mary Fowler, Ron Rees, Marjorie Kennedy, Lloyd Johnston, and Eoin Mackay. Lyne Saunders's expertise in translation, Gwen Peroni's skills on the computer, Dwight Lubiniecki's thoughtful advice, and Ged Martin's enthusiasm and encouragement contributed to the final version.

Introduction

R.B. Fleming

Biographers have only recently become self-conscious. Only in the last fifteen years or so have methods and intentions, techniques and choices, come under scrutiny. The biographer can no longer conceal herself completely beyond or inside her subject, like a child dressing up in an adult's finery. We have had to ask ourselves what the hell we think we are doing, because other people are asking that question. The Berlin Wall between fiction and biography, between autobiography and biography, between politics and biography, has huge breaches in it.[1]

           – Victoria Glendinning, October 1990

During the last dozen years, biography has emerged as a distinct genre, enjoying sovereignty-association with literature, history, political science, and economics. The genre has its own journal, called, appropriately enough, *Biography*. And journals devoted to other disciplines are taking greater interest. In its winter 1989–90 number, the *Dalhousie Review* published P.B. Waite's "Invading Privacies: Biography As History," in which the biographer of Sir John Thompson and Larry Mackenzie argues that biography is not on the edge of history, but directly in its midst. In its June 1990 number, the *Canadian Historical Review* (*CHR*) published Katharine Ridout's biographical study of missionary Agnes Coates, in which the author illustrates Susan Mann Trofimenkoff's contention that an individual's life can act as a "laboratory for testing certain generalizations about a given society, a given social movement, the process of social change," an argument also made in Trofimenkoff's article entitled "Feminist Biography" published in *Atlantis* (spring 1985). More recently (September 1991), the *CHR* published Ken Dewar's analysis of Donald Creighton's use of narrative in his biography of Sir John A. Macdonald. The debates continue. A professor of history based in Erie, Pennsylvania, is researching nineteenth-century British political biography written by contemporaries, which suggests that biography is developing its own sub-genres.

The Biography and History Conference sponsored by the Centre of Canadian Studies, University of Edinburgh, in May 1991 contributed to the debate. Forty-two papers were presented, including four during a witty panel discussion whose subject was biographical truth. The conference was brought to a fitting conclusion by Ken Mitchell's biographical drama on Norman Bethune.

This publication is a selection of the papers. By their methods and conceptions, some papers imply that lives can be told objectively, without authorial interference. Other papers, influenced by Hayden White and Michel Foucault, explore the delicate balance between biographer and subject. Truth for these biographers is multifaceted and evasive.

In order to clarify the debates, I have chosen to group papers by common themes, methods, or approaches. There are seven sections. Part 1, "Expectations," contains the paper which officially opened the conference. In it, Francess Halpenny provides an overview of biography, with some emphasis on biographies of Parnell and Macdonald. Biography, she argues, must ask questions about how biographers conceive, structure, and put into words their facts and interpretations of their subjects.

Part 2, "Truth in Biography," includes three papers on the subject of biographical truth, the topic of the panel discussion during the conference. Elspeth Cameron, David Nock, and Ken Mitchell discuss the role of facts, the relationship between biographer and subject, and patterns and craft in the quest for biographical truth. (Unfortunately, Owen Dudley Edwards's intelligent and entertaining panel presentation was not converted to print.)

Part 3 deals with the relationship between subject and biographer, or in biographical terms, engagement and disengagement. In writing a biography of evangelist Aimee Semple McPherson, Janice Dickin McGinnis wrestles with inventions and myths, her own and those of McPherson. Anna Makolkin focuses on the shifting relationship between Lord Byron and his biographer, John Galt. The final paper in this section deals with Georges Henri Dagneau's connections with several topics, including the O'Learys of Quebec City, the controversial relief model of that city, and the fate of Francophones outside Dagneau's home province.

In Part 4, entitled (*pace* Waite) "On the Edge of History," six biographers deal with people who played roles on the periphery of history. The lives of these minor characters help to modify accepted views of major figures, as is the case with Chris Raible's piece on James Mackenzie, illegitimate son of William Lyon Mackenzie, who can now be seen, thanks to Raible, as a man of considerable sensitivity. Minor characters can also modify accepted interpretations of history, as demonstrated by David Rollo's version of the Reverend William Patrick, who helped found the United Church of Canada. Ron Stagg's research into Silas Fletcher and Jesse Lloyd shows how a study of two minor characters can cast new light on an already well-known event, in this case the Rebellion of 1837. While not modifying history to any extent, John Connor's portrait of Henry Childers gives us a glimpse of the remittance man who gravitated to the edges of the empire in the earlier part of this century. Donald Simpson separates truth and untruth by examining relatively minor players whose reputations have been inflated by themselves or even by gullible biographers. And Claire England's research into Canadians in the British *Dictionary of National Biography* reveals that as far as the *DNB* is concerned, Canada was "discovered" and developed not by hardworking mariners and settlers but by explorers, patrons, politicians, and a few uncomfortable writers – in other words, by those who had connections with power. Although some of these people are central to Canadian history, when viewed from the old imperial centre, they remain peripheral.

Part 5 deals with the topic of cultural migration. Does the migrant carry cultural baggage to the new land? Probably not, argues Leon Litvack in his paper on retailer Timothy Eaton, whose apparent fondness for the "auld sod," Ireland, was a convenient invention of company historians and executives. On the other hand, Barbara Murison's paper on migrant Scots of the 1820s and 1830s demonstrates that migrants do cross the ocean with trunks full of attitudes that are reshaped by the New World. (Bill Baker's paper on Timothy Anglin, in Part 7, tends to be in agreement with this idea, while J.R. Miller's paper in Part 6 casts doubt on the notion of cultural migration.)

Part 6 addresses the Manitoba Schools Question, a key event in the lives of both D'Alton McCarthy and Sir Wilfrid Laurier. Was McCarthy the villain of the Manitoba Schools Question? According to J.R. Miller he was no anti-Catholic bigot. And what of Laurier's role? In reaching out to the whole of Canada, did he sell out French Canadians? Yes, argues Réal Bélanger (whose paper also examines the larger question of why biography has attracted so few Quebec historians). The compromise with Premier Greenway threatened the linguistic dualism implied in the British North America Act, and provoked frustration and disenchantment among French Canadians. Ironically, had McCarthy's life not ended suddenly in 1898, he might have become Laurier's minister of justice, which proves Bélanger's contention that two of Laurier's strengths were moderation and tolerance. Biography can bring these ironies and paradoxes, these solitudes, into sharp relief.

The papers in Part 7 demonstrate how biography can enrich history. Curiously, although we have had governors since Samuel de Champlain in 1605, their role as representatives of the Crown in Canada has attracted few Canadian historians. John Gordon's study of Lord Lansdowne shows us that the role of governor general in the last century was more than ceremonial. George Davison uses the life of Sir Francis Hincks to cast light on a somewhat misunderstood corner of Canadian history, the Union period from 1841 to 1867. Michael Hopkinson reassesses the role of Michael Collins in the context of Irish revolution and civil war after 1916. Bill Baker and Rae Fleming agree that history and biography cannot live without one another. Baker demonstrates his contention by focusing on politician T.W. Anglin and his concept of nationalism. Fleming's illustration is Sir William Mackenzie and his connection with politicians and other businessmen during the days of Sir Wilfrid Laurier and Sir Robert Borden.

One regrets absences. I have mentioned Owen Dudley Edwards. Before work on this publication began, several potential contributors – T.D. Regehr, Colin Read, Peter Way, and David Nock – had committed papers to other publications. Read's fine piece on Edward Alexander Theller has been published in *Ontario History* (March 1992), and the collected work of both Way and Nock will appear in 1993. Other speakers – Catharine Wilson and W.A. Waiser, for example – preferred to direct readers to larger works, of which the paper given in Edinburgh was an excerpt.

Papers are published in the contributor's mother tongue. To encourage readers who may be not be completely fluent in French, those by Réal Bélanger and Georges Henri Dagneau are introduced briefly in English.

May the reader enjoy this collection of self-conscious biographical expectations, written and edited by spiritual descendants of James Boswell, Edinburgh's greatest biographer.

R.B. Fleming
Argyle, Ontario
August 1992

Note

[1] Victoria Glendinning, "The Truth about Biography," in Linda Spalding and Michael Ondaatje, eds., *The Brick Reader* (Toronto: Coach House Press, 1991), 113.

Part 1

Expectations

Chapter 1

Expectations of Biography

Francess G. Halpenny

The plan of this essay was largely determined by the outlines for the Edinburgh conference prepared by Ged Martin, director of the Centre of Canadian Studies, and then implemented by Rae Fleming as program director. The announced title was "Biography and History" and Dr. Martin's letters to me expressed his interest in a general discussion of the nature of biography and its relationship with history and literature as a prelude to the examination of particular biographical undertakings in the papers proper. The subtitle of the conference was to be "A Canadian/Irish Colloquium," and it was intended that the conference would concentrate on periods since the late eighteenth century. Dominating the poster for the event were the figures of John A. Macdonald and Charles Stewart Parnell, for both of whom 1991 was a centenary year. Accordingly, this paper offers some reflections on expectations of biography as developed by a number of commentators, and its choice of examples of biographies takes some note of the subtitle and the two anniversaries. The list of commentaries on biography continues to grow, and the pace of publication of biographies never slackens; inevitably, therefore, this paper must be selective and reflect my particular bent as I have followed the genre for reasons of professional and personal curiosity and have chosen titles for my bookshelves.

We are surrounded by "biography." It fits itself even into the routine of our daily lives. A voice announces over the radio that "on this day" X or Y was born or died; the item may be a handy way to provide a filler between snatches of music, but the choice of filler seems to suggest that marking time's progress by the lives of individuals is likely to catch listeners' interest. Anniversaries can indeed have a significant effect on public life, ordering events for many persons. The splendid exhibition at Greenwich in 1991 reinterpreting Henry VIII on the 500th anniversary of his birth advanced scholarship, caught the imagination of visual artists, and drew thousands of viewers. And 1991 was moulded for programmers, performers, and the public by the 200th anniversary of Mozart's death; we have learned much about his music and also about his life in Salzburg, Paris, Prague, Vienna. Then again, we all write bits of biography about others and about ourselves even in casual conversation. It can come to us in a restaurant as we hear a voice saying: "Yes, of course, I knew her – but let me tell you about the time ..." Many of us are busily looking up our family ancestors, seeking a sense of participation in their lives and an assurance of continuity against time. We attend a memorial service where the immediate past is once more given definition and both individual and general meaning as the pattern of the life is set out. A valued service of the Royal Society of Canada is the continuing group biography of its fellows in the published memorial notices; writing them is a challenge of portrait and assessment. I went back to P.B. Waite's notice for Donald Creighton as I worked on this paper, and remembered the concern he had expressed to me about rendering the man and the historian: both are in his piece, made vivid with his flair for anecdote, and he sets out the fruits of the life for a generation of historians and readers.

Biography – supermarkets, bookracks, bookstores, and libraries know its appeal well. It pours out in print in divers forms. A flood of graceless "life stories" of popular figures exploits their subjects for a mass market "with little authority or restraint." At higher levels of insight and knowledge are the thousands of biographies that are staples on the yearly lists of many publishers. Cultural importance and professional standards of scholarship are expected of historical, political, or literary biographies written for good regional publishers or trade houses and university presses; these biographies are widely reviewed and discussed. Harbourfront at Toronto, which conducts a now-famed international series of readings by contemporary authors, has in the last several years added biographers to the program. They have turned out to be highly popular, for they not only read but also discuss their biographical challenges: the choice of their subjects, their relationships as authors with those subjects, the subjects in their social settings.

Biography – we are endlessly curious about people, both in the immediacy of Russian women hurling their personal stories of food queues onto the television screen or in books stretching over the long saga of past years. We expect that biography will bring us people who have actually faced the uncertainties, the dangers, the successes, and the failures that we all face. And, what is important for our satisfaction, it will present these experiences within a pattern; in contrast, we cannot observe pattern as we proceed through our own lives; we dwell with questions. The defining points of a biography, as for a life, are birth and death. When we finish reading, one life has ended, an influence persists. It is no accident that the biographies we most appreciate so often begin with origins and in the elegy of the close look back but also forward. The structure has aesthetic congruity, which at the deepest level responds to human curiosity and human need.

Over the centuries many forms of serious biographical writing have been created in awareness of human interest in the lives of real people. The earliest of these are now studied largely for reasons other than strictly biographical information. The emergence of biography in English has been attributed to the Renaissance interest in the individual man, and commentators pick out examples here and there, from More's *Richard the Thirde* (1513) through Isaak Walton, John Aubrey, Clarendon, and Margaret Cavendish in the seventeenth century until they arrive at "the coming of age" with Johnson and with Boswell in the eighteenth century. From then on, the field is full and approaches to biography arise and recede as convictions about its content and form, emphases in concurrent writing of history and literature, developments in social forces, knowledge of the past, sources of documentary material, and attitudes to such material shift and acquire greater complexity. Sustained critical analysis of biography as a genre in its own right, independent of history and literature but with close links to both, and of biographical examples has been largely an undertaking of the twentieth century, with literary biography first receiving attention, no doubt, as Richard D. Altick has suggested, because of a transfer of the excitement generated through studies in the 1920s of "the Art of the Novel" (borrowing here a Henry James title), such as those by Percy Lubbock and E.M. Forster. Analysis has become more and more copious, particularly since the 1950s. Biographers, critics, historians, literary historians, and theorists in Britain, the United States, and Canada have contributed. Today the legitimacy of this interest is acknowledged by its being structured in academic discourse, in theses, and in courses, and the subject has a scholarly journal, *Biography*. The bibliography resulting from all this attention has continued to grow. I would suggest consultation of the generous lists and the examples in Altick's *Lives and Letters: A History of Literary Biography in England and America* (New York: Knopf, 1966); Ira Bruce

Nadel, *Biography: Fiction, Fact, and Form* (London: Macmillan, 1984); Ruth Hoberman, *Modernizing Lives: Experiments in English Biography, 1918–1939* (Southern Illinois University Press, 1987).

The discussion has shown a number of common threads. It has, for instance, been separating out and characterizing approaches to the genre taken by biographers in earlier periods and in the nearer present. It has used such surveys to identify elements that enter into a particular biography: life facts, social setting, interpretation, aesthetic pattern. It has pointed to the nature of the contribution authors make in giving "order, shape, and coherent meaning" (Altick's phrase) to the data they assemble about their subjects. Nadel quotes a fine remark by Pirandello: "A fact is like a sock which won't stand up when it's empty. In order that it may stand up, one has to put into it the reason and feeling which have caused it to exist." A.O.J. Cockshut, in the opening chapter of his *Truth to Life: The Art of Biography in the Nineteenth Century* (London: Collins, 1974), echoes many other commentators in seeing biography as having its "great strategic difficulty" in solving tensions between the writer's necessary adherence to facts and the need to reach an interpretation of the subject. A "tactical" problem he identifies is the handling of time, not just in presenting its passage as the reader follows the career, but in rendering "the complex way in which [time] is experienced by the subject" – mixing "continuity, memory, anticipation, routine, and surprise." A second tactical challenge Cockshut, like others, distinguishes is the biographer's personal relationship with the subject. That relationship, as it is felt and as it is reflected in the work, can be affected by proximity: the biographer may have known the subject when alive or the subject may still be alive – special challenges lie here. Taking the more usual case, no matter how shortly or how long gone the subject, an inescapable relationship of the biographer with the person develops and changes even as the subject is chosen and while the research proceeds. The relationship will affect the credibility of the interpretation embodied in the written work, the handling of incident, indeed the work's very style. (Recently an interesting explosion of novels has taken the potency of biographer/subject relationships as theme, including, to mention only a few – and remembering an ancestor, Henry James's *Aspern Papers* – John Banville, *The Newton Letter*, 1982; Penelope Lively, *According to Mark*, 1984; Julian Barnes, *Flaubert's Parrot*, 1984; Alison Lurie, *The Truth about Lorin Jones*, 1988; Daphne Marlatt, *Ana Historic*, 1988; A.S. Byatt, *Possession*, 1990; Celia Gittelson, *Biography*, 1991. One is tempted to speculate why, but I must refrain!)

How authors choose finally to present themselves to readers in relation to their accounts of their subjects will ultimately affect the structure of the biographies. Hoberman makes this aspect the organizing function in her discussion of "experiments" in English biography in the twenties and thirties. She uses three general categories of narrative variations: novelistic, where the narrator is virtually omniscient (Strachey, for example); mediated, "where the biographer's own perceptions are dramatized" and insight is limited by "his own particular viewpoint" (examples are Lubbock's *Edith Wharton* and A.J.A. Symons's *The Quest for Corvo*); psychosociological, where the aim is to "open up the self" and "to dramatize its multiple elements as they interact, fragmentarily, with elements of other selves and with the environment" (Strachey's *Elizabeth and Essex*, Virginia Woolf's *Roger Fry*). To these three variations, each of which has a chapter, Hoberman adds a discussion of feminism, which centres on Woolf's concern to alter the relation of women to history and biography. The importance of the decision biographers make about themselves as narrators is emphasized also by Nadel. Having the freedom "to create the story and shape the presentation of facts ... establishing a pattern of significance" is a privilege for the biographer, but it is also a responsibility because "the narration must be accurate, reliable and correct" in order to result in "a truthful portrait." He identifies three dominant types of narration, which have appeared in no historical order and which may coexist at any one period or even in any one work: the "dramatic/expressive," emphasizing "participation" (Boswell, Mrs. Gaskell, Johnson's *Savage*); the "objective/academic," emphasizing "detachment"; and the "interpretative/analytic" (Walter Jackson Bate's *Johnson*). Richard Ellmann's *James Joyce* illustrates coexistence in its combination of the detached, objective style and the interpretative.

Nadel is particularly emphatic about another challenge of biography: the relation of "fiction" and "form" to "fact" (the three words in his subtitle). Biography is a "factual narrative," and if we assume that it is responded to as literature, we should be aware of the way in which the biographer, as writer, uses literary effects in presenting the details of a life; the methods available are not only selection, ordering, and emphasis of detail, but also the building of successive scenes around incidents, the varying of pace and tension, the deployment of simile and metaphor and of metonymy, the calculation of "the tone of every sentence" (Edmund Wilson's phrase). Too much criticism (certainly, one might add, too much reviewing) still concentrates on accuracy of materials. Yet, because biography has been "fashioned by developments in other genres," notably the novel, it is misleading, Nadel insists, to try to separate fact from fiction and form in considering the results.

These common themes about the genre have been presented almost as challenges to biographers. But they are also, from another viewpoint, expectations readers may have as they approach works. I turn now to consider what a number of readers have seen in a selection of works.

Given the conference's interest in the nineteenth century, it seems appropriate to look at A.O.J. Cockshut. Cockshut is a literary historian and his title *Truth to Life: The Art of Biography in the Nineteenth Century* announces his emphases. A long reticence he points to among literary critics in the face of what he calls a golden age of biographical writing, beginning for him with Johnson's *Savage* and the inimitable Boswell's *Johnson*, that "Flemish picture" (to use Boswell's own description), Cockshut puts down to a usual treatment of biography as a historical record, dealing with facts and their interpretation. Accuracy and insight were the touchstones. What was neglected, Cockshut states, was the question of form, of biography as being also a work of art. What, he asks, is "the biographer's informing principle" as the author of a work of art, and since a historical record is indeed involved, how does that principle relate to accuracy? Cockshut pursues his exploration by looking at a nineteenth-century British tradition in general and then by examining examples in detail. Over the century the "tradition" meant, first, that lives were written "in a persistent attempt to establish heroism"; "the fundamental reason for writing a man's life was that he was admirable." (I should acknowledge here a valuable article by Ronald Rompkey in *Prose Studies*, September 1981, on "Heroic Biography and the Life of Sir Wilfred Grenfell.") Cockshut takes as the tradition's second characteristic "a universal trust in documents"; written evidence abounded (witness the long letters people wrote, and kept) and selection could be unwise; hence "the life and letters" school. What this reliance on written evidence meant, Cockshut suggests, was an emphasis on conscious, deliberate activity. In a time and place with a sense of national greatness, of destiny, and in years of intellectual brilliance, this force of will may have characterized the elite, he admits, but perhaps not to the extent nineteenth-century biography would suggest. What is missing is the force of impulse – reflected in personal relations, in emotions, in flashes of moral inspiration such as Wordsworth pictured. Cockshut points to a larger, overarching framework, however. Most biographers of whatever time see their subjects as people "struggling to achieve something and being helped or hindered by forces separate from them," but in the tradition Cockshut is exploring, he finds the idea, overt or shadowy, of "spiritual formation by forces beyond man's control and beyond his full understanding." "The biographer reads the *evidence* of the life as if it were a novel, and God were the novelist"; he or she performs a task of "literary criticism," reporting upon "an obscure but momentous work of art." There is more to be said of the tradition. When most of us think of nineteenth-century biography, we may be apt to think first not so much of the handling of public life as of prudence and restraint with private matters. Cockshut sees this tendency as particularly marked between 1840 and 1875; certain topics became un-mentionable. It is easy, he claims, to write this mid-Victorian "ethos of decency" off as a hypocritical façade, but he considers it must be seen as "something felt and lived by," influencing even a sceptic such as Leslie Stephen more than he knew when he came to question details of a Thomas Hardy novel running in his *Cornhill Magazine*. Cockshut goes on in his study to provide close analyses of nineteenth-century lives – for example, Trevelyan's *Macaulay*, Froude's *Carlyle* (his high point), Morley's *Gladstone* – in which he lays out subtleties the biographers managed to achieve within the tradition and identifies the puzzles in their subjects that they recognized, but could not or would not treat, and the puzzles they did not see. Cockshut's chapters make good reading. Are the biographies he chooses, and, say, Lockhart's *Scott*, now read? Are they readable?

Paul Murray Kendall, a historian and biographer, had earlier claimed in *The Art of Biography* (New York: Norton, 1965) that "the cultural-social forces of the age [1840s and up] had throttled the development of biogra-phy," that, to use Harold Nicolson's phrase, Victorian earnestness led to hagiography "scribbled ... by the light of shaded lamps." "A gap opened then between what man knew of man" after some centuries and "what man permitted himself to know." Pseudobiography took the place of biog-raphy. Today, Kendall says, even the well-known titles "are embalmed in our literary histories, a petrified forest." But the life-writing impulse, which, he is clearly convinced, can never be thwarted, he sees as finding its outlet through the nineteenth century by other means. Fiction was one – witness novels such as *David Copperfield, Pendennis, Jane Eyre*. Another was autobi-ography in several guises: *The Prelude, Childe Harold*, and *In Memoriam* move through the life pattern of idealism and hope, disillusion and de-spair, maturity and re-entry; thematic autobiography is striking in Newman's *Apologia*, John Stuart Mill's *Autobiography*, and also Edmund

Gosse's *Father and Son,* upon which, in 1907, Victorian scruples could still turn enraged. Granting what Kendall says about where the life-writing impulse flourished, one may still wish, especially if one is a student of the Victorian age – Kendall was the biographer of Richard III and Louis XI – to listen to and reflect upon what Cockshut has to say, and perhaps sound the volumes.

Whatever one's conclusions, for my purpose here it is important to stress how the spirit of the age is reflected in what is written and how it is written. A sea-change has come over history, literature, and biography in a hundred years. In the 1990s, convictions about life itself and about society, conventions about what is appropriate for the printed page, have fundamentally altered. We see dilemmas rather than certainties; the private has been taken over for the public page. Yet questions remain that are as cogent as ever. What is the centre of a life that is told? Where does that centre have its being? Do taste and artistry have a role to play in dealing with kinds of material that could otherwise be, as they have been, piled up in sensational and unbalanced detail?

The sea-change began for Kendall, as for most historians of biography, with the guns of the First World War and in the aftermath of its "volcanic forces." It is this change that Hoberman takes as her subject in *Modernizing Lives.* At the forefront was Lytton Strachey with *Eminent Victorians* (1918) and *Queen Victoria* (1921). The gleeful enthusiasm with which iconoclasm was at once taken up by many imitators, and the fervent excitement with which psychoanalytic factors were seized upon, subsided and these novelties acquired a different tone and capacity of application. They were not to disappear – for many good results but, when badly used, for ill. Leon Edel's metaphor for hidden personal myth, the "figure under the carpet," is now widely accepted as more than a figure of speech. Strachey's influence went, of course, beyond matters of content to matters of structure and approach: the use of irony, "delicacy of selection" (Kendall's phrase), a dramatic touch and flair for incident, a personal entry into the work. All these qualities were "diffused into the biographical atmosphere" (Kendall again, an appreciation echoed by Frank E. Vandiver in an article, "Biography as an Agent of Humanism," included in a collection of essays, *Biography as High Adventure,* edited by Stephen B. Oates, University of Massachusetts Press, 1986). Strachey's qualities have, indeed, become in one way or another, directly or indirectly, some of the expectations of biography. Michael Holroyd in his introduction to the Penguin edition of *Eminent Victorians* (1986) quotes Edel about the quality of irony in particular, a quality pervasive in our time and perhaps inescapably part of the approach to character: "A biographical subject is consistently ambiguous, irrational, inexplicable, self-contradicting; hence it truly lends itself to irony and to delicacies of insight and sentiment." And there was Strachey's prose, the power of image and metaphor, for example (one of Nadel's touchstones of style). The Duchess of Kent bustles through his pages "with bulky vigour," "swelling in sweeping feathers." He reflects on the young Victoria writing in her journal about her confirmation: "One seems to hold in one's hand a small smooth crystal pebble, without a flaw and without a scintillation, and so transparent that one can see through it at a glance." The cadence of Strachey's phrasing was to haunt the passages of many authors, even if written years later – that cadence he used to evoke the drifting shadows of the past that "perhaps" (Strachey's word) floated in Victoria's fading mind at her end or to place us with the participants at her first council in 1837.

> The great assembly of lords and notables, bishops, generals, and Minis-
> ters of State, saw the doors thrown open and a very short, very slim girl in
> deep plain mourning come into the room alone and move forward to her
> seat with extraordinary dignity and grace; ... they heard a high unwavering
> voice reading aloud with perfect clarity; and then, the ceremony over, they
> saw the small figure rise and, with the same consummate grace, the same
> amazing dignity, pass out from among them, as she had come in, alone.

Kendall mapped the excursion he took through the wide range of modern American and British life-writing by using a spectrum of biographies "from the most literary–least factual to the most scientific–least literary." His spectrum can be useful in pinpointing what the outburst of contemporary biography is doing, wittingly or not. On the far left of the scale Kendall puts "the novel-as-biography, almost wholly imaginary" (imaginary perhaps but not without imagination; for example, in Mary Renault's *The King Must Die* or Hope Muntz's *The Golden Warrior*). Next on the spectrum comes "fictionized biography," including outright romancing but also works with some serious intention. On its right he puts "the more carefully controlled and sometimes able" interpretative biography, commendable examples of which can take us up to the centre of the spectrum. Interpretative biography may rely on psychology or it may use literary techniques, drawing on invention "to flesh out a scene" or "read the subject's mind." Catherine Drinker Bowen's *Yankee from Olympus* has often been thought a responsible follower of this mode. Kendall, however, challenges here the claim of Hesketh Pearson that the truer sketch of a person is not the one with most facts but the one which paints the more living picture or, to put it another way, Pearson's claim that his invention of a subject's inner life cannot be proved to be less true than the biographer's suggestion of it. To this Kendall replies that the biographer's true objective is not simply a living picture but a living picture made from the materials at hand, judiciously weighed and then used with insight.

Immediately right of centre on his spectrum Kendall places the best scholarly biographies. Beyond them is the denser "research" biography, the "Behemoth biography," and at the far right edge "works of such high specific gravity that they are mostly compilations of source-materials." Some of the denser modern works he puts down to a "self-conscious dedication to accumulation of facts," encouraged by the contemporary confusion in many fields of "research" with "scholarship," under the influence of attitudes proper to the physical sciences. As readers we have seen that this magpie habit can, unfortunately, smother the subject itself, and we may search wearily and in vain for the theme, for the meaning of the life, or, in a biography of a writer, for the poetry or fiction he or she created. Even when put together with some skill and sympathy (and not inspired by reductionism), such works, though they may open up recesses of a life, are, according to Kendall, "biographical scholarship" rather than biography. He mentions Newman Ivey White's two volumes on Shelley, which have been called an "accepted authority." The work was published in 1940 and the form continues to appear from university presses and even trade houses. Despite the prestige these publications can acquire – and they have value as reference – are they *read*, read as biography? When I came to peruse Robert Holmes's *Footsteps: Adventures of a Romantic Biographer* (1985), I could see why, as he set out to move through Italy in pursuit of Shelley for his biography (1987), he deliberately did not read White. In the preface to volume 1 of his *Coleridge*, published in 1990, Holmes tells us that he had turned away from those who saw Coleridge's "imaginative existence" as "a gigantic booklist" in order to try to recapture Coleridge's fascination as a human being, what made him "for all his extravagant panoply of faults" the person whom Wordsworth could describe as "the most wonderful man" he had ever known. Attempting "the most traditional form of popular narrative biography," he relied for evidence and illustration on Coleridge's own voice as presented in exemplary works of scholarship, Griggs's edition of the Coleridge letters and Kathleen Coburn's of the notebooks. (A tribute to the resource value of such contemporary large-scale editorial projects appears in John Wain's "Note on Sources" to his *Samuel Johnson* [1974], where he says firmly, "There is no original research" in his work, and points, among the basic research of others, to the Yale edition of the *Works*. One confidently hopes that the Toronto edition of the *Collected Works* of John Stuart Mill, just crowned in its thirty-third volume by comprehensive indexes, will now be put to good biographical effect.)

Thus far we have been looking at the left and right of centre ranges of Kendall's spectrum. Floating uneasily above where left merges into right is what he calls the "superbiography," a twentieth-century phenomenon that exploits literary devices and scientific probings but claims to use no outright invention. He needs this category to explain Leon Edel, his eminent representative of it. Edel had said in his *Literary Biography* (University of Toronto Press, 1957) that "the biographer may be as imaginative as he pleases – the more imaginative the better – in the way in which he brings together his materials, but he must not imagine the materials." Kendall goes into a long, vigorously critical analysis of Edel's handling of one particular incident in his five-volume *Henry James* (1953–72). Reporting a visit the young Henry James paid to Emerson in 1870, Edel at this point brings in matter from encounters in the future, including Emerson's funeral in 1883 and an article by James in 1887. The effect is that we are in Edel's time, not the time that is James's at this moment in his life, and we are watching not only the omniscient author, master of his subject's time, but also the omnipresent author taking hold of the reader's concentration. Skilful, yes – but, to this reader at least, confusing. And, asks Kendall, is it biography? A good question to ponder. (A 1991 biographical work, much praised for its story, David Macfarlane's *The Danger Tree* about a Newfoundland family that lost three sons in the First World War, uses this technique to extremes that I found finally destructive of a reader's concentration.) Penelope Lively's narrator in her novel *Moon Tiger* (1987), debating the virtue of "linear history," cries out: "Chronology irritates me. There is no chronology inside my head ... The pack of cards I carry around is forever shuffled and re-shuffled; there is no sequence, everything happens at once." How far can freedom from linear plot go in biography? The leading characters in a novel are totally the author's creation (for instance, Peter Ackroyd's 1987 novel, *Chatterton*, based on Thomas Chatterton, moves in and out of three centuries). The novelist holds the pack of cards and shuffles them. Is a biographer ever omniscient in this sense?

We arrive finally at the centre right of Kendall's spectrum, where he places his nominations for best contemporary biographies. Among them he finds something like a common approach, though style and technique may differ. Here the literary and the scientific elements have drawn together "beneficently." This drawing together involves an ambition for literary grace and a nourishment of insight on rigorous research. At a deeper level, and as a result, is a perception, a link of biographer to subject that informs the projection of experience and supports a dramatic unfolding of action; the reader can rest assured in the validity of the link the biographer has forged. Kendall's British examples of this biography include Churchill's *Marlborough*, Cecil's *Melbourne*, Hart-Davis's *Hugh Walpole*, Harold Nicolson's *George V*, and his American, Andrew Turnbull's *Scott Fitzgerald*, D.S. Freeman's *R.E. Lee*. With titles such as these as touchstones, each of us will be able to add examples from the decades since Kendall made his selection. At a conference of the Victorian Studies Association of Ontario in April 1990 I buttonholed people with a question about nominations they would make for late nineteenth-century lives. Several historians of British history at once chorused: Robert Blake's *Disraeli* (1966); long though it is, it moves at ease and with grace, re-examining especially "the political side of his career," being judicious but giving proof of the fascination of this "brilliant eccentric," one of the few, as Cockshut puts it, who, amid Victorian high seriousness, could "regard the wickedness of the world with equanimity." (Of my responding historians, one has been on the advisory board of the edition of Disraeli's letters going forward at Queen's – as has Lord Blake – but he considers the edition as it proceeds enhances the picture in the biography and does not frustrate it.) Other respondents to my asking for recommendations identified Ellmann's *Oscar Wilde* (1987). A structural aspect of it caught my eye and I volunteer it for study of the possible effect upon an entering reader of the two-page introductory assessment of Wilde's career with which Ellmann decided to launch his 550-page text – a not uncommon strategy. Once launched, the text follows the chronology of the life, a pattern many practitioners stress for surest reconstruction and best transference of that reconstruction to a reader. Some biographers take a risk, however, beginning with a vivid scene somewhere in the life and then moving backward. In *Nora* (1988), Brenda Maddox introduces us to her subject as she goes on board ship to leave Ireland with James Joyce. Rosemary Sullivan in *By Heart* (1991) brings on Elizabeth Smart at age twenty-three as she stands fatefully in a Charing Cross Road bookstore reading George Barker's poetry. The choice of incident will certainly reveal much about the author's sense of the life's pattern and will influence a reader's response to all that follows. We are familiar with such a technique in film and in fiction – its results in biography would bear analysis. (Rosemary Sullivan speaks out on this very point, and on other biographical challenges, in "Writing a Life," *Books in Canada*, April 1991.)

Biographies of nineteenth-century figures germane to this conference beckon, but in approaching them I found helpful yet another formulation of the biographer's relation to and presentation of his or her account, and note it here briefly. It comes in Oates's prologue to his anthology of articles by biographers, *Biography as High Adventure*. He distinguishes three approaches. The "critical biography" he sees as having analogies with an academic lecture. The author "analyzes his subject with appropriate detachment and skepticism," "offering judgments about significance and consequence"; "the action here is almost entirely intellectual"; "our focus is on the author, not the subject"; the author "is involved in critical discussion, not in art." A second approach results in "the scholarly chronicle," "a straightforward recitation of facts"; "we read [it] to gain information about its subject, not to be swept up in a powerful story." (Kendall's phrases echo here.) The third approach Oates calls "pure biography," the kind that "employs fictional techniques without resorting to fiction itself." The life-writer who chooses this mode is "an artist on oath" (Oates takes this phrase from Desmond MacCarthy). "He cannot invent facts but he can give them narrative form to tell a story." He must have psychological insights; nevertheless the emphasis is on presentation of the subject as the life was lived so that readers identify with it and thus make discoveries for themselves as they move along. The life-writers anthologized in Oates's book are attempting this form of biography, but he acknowledges that many biographies "contain elements of all three approaches."

Where in Oates's paradigm and on Kendall's spectrum would we put F.S.L. Lyons's *Charles Stewart Parnell* (1977) and Oliver MacDonagh's first volume (1988) on Daniel O'Connell, *"The Hereditary Bondsman" 1775–1829?* This reader, who is most certainly not, however, a familiar of Irish history, read them as candidates for the centre of Kendall's spectrum. These are biographies that to me seemed to have been deep into their sources, deep into the personalities crowding their pages, deep into the social contexts. The biographers were absorbed by the two leading characters. They for me had the power of re-creating great events and small. One lived through O'Connell's handling of the Rent issue in 1827, the election in County Clare, his triumphal return to Dublin, the achievement of Emancipation in

1829; one felt the relationship with his wife and the constant private struggles over money (the very fact that O'Connell was away from her a good deal on circuit or on political business provided the letters to serve as documents).

Coming to the *Parnell* at the same time, I found myself reading side by side two biographies about leaders combatting the intransigence of the English by using their own parliamentary system to beat them. The depiction in both of an onrushing hurly-burly and crescendo of events had a similar thrust of narrative movement. Into the events of *Parnell* came "the dark and complex relationship between physical force and constitutionalism which was to haunt" this leader all his life, and the threatening relationship with Mrs. O'Shea that he vainly tried to keep private. In these two books one felt the stuff of the past, the pulse of life. They seemed to be informed by the skills of "pure biography." Yet there were also elements of critical biography when each author turns to reflect upon the meaning of events and upon the development of the central character: thus MacDonagh in an interesting passage relates the methods and attitudes of a skilled courtroom lawyer to O'Connell's political techniques; and thus Lyons evaluates the notorious alleged reference by Parnell in the United States to destroying the "last link" between Ireland and England, because he needs to discuss whether Parnell or a newspaper reporter was responsible for the remark and to render the effect upon Parnell of the aroused crowd in their thousands. Again, at the end of his book, Lyons, having brought us the story, turns to examine in the chapter "Myth and Reality" this "strange personality," this "enigma which baffled contemporaries and has baffled posterity ever since." The biographers have placed themselves, and us, at a point outside the story. The shifts are obvious, but skilful. MacDonagh has this to say about his approach: "I have tried to write a biography of O'Connell to 1829, which is also a study of the early formation of modern Irish culture and nationalism. My biography is not a 'life and times,' or a 'portrait,' or a psycho-history, and my study of cultural formation is implicit rather than specific. But these are not, I trust, things which, intrinsically, either secure merit or require excuse." Agreed.

The other anniversary of this conference was for Macdonald, which brings us inevitably to Donald Creighton's biography, long a landmark for Canadian historians, students, writers, and readers, what Peter Waite in his Royal Society obituary of 1980 claims "still remains the greatest biography ever published in English in this country, written from immense research, and with a remarkable sense of the period, so vivid as to be almost palpable." The biography's two volumes came out in 1952 and 1955, based, Creighton said in the prefaces, on "contemporary sources," that is, on the documents of the period, and not taking up secondary research. Those documents Creighton had thoroughly absorbed; his are not life-and-letters volumes. He tells the story – and the biography is indeed primarily a narrative, a story, not a "critical" account – looking out from the place where John A. stood, and the perspective holds steady throughout. That is the strength of the handling; Creighton knew his man so well that the two blend, perhaps more than the biographer's necessary participation with the subject might call for. At times one is not sure whether it is a perspective from Macdonald alone or with the addition of Creighton's own preferences that explains the way in which, say, the whole matter of Riel is handled or the prominence given to the nagging negotiations of the Treaty of Washington, where the balance of Great Britain, the United States, and Canada was so much at stake.

Creighton had a finely tuned sense of pace and scene, literary gifts that enhanced his historian's evaluation of the significance of events. His *Macdonald* moves through routine happenings into the great set pieces of the Charlottetown, Quebec, and London conferences with a relish for the strategies of the participants and a strong sense of the drama of what was at stake. I cannot resist, in the light of Canadian political events of 1990, choosing as a modest example the account of how the completion of the drafting of the British North America (BNA) Act with the British officials and Carnarvon was nearly frustrated when the British suggested some provision should be made for escape from a possible deadlock between Senate and Commons, and Macdonald found himself once more in an operation "almost as delicate as the removal of a thorn from the injured paw of a lion." That is Creighton's telling phrase (and an example of Nadel's simile). His sense for a document is able to make even more vivid the tenseness of Quebec and Maritime delegates watching over their own interests. He makes use of a letter written later by the under secretary of state. Macdonald, the secretary wrote, was trying to argue with the British while among the colonial representatives now the English, now the French watched "as eager dogs watch a rat hole; a snap on one side might have provoked a snap on the other, and put an end to the accord." Thus Creighton marshals many scenes up to the hush of a waiting country as the candle of Macdonald's life flickers and dies. Even the weather plays a part. The rain falling steadily at Kingston reinforces the sadness of the city's loss of the site of the capital of the united province; the warmth and high sun of a

Canadian summer bathe the lustrous account of the celebrations of 1 July 1867 in glowing splendour.

The value of a sense of place as a setting for personal and public drama is something stressed by all the commentators on biographical method I've been looking at – so Holmes searching out the Paris of Mary Wollstonecraft and the northern Italian cities of the Shelleys, or Kendall the Yorkshire moors of Richard III . Creighton came to his biography with his sense of the dynamic of Canada's geography set by Innis and argued in *The Commercial Empire of the St. Lawrence*. It takes visual form in the opening of volume 1 of the *Macdonald*. You remember: "In those days they came usually by boat." And we too are on the craft that comes up from Montreal by the long water system, through the thrust of the "huge knotted fist" of the Shield to the town where great lake and mighty river meet. (I should note here that after this paper was presented in Edinburgh, May 1991, the *Canadian Historical Review* in September published an engrossing article by Kenneth C. Dewar, "Where to Begin and How: Narrative Openings in Donald Creighton's Historiography," which relates Creighton's work to recent discussions of narrative in historical theory.) The places of Canada on 1 July 1867 sound their drums, run up their flags, race in village games, blaze out in bonfires on the hilltops. The country surrounds us. Then: "Parliament Hill was crowded once again with people who had come to watch the last spectacle of the day. The parliament buildings were illuminated. They stood out boldly against the sky; and far behind them, hidden in darkness, were the ridges of the Laurentians, stretching away, mile after mile, towards the north-west." In that last evocation of volume 1 is the theme of the second volume, and when it too comes to its conclusion a river still flows. The life, and its passions, are passing. "When once more the sun had gone down behind the long blue line of the Laurentians, the last change came. Up to then his breathing had been shallow and rapid. Now it grew slower, slower still, and, as the watchers clustered around him, died away in the last, faint, lingering prolongations. He was going now. He was borne on and outward, past care and planning, past England and Canada, past life and into death." Creighton's response to music and his memory for the words and rhythms of English poetry unite the enduring hills and the ebbing life.

One might be curious, since Creighton's is so much a "literary" biography, about how any one specific incident is handled. I can deal with only one aspect here. In volume 1 when the author is building up one of his great scenes, say, at Charlottetown, the expression "may have been" appears in the reconstruction of events or Macdonald's intentions. In volume 2, reading the account of the electricity in the House of Commons in October–November 1873 during the debate on the Pacific Scandal, I came upon something different. The debate has dragged on and the government's majority dwindles day after day; Macdonald sits in silence or replies ineffectually. What "revelation" might Edward Blake bring forward? He does not make a move. And then Macdonald finally rises. "He would show Blake that a moral victory was not so easily gained as that."

> He felt returning confidence, like a great masterful wave of water, roaring through his body. The packed House lay spread out round him, the packed galleries soared above his head. They were waiting, waiting for him, and for him alone. They would not be disappointed. He would speak and speak his best. He was on his feet now, his face drawn and white, his body slight and curiously frail. The applause swelled into a roar which maintained itself for long clamorous moments, and then died slowly and utterly away. He could feel the silence of acute physical tension settle like a burden upon the great room. He could see the last laggard member tiptoeing softly to his place, the reporters settling down to their note-books, Lady Dufferin bending eagerly over the railing, and Agnes watching him, her dark features strained with painful expectancy. He wetted his lips in the nervous, involuntary manner that had become habitual with him. Now.
>
> It was nine o'clock.

And with that almost audible chiming of a dramatic clock, the chapter section ends. Macdonald was to speak, achieving "a personal triumph," for nearly five hours. Creighton opens the next section with his eloquent peroration. But the effort was not sufficient, and a few days later the government resigned.

How is the passage quoted from chapter 5 built up? The details of the tense scene in the House – the crowded benches and galleries, the reporters, the hush of expectation – could be imagined through likeness. But the factual elements of it are verified in two sentences about the setting in *Memoirs of Sir John A. Macdonald* by Sir Joseph Pope, who also chooses the peroration to conclude his account (see Creighton's footnote 97). The *Mail* of 4 and 5 November (footnotes 97, 98) has long accounts of the debate itself, and though the paper was hardly an impartial witness, its commentary pointed to the "force and effect," "eloquence and power" of Macdonald's oratory, and to the circumstances that called forth "the use of his utmost strength," rousing him from the seat where he had sat "un-moved and immoveable under the seven days' torrent of abuse and vile inuendo [*sic*]." A most interesting background of fact is in a private letter of 6 November from the governor general, Lord Dufferin, to the Earl of Kimberley in the Colonial Office (footnotes 95, 96, 99) in which Dufferin relates the progress of the long debate, Sir John's response to the strain, the reason for the prime minister's watching Blake, the gradual defection of those who "day after day, like autumn leaves in the valley of Vallombrosa" "kept falling from the Ministerial side," and Lady Dufferin's description to him at 3 a.m. of the effect of Macdonald's lengthy defence. Creighton does not use the autumn leaves image in a quotation, but he does quote Dufferin's marvelling at how Macdonald could look "as though a feather would knock him down" and then could "pull himself together" to deliver such a sustained address. Yet when all is said and done about the documents, in the quoted passage the reader is put inside Macdonald's own conscious-ness and his thoughts and feelings as he brought himself to face an expect-ant House.

The point is of great interest because it is frequently discussed in comments on Creighton's methods and in the critiques of biography I've been examining. Can one, the question is raised, know what was in a subject's mind without some sure indication from that subject – in a letter or recorded conversation or speech? How far can a biographer's immer-sion in the character and personality of the subject be taken? Frank Vandiver, in Oates's anthology, refers to Freeman. "Freeman, who lived with Gen-eral Lee for nearly twenty years, confessed that he never knew what was in Lee's mind unless he found the thought expressed somewhere." Vandiver says categorically, "Of a subject's thoughts or beliefs nothing can be as-sumed." That is not to say, he goes on, that "familiar things" in the unfold-ing of events may not be made "givens," that verisimilitude cannot be achieved "without racing for a footnote." Hence the possibility of creating the general atmosphere of the Commons on that night of high drama in 1873. I came upon Vandiver's point again quite recently in John English's first volume on Lester Pearson (*Shadow of Heaven*, 1989). He had resources of letters, Pearson's memoirs, reminiscences of friends and colleagues, yet they could take him only so far. He says in his preface:

> Lester Pearson has not been easy to know. He had a Victorian reserve that made revelation about one's private life difficult. In writing this biogra-phy, especially when I had to divine Pearson's private thoughts and mo-

tives, I often recalled Virginia Woolf's comment about her sighting of a kingfisher on a cold September day that awakened a special feeling in her. No biographer, she rightly warned, could ever know that important fact about her life in the late summer of 1926 and no biographer should pretend to do so.

As one comes to recent decades and the flux of contributions to biography, one must take account of the directions and emphases of the large number of women biographers of skill and stature. Political biography is not a dominant interest here. Literary biography is a favourite, but they have introduced new approaches. In charting their part, one must go back to Mrs. Gaskell and must reckon with the mesmeric influence of Virginia Woolf in her critical writing and correspondence or in works such as *Orlando*. For my present purpose, I scouted prefaces to works on my shelves to get a sense of the preoccupations of contemporary writers. Worth study as a sign of different times is Phyllis Rose's preface to her interpretative biography of Virginia Woolf (1978). She had, of course, to take note of the previous writings of Leonard Woolf, Nigel Nicolson, and Michael Holroyd, and especially of Quentin Bell's "urbane and masterful" (her words) two volumes, which she says will "deservedly" remain the definitive source of information about Woolf (a statement needing qualification in the 1990s). But she herself began because of what had *not* been written; Bell had used Woolf's memoirs, journals, correspondence – the documents – but, according to Rose, he had not explored the ways in which Woolf's life, her life as a woman and as a writer, "fed her fiction and in which her fiction may illuminate aspects of her life." Rose returns to the original sources used by Bell, in a different way, summed up in her title *Woman of Letters*. Take also Claire Tomalin in the foreword to *Katherine Mansfield: A Secret Life* (1987). Two important books on Mansfield, by male authors, had appeared in 1978 and 1980, both based on wide reading and research, both of which she admired. Was there more to say? Ongoing new scholarly editions of letters provided an impetus to Tomalin, but even stronger was her gradual conviction that aspects of Mansfield's life had been scanted. Beyond this challenge, felt by many biographers of either sex in the face of the eternal mystery of human personality, was the fact that she would be a woman writing about another woman. "I can't help feeling that any woman who fights her way through life on two fronts – taking a traditional female role, but also seeking male privileges – may have a special sympathy for such a pioneer as Katherine, and find some of her actions and attitudes less baffling than even the most understanding of men." Moreover, Tomalin's mother and mother-in-law were both "gallant and gifted outsiders" and through them she felt she "approached Katherine Mansfield's experience at certain points." Then, Victoria Glendenning. Since 1978 she has published four important biographies of women. Her preface to *Rebecca West* (1987) explains that here she found a personal story that is also the story of twentieth-century women, of one who was an agent for change and a victim of change. When West became a writer on world affairs, she entered upon what had been a masculine profession and she experienced the patronage that went with her challenge. "There is little that a woman could have achieved, enjoyed, and suffered during decades when women's lives were being transformed that she did not achieve, enjoy, and suffer." Yet Glendenning took on the biographical commission to create not an "emblem," but a person.

These women biographers and their companions are, it will be seen, using the basis of biography in well-versed fact and employing the various techniques of biography we have been examining to give the fact shape and meaning in the frame of a personality and a life. What they are giving from themselves is a different kind of sensibility and sensitivity, and the relation between subject, biographer, reader is correspondingly affected. In the course of their experiments they have brought to biographical attention the kind of women subjects that have long been overlooked: witness Claire Tomalin's turning to *The Invisible Woman: The Story of Nelly Ternan and Charles Dickens* (1990). The sweep of this new concern with women's lives has been wide, stretching across disciplines. To pick only two very recent Canadian examples at random, one can cite *Re(Dis)covering our Foremothers: Nineteenth-Century Canadian Women Writers*, edited by Lorraine McMullen (University of Ottawa Press, 1990) or Joy Parr's *The Gender of Breadwinners: Women, Men, and Change in Two Industrial Towns, 1880–1950* (University of Toronto Press, 1990).

Making my way through works of analysis of biography itself, browsing in biographies, reading prefaces, critical surveys, reviews, and hearing current biographers interviewed have given me a powerful urge to see proper attention given to the achievements *as writers* of the authors of the long list of excellent biographies in English published by Canadians, whether on figures who contributed to the Canadian story or lived elsewhere, whether on public, literary, artistic, or other figures, whatever the approaches to character, whatever the structures chosen. The record is indeed substantial – and it should be compared and contrasted with another list in French. It can be followed in the surveys of the *Literary History of Canada*, in writings by Carl Berger and Shirley Neumann, in historical and literary periodicals, in series such as those by ECW Press and Twayne, in essays such as that by biographer Robert Craig Brown in his presidential address to the Canadian Historical Association in 1980, in proceedings of conferences on biography. Cameron, Tippett, Thomas, Pitt, Grosskurth, Millgate, Eccles, Careless, Neatby, Waite, Bliss, Brode, Flanagan, Donald Smith, Richard Gwyn – the contributions continue into the 1990s. Berger has seen, since the late 1970s, a recoil among academic historians from political biography, a turning away from the art of narrative as a model, and a shift to social history, with an interest in groups such as workers, immigrants, native peoples, and women. A popular fascination with the past he has pictured as being responded to by genealogy, the "living history" of regional accounts, museums, and parks, the dramatic stories of journalist biographers of individuals or groups. And yet the interest in public individuals persists, as English, Marrus, and Clarkson and McCall have been demonstrating. Biography, that presentation of "the activities of men and women, of their hopes and of their fears, of their triumphs and of their failures" (Craig Brown), draws those who study the human record and gives them readers. What is due our biographers in this country now is attention not just to the content they have mastered but to the craft by which they have striven to give it living form.

By some quirk it is not always recognized by those who talk about "biography" in Canada that an enormous effort in this form, by authors in English and in French, has been going on in the *Dictionary of Canadian Biography/Dictionnaire biographique du Canada* since the 1960s. The chronological structure of the enterprise is reflected in the structure of most biographies but, that being said, many kinds of biographical interests and approaches can be found, as well as an infinite variety of subjects. A historiography of the whole and its parts would repay the doing. The slow progress of the centuries enfolds the six thousand persons in the twelve published volumes: time that runs hurriedly through great events and slows to the quieter run of practicalities; moments that change persons and communities; relationships that build up over years. In the midst of our current constitutional debates, many voices have been heard calling out that we need to know who we are and where we have come from. We need to hear our stories. Those stories are in the *DCB/DBC*. Without ever setting out to do anything but tell one story as he or she thought fit, each and every author has added a segment to what now constitutes a monumental yet pulsing biography of Canada.

Stephen Oates provides me with a fitting close. "The people of the past have never really died. For they enjoy a special immortality in biography, in our efforts to touch and understand them and so to help preserve the human continuum. Perhaps this is what Yeats meant when he said, 'We may come to think that nothing exists but a stream of souls, that all knowledge is biography.'"

Dr. Francess Halpenny is professor emeritus, Faculty of Library and Information Science, University of Toronto. From 1972 to 1978 she was dean of the same faculty. She obtained a B.A. from University of Toronto in 1940, and an M.A. from the same university in 1941. That year, she began a long association with University of Toronto Press; she was its editor from 1957 to 1969, managing editor 1965 to 1969, and associate director (academic) 1979 to 1984. From its inception in 1959, she was associated with the *Dictionary of Canadian Biography/Dictionnaire biographique du Canada*, of which she was general editor 1969–88, responsible for volumes 3 to 12; since 1988, she has been the *Dictionary*'s general editor emeritus. She has been active in the Book and Periodical Council and its Committee on Library Information, and has published and given lectures in the area of publishing in Canada, especially scholarly publishing, as well as library relations with the book trade, Canadian collections in Canadian libraries, biography, bibliography, the *DCB/DBC*, and the humanities in Canada. In 1977 she was made a fellow of the Royal Society of Canada, and she has received honorary degrees (LL.D., D.Litt., and D ès l) from ten Canadian universities. Other honours include the Molson prize (1983), Companion of the Order of Canada (1984), the University of Toronto Faculty Award (1985), and the University of British Columbia Medal for Canadian Biography (1986). Dr. Halpenny has long been interested in theatre, both as actor and as playwright. In May 1991 she was special guest speaker at the conference on biography and history at the Centre of Canadian Studies, Edinburgh, Scotland.

Part 2

Truth in Biography

Chapter 2

Truth in Biography

Elspeth Cameron

And to think we supposed we knew her; we knew all there was to know ...

We never know it all; we only make up stories about it, and sometimes our characters seem fully developed; but they have only fooled us again. And if we call ourselves biographers, we call the stories and the characters we have invented biography.

– Amanda Cross, *Sweet Death, Kind Death*

Freud was of the opinion that there was no such thing as biographical truth. In a letter to a friend in 1936, he wrote, "Anyone turning biographer commits himself to lies, to concealment, to hypocrisy, to flattery and even to hiding his own lack of understanding, for biographical truth is not to be had, and even if it were it couldn't be used. Truth is unobtainable."[1] Certainly Freud's 1916 biography of Leonardo da Vinci is a case in point.[2] Subsequent scholarship has demonstrated that there is not much biographical truth to be found in it.[3] Ironically, the father of the school of psychological investigation that has revolutionized biography in this century was himself an irresponsible biographer.

Freud's dismissal of biographical truth alerts us to the folly of naivety; but it is, surely, an overreaction amounting to cynicism. Though truth in biography is difficult to corner, biographers succeed in a number of ways in at least approximating the reality of other lives.

Virginia Woolf, in her short analysis of the "new biography,"[4] grappled with some of the difficulties biographers face in essaying what biographer Sir Sidney Lee called "the truthful transmission of personality." "We think of truth," Woolf wrote, "as something of granite-like solidity and of personality as something of rainbow-like intangibility." Though

Woolf's images of granite and rainbow oversimplify the matter, no biographer can fail to feel a frisson of recognition on encountering them. Truth in biography is elusive, partly because, as Woolf intuitively sees, "the truth of fact and the truth of fiction are incompatible, yet [the biographer since the early twentieth century] ... has been urged ... to combine them."

It is scarcely original to observe that one kind of truth – what Woolf would call "the truth of fact" – is dependent upon the materials available to the biographer. Sometimes these are too meagre; at other times far too profuse. What is to be done with a life about which nothing is known for some significant three-year period? A digression? A fictionalized bridge of probabilities based on the biographer's educated guess? The opening of a bold new chapter that distracts the reader from realizing that three years have been omitted?

And what about the opposite problem: a morass of materials that lead this way and that, from which it seems impossible to select a focus decisively without doing an injustice to other threads? – an overloaded narrative that fails to sweep the reader along in the way the subject felt carried purposefully through life? – an arbitrary emphasis that runs the risk of reflecting the tastes and interests of the biographer more than the priorities of the subject? In short, even the biographical paths dictated by the nature of available materials (to which must be added the stipulations of editors and publishers as to length, illustrations, title, and cover) affect the nature of each biography's "truth."

In a more complex way, biographical truth depends also on the nature of the relationship between the biographer and the subject, whether the subject is living or dead. That relationship is not fixed, as Woolf's analysis seems to assume, but is a dynamic intertwining of two personalities, two life experiences. For this reason, there is no such thing as a "definitive" biography. Any two people – even identical twins – having access to exactly the same sources, would produce different versions of the same life. Even the same person writing at different stages of life about the same subject will reassess and shift interpretation, as Leon Edel's revised and condensed version of Henry James's life bears ample witness.[5]

This dynamic intertwining of biographer and subject takes the form of a dialectic between engagement and detachment. There must be a significant number of "hooks" by which the biographer can engage with the subject. These hooks consist of an unlimited array of possible common denominators between the two: whether temperamental, physical, and emotional traits; similarities of gender, class, religion, and ethnicity; or interests in various activities that might be cultural, political, athletic, and so on. It is not at all uncommon to find a biographer acquiring temporarily some of the subject's tastes, mannerisms, ideas, or even emotions as something akin to the psychological phenomenon called transference takes place. The biographer must be able to let go of himself or herself in order to empathize or identify in significant ways with the subject, not only with that subject's socially constructed selves and deliberately invented public personae, but also with that more elusive "hidden personal myth" Edel aptly compared to "the figure under the carpet."[6]

But disciplined detachment is also necessary. A biographer who can enter the subject's world, but cannot make a seemly exit when the time comes for analysis, assessment, interpretation, selection, and arrangement – indeed the judicious application of the forms of training most useful to biography, whether psychological, historical, bibliographical, or literary – will be ghost-writing an autobiography or constructing a eulogy, not presenting biographical truth. In other words, a biographer must be able to feel in some significant respects what it is like to *be* the subject, yet be able to stand back, be him or her own self, in order to neutralize bias as well as assess and transmit the truth of personality. Leon Edel puts it well: the biographer "must be warm, yet aloof, involved, yet uninvolved. To be cold as ice in appraisal, yet warm and human and understanding."[7] As Edel also recognized, this dialectic of merging with and abandoning the subject has much in common with method acting, though the "performance" will ultimately take written rather than dramatic form. Having assumed what might be called a series of subject positions approximating as closely as possible those typical of the personality in question, the biographer returns, like the Ancient Mariner, compelled to recount that astonishing and exciting voyage into another self in narrative prose. This is what James Boswell (who, we must remember, had no recourse to psychological theory) meant when he bragged excitedly that his Dr. Johnson "will be seen more completely that any man who has ever yet lived," because the reader could "'live o'er each scene' with [Johnson], as he actually advanced through the several stages of his life,"[8] though at the writing stage Boswell needed the objectivity of a great scholar, Edmund Malone, to extricate himself from his engagement with Johnson.

But the deepest truth of biography comes as a result both of a long-term immersion in whatever materials are available to the biographer and of an in-and-out immersion in the personality of the subject. Over time, patterns emerge, patterns all the more valid if they are in no way precon-

ceived by the biographer. An example of the kind of pattern recognition I
have in mind comes not from literature or psychology, but from botany.
The pine tree is commonly depicted with its branch tips pointing upwards,
as if each branch were a wide-swept "U." In fact, the branch tips of pine
trees point down in the opposite direction. That downwards-pointing structure can be observed to resemble the structure of the pine cone, whose
seed-containing flaps open in microcosmic imitation of the tree's shape. So
it is with people. Patterns of behaviour on a large scale are echoed in their
enterprises: the way a politician plays bridge is likely to reflect the way he
conducts his political business; situations depicted in art will reflect in
some way the artist's life; even linguistic patterns and the use of special
words with private connotations resemble larger life patterns. Though
novelists may routinely make such disclaimers as "Any resemblance to
persons living or dead is purely coincidental" in order to dodge potential
libel suits, it would be more truthful were they to say something like this:
"If I had not been the person I am and lived the life I've lived and met the
people I knew, I could not have written this book." To turn to sculpture for
a striking example of repeated patterns, Henry Moore, by his own admission in the film documentary of his life and work, grew to love the massive, rounded shapes so typical of his work partly because the act of
rubbing medication on his mother's back and shoulders when he was a
small boy became invested with special tenderness.[9] Openness and alert-
ness to the recognition of such patterns are crucial aspects of the biographical endeavour to locate truth.

    And what of the "truth of fiction," that means of conveying what
Woolf called the "rainbow-like intangibility" of personality? No biographer could underestimate the difficulty of *transmitting* personality. No
matter how satisfactory the materials; no matter how fulsome the empathy
with the subject; no matter how sophisticated the analysis and assessment;
no matter how rigorous the self-examination for bias; and no matter how
insightful the recognition of patterns among these many overlapping lay-
ers, the truth readers encounter must be found in the written work itself.
Woolf recognizes this: "In order that the light of personality may shine
through, facts must be manipulated; some must be brightened; others
shaded; yet, in the process, they must never lose their integrity."[10] And
Boswell, much earlier, realized the same thing: "Johnson and I dined together at several places; but of his conversation during this period, I neglected to keep any regular record, and shall therefore insert here some
miscellaneous articles, which I find in my Johnsonian notes."[11] Boswell

felt certain that his mind was so "strongly impregnated, as it were, with the Johnsonian ether, [that he] could with much facility and exactness, carry in [his] memory and commit to paper the exuberant variety of [J's] wisdom and wit."[12] Like Woolf, he believed in the delicacy of his task: "The incidents that give excellence to biography are of a volatile and evanescent kind, such as soon escape the memory, and are rarely transmitted by tradition. We know how few can portray a living acquaintance, except by his most prominent and observable particularities, and the grosser features of his mind."[13]

Truth in biography must therefore remain an approximation of varying degrees of credibility partly because different kinds of truth are appropriate for differing aspects of the preparation of a life. The truth of fact must be diligently recorded and checked in research. The truth obtained by a series of engagements with and disengagements from the subject – a kind of truth dependent on the degree to which a biographer can paradoxically identify passionately and assess ruthlessly – must emerge over time, each biographer experiencing the subject differently. The truth that results from pattern recognition after long absorption in the same subject matter must be allowed to filter into consciousness slowly. And, finally, the truth that comes from felicitous shaping and the canny employment of fictional techniques will depend on the biographer's skill in handling narrative prose.

Elspeth Cameron is an associate professor with Canadian Studies and the English Department, University College, University of Toronto. She is the biographer of three Canadian writers, Hugh MacLennan (*Hugh MacLennan: A Writer's Life*, 1981), Irving Layton (*Irving Layton: A Portrait*, 1985), and her current project, Earle Birney. She is also working on a book that will explore the cultural history of Montreal between 1926 and 1945. In total, she is the author and/or editor of seven publications, in addition to some one hundred published articles, essays, and reviews whose topics range from Sartre and Atwood to Murray (Anne) and Newman (Peter). The recipient of numerous awards, including the University of British Columbia's Canadian Biography Award (1981) for her biography of MacLennan, she is a member of the editorial boards of two academic journals and *Saturday Night*, and has been a member of several juries, including the Canada Council Non-Fiction Writing Awards Jury (1986). She speaks regularly at conferences in Canada and internationally, most recently in Cadiz and Madrid, where she gave papers on Canadian Literature, and women writers in French Canada, and at the University of Calgary, where her topics were "Libel Law and the Ethics of Biography" and "Biography: Interdisciplinary Alloy." In May 1991 she was visiting professor, Michigan State University. In her spare time, she has contributed to CBC radio and television and to the National Film Board.

Notes

1 Sigmund Freud to Meister Arnold Zweig, who had proposed writing Freud's biography, 31 May 1936, in *Letters*, edited by Ernst Freud, translated by Tania Stern and James Stern (New York: Basic Books, 1960), 430.

2 Sigmund Freud, *Leonardo da Vinci: A Study in Psychosexuality* (New York: Vintage Books, 1947).

3 Meyer Schapiro, for example, in his excellent analysis of this biography ("Leonardo and Freud: An Art-Historical Study," *Journal of the History of Ideas* 17, no. 2 [April 1956]: 147–78), convincingly negates most of Freud's conclusions.

4 Virginia Woolf, "The New Biography," in *Collected Essays*, edited by Leonard Woolf, vol. 4 (London: Hogarth Press, 1967), 233–34 (first published in the *New York Herald Tribune*, 30 October 1927).

5 See Leon Edel, "Biography and the Sexual Revolution – Why Curiosity Is No Longer Vulgar," *New York Times Book Review*, 24 November 1985, 13–14. Edel admits that he originally wrote under constraints that stemmed from "the genteel tone of the former time and also ... my residual prairie puritanism." His revisions of the five-volume life of Henry James (1953–72), he says, "benefitted from the new candour. I could speculate more freely and with wider latitude on subjects we treated rather daintily in earlier years." The result was an "extensive revision of the psychosexual portions of James' life."

6 See Leon Edel, "The Figure under the Carpet," in Marc Pachter, ed., *Telling Lives* (Washington: New Republic Books, 1979), 17–34.

7 Leon Edel, *Literary Biography: The Alexander Lectures* (Toronto: University of Toronto Press, 1957), 8.

8 James Boswell, *The Life of Samuel Johnson*, vol. 1, edited by Roger Ingpen (Bath: Baynton Press, 1925), 1–5.

9 "Sculptor Henry Moore," a film by Julius Kohanyi (1968).

10 Virginia Woolf, "The New Biography," 233–34.

11 Boswell, *The Life of Samuel Johnson*, 279.

12 Ibid., 373.

13 Ibid., 1–5.

Chapter 3

Biographical Truth

David A. Nock

One traditional representation of scientific work may be portrayed by the image of the researcher with flashlight in hand (which may be interpreted as one of several ever more sophisticated research methods) uncovering new facts of nature that sit passively on the shore awaiting discovery. Barry Barnes refers to this as "the contemplative account" of knowledge accumulation, in which it is supposed that knowledge is accumulated by "disinterested individuals, passively perceiving some aspects of reality, and generating verbal descriptions to correspond to it."[1]

One key assumption is that individuals "intrude minimally between reality and its representation," and this is encouraged by the fostering of detachment and value neutrality in the scientist. The development of scientific knowledge is seen to be cumulative, with researchers each contributing to the completion of a giant jigsaw puzzle. It is seen as directed by the nature of nature. As Barnes puts it, this account puts a stress "on the objects of knowledge almost to the extent of excluding the role of the knowing subject."[2] In this traditional account, it is held to be possible for the scientist to approach the object of knowledge without preconception or prejudgment, without prior values, and without consideration of the standpoint of the researcher.

In relating this to biography, the expectation would be that the more the biographer minimizes his or her authorial voice and depends on collecting more and more facts, the more likely it is that a "true" portrait – that is to say, one true portrait – can be achieved. Such ideas lead to the conclusion that there can be such a thing as a "definitive" biography.

In countering such a notion of the biographical enterprise, imagine a thrust stage as found at Stratford's Festival Theatre. The stage juts out in a semicircle, and thus what the individual audience member perceives depends not just on distance from the stage but on where on the arc of the semicircle he or she is located. And one must remember that the seats are on two levels: balcony and orchestra. When I have been seated apart from a friend or relative, I am amazed at the differences in our perceptions of a production.

What we see and how we interpret it at the theatre depends not just on where we are seated but on the values and moral ideas of both the spectators and the theatrical community at a given time and place. Take Shakespeare's *The Taming of the Shrew*. In the sixteenth century, it was only natural that Katherine would eventually submit to her husband, since that subordination represented a natural law that was underwritten by Church and State. Although the play is irresistible today because of its strong leading characters (including Katherine until her final submission) and dramatic conflict, its final resolution is an affront to modern audiences reared in the aftermath of the feminist revolution, a reaction no doubt at odds with original audiences for whom the resolution would have seemed natural. In order to placate modern audiences, uneasy at viewing what is arguably a patriarchal play, Kate will often wink or grimace or otherwise use stage business to indicate to us that her submission is simply a ploy to let her husband win a contest and not a real conversion to traditional roles.

With respect to biography, I would deny that there is any such thing as a definitive biography that simply depends on accumulating "fact." Any biography depends on the "knowing subject," that is, the biographer and his or her social location within a society. In addition, it will depend upon the assumptions of a society that are shared by a biographer. One does not want to be too mechanical about this because whatever the cultures, subcultures, and societies we live in, we do not just reflect outer influences. We do have some space in which to construct our personal selves and even, to some degree, to choose which social influences we will allow to influence our individual persona. However, no individual represents an inner individual self apart from his or her social location and society and epoch.

Thus, we must expect that prominent figures will always attract numerous biographers at one time and over periods of time. Perhaps Jesus of Nazareth is a prime example of this. Each generation of scholars produces a different portrait of Christ. The zealot revolutionary patriot of the 1960s, in tune with the spirit of that decade, has disappeared.[3] Nor is it a surprise that numerous studies make much of Jesus' favourable treatment of women, a topic that drew little interest before the recent great changes in women's status.[4]

Such ideas may dismay some readers who still hope that one good book will "sum up" once and for all a particular individual. After all, such a notion appeals to most of us who wish for stability and finality and assurance. However, my own experience is that when we come to a conclusion that we have read a "definitive" biography, we have been seduced by the craft of the biographer. My own work on E.F. Wilson demonstrates that even a lesser-known historical figure can inspire rather different portraits, depending on the social location and generation of the biographer.[5]

In addition to the effects of the sociology of knowledge on biography, there also has been the influence of postmodernism, which diminishes the sacrosanct distinction between "fact" and "fiction." Readers are directed to Hayden White's landmark volume, *Metahistory: The Historical Imagination in Nineteenth-Century Europe* (1973). Whether or not one is interested in nineteenth-century historiography is not the point, for White transcends the particular authors under discussion and shows that the narratives produced by historians and usually presented as uncontroversial scientific "facts" are, in truth, carefully designed constructs that employ literary devices usually reserved for fiction to achieve their effects. All historical writing is sustained by an argument and invariably political implications arise, even when the historical authors are themselves unaware of their use of literary artifice and political message.

The implications of such discussions are contained in Peter Novick's prize-winning *That Noble Dream: The 'Objectivity Question' and the American Historical Profession* (1988). The results of such analyses may be doubt, self-questioning, a lack of finality in analysis, in short, a certain ephemerality. The positive contribution will be the destruction of the author as god-like scientist and the proliferation of multiple perspectives.

David A. Nock teaches sociology at Lakehead University. He received his B.A. and M.A. from Carleton University (the latter from the Institute of Canadian Studies), and a Ph.D. at the University of Alberta's sociology department. Professor Nock has always been keenly interested in social history, historical sociology, and the interconnections between the two disciplines. His B.A., for example, was in history and sociology. He has published a number of articles dealing with E.F. Wilson (1844–1915), missionary, educator, and anthropologist, who once lived on a piece of property in Sault Ste. Marie, from 1874 to 1893, next to where David Nock lived in the 1960s. This interest resulted in his book *A Victorian Missionary and Canadian Indian Policy* (Waterloo: Wilfrid Laurier University Press, 1988), which comprises a partial biography of Wilson. Nock has published other articles dealing with Anglican bishops, the sociology of religion, and the intellectual history of Canadian sociology, to name a few areas. He remains convinced that theories and narratives cannot be understood from their formal content alone but must be analyzed in terms of the motives and social position of the authors. Nock is an active tournament chess player. In chess there are numerous choices to be made, many of them quite different but of equal value. The choice depends on the style of the player (active, passive, tactical, strategic, a preference for end-games rather than middle-games). Nock compares this pluralism of choices dependent upon personal style to the many choices of theme and selection of "fact" facing the historian and biographer. The choice of opening moves tends to be greatly influenced by the decade in which the player/historian/biographer lives. Game strategy tends to be a compromise between vogue and personal style.

Notes

1 Barry Barnes, *Interests and the Growth of Knowledge* (London: Routledge and Kegan Paul, 1977), 1–2.
2 Barnes, *Interests*, 10.
3 S.G.F. Brandon, *Jesus and the Zealots* (Manchester: Manchester University Press, 1967).
4 Tom Harpur, *Harpur's Heaven and Hell* (Toronto: Oxford University Press, 1983).
5 See Nock, "E.F. Wilson and the Social Construction of Text," in David Nock, *Star Wars* (Halifax: Fernwood, 1993 [pending]).

Chapter 4

Living the Biography, or,
the Importance of Being Norman

Ken Mitchell

As a professor of literature, my perspective is necessarily a literary one. I believe that to reach the heart of biographical "truth," one must rely less on the dictates of historical accuracy and documentary truth and more on a comprehension of character, which is preceded by a fusion of writer and subject, perhaps an immersion in the subject's historical experience.

Of course we can not require the biographer of Lenin to lead a Soviet revolution, and what point would there be in reliving the lives of most of our century's most popular biographical subjects, most of them very self-destructive people?

Let me speak from personal experience about my work on Dr. Norman Bethune, the subject of a biographical drama I have performed in theatres from Beijing to Edinburgh to Bethune's birthplace of Gravenhurst, Ontario. I first became interested in Bethune on reading *The Scalpel, The Sword*, a biography by Ted Allan and Sidney Gordon. In spite of the Marxist overtones of the book, a kind of political hagiography, Bethune's character – rebellious, quixotic, dynamic, and vital – emerges strongly. And although Bethune has become a latter-day Canadian hero, at first glance he seems very un-Canadian – an alcoholic playboy, a philanderer, and a very egotistical man.

Many writers are attracted to Bethune. Since 1953, when *The Scalpel, The Sword* was published in New York, a multitude of biographies have appeared, mainly in Chinese and English. He was the model for Hugh MacLennan's Jerome Martel in *The Watch That Ends the Night*. There have been six films, including the Phillip Borsos epic released in the fall of 1990, starring Donald Sutherland. To my knowledge, there are four stage plays, including my own, *Gone the Burning Sun*.

So why would I bother adding to the pile? There are two reasons. First, the existing biographical information is insufficient and often historically inaccurate. The official Chinese version, for example, refuses to acknowledge Bethune's legendary consumption of alcohol or his flagrant womanizing.

Secondly, I discovered that he was a relative of mine. This happened a

Ken Mitchell as Norman Bethune in Mitchell's Gone the Burning Sun: *"No laddie — medical inventions will not make you rich. Unless you're a psychiatrist. Or a plastic surgeon." (Courtesy Ken Mitchell.)*

few years ago in Edinburgh when I was researching my family's genealogy. My great-great-great-grandmother was one of seven sisters belonging to a celebrated family called Beaton from the Isle of Mull. Along with the Bethunes and Beatouns, they constituted a clan of hereditary physicians to the Lords of the Isles. Their role in Scottish history is astonishing, going back to the tenth century and presumably to the founding of Iona. The most common explanation of their name is that they arrived originally as healers from a great monastery at Bethune, in present-day Belgium.

But their medical lore, as I discovered in ancient documents in the Scottish National Library, was Persian and Arabic. This knowledge was passed on through the Beaton clan for centuries, long before universities existed in Britain.

It was important for me to discover in Bethune's heritage this base of Christian humanism, which he may not have known, for it is barely mentioned in existing biographies. He did know that one of his clan was David Cardinal Beaton, the controversial primate of Scotland. Norman's great-great-grandfather, John Bethune (christened Beaton), established the Church of Scotland in British North America in the eighteenth century. Norman's grandfather, also Norman, went back to Scotland to become a surgeon and, almost incidentally, one of the volunteer doctors memorialized by Jean-Henri Dunant in *Memories of Solferino*, the book that led to the founding of the International Red Cross.

But even more productive than this assembly of data were my adventures in Skye and Mull, searching out the Beaton roots to Iona and beyond, taking Norman with me into the past (and discovering along the way that the name Macbeth derives from the same family).

While working in Scotland, I was given the opportunity to go to China the following year with my family as a university teacher. I leaped at this chance to travel to the land that had made Dr. Bethune's reputation, to the exotic continent where my distant cousin became a martyred hero of the Chinese Revolution. I believe that had Mao Tse Tung not eulogized Bethune upon his death in November 1939, and had billions of Chinese not memorized his essay "In Praise of Norman Bethune," none of this historical attention would have occurred. Norman Bethune would have died an ignominious death, a rebel and a misfit, a reject of Canada's medical establishment.

By 1937, he had turned his back on Canada, blacklisted as a Communist agitator by his own profession. Even as a Communist hero, he had been sent home in disgrace from Spain, where he had single-handedly invented battlefield blood transfusions. In China, he met destiny.

And in China, where I followed in his footsteps, I had the uncanny experience of being pointed out on the streets as Bethune himself. As I grew bald, there developed a physical resemblance. (In fact, I look more like V.I. Lenin, but Chinese iconography being what it is, or was, Bethune's image there had come to resemble Lenin's.)

It hit me with the power of a lightning bolt, on the streets of Nanjing. I would write a one-man play about Norman Bethune! And perhaps – since he had been such a popular hero – I could perform it around China. I travelled into the Chinese countryside, writing the first draft of my play during a two-week train journey to Kunming.

If Bethune had discovered himself in China, my task was to repeat the experience, to travel and act like Bethune. Needless to say, I met many friends. I fell in love with China. And I came away burdened not so much with facts and statistics and place names, as with historical experience – the heart of the story.

It's fair to say that I have tried, with my limited resources, to become Norman Bethune, to think the way he must have thought – to merge into the character sufficiently to write a drama from the inside, as it were, yet to maintain historical accuracy. The result was a prize-winning script that seems to have captured this complex character in the way that a conventional docu-drama never could. The experience has not only gone into the script, of course, but, since I took up acting the role about three years ago, into the performance as well.

In the end, who could claim that this creative interpretation of Bethune's life is not more truthful than the photographic and documentary memorabilia of archival documents?

Norman died in China of septicemia from an infected cut on his index finger. His distant cousin from Regina cut his finger on a broken glass during rehearsal for the play in May 1991 in Edinburgh, but survived to perform the play that evening, and many times thereafter.

Ken Mitchell's performance of *Gone the Burning Sun*, on Saturday, 4 May 1991, provided a fitting conclusion to the conference on biography at the Centre of Canadian Studies. In addition to teaching English literature at the University of Regina, Professor Mitchell is the author of three novels, *Wandering Rafferty* (1972), *The Meadowlark Connection: A Saskatchewan Thriller* (1975), and *The Con Man* (1979); a story collection, *Everybody Gets Something Here*

(1977); and several plays based on prairie characters, including Tommy Douglas, Nicholas Flood Davin, and Tom Sukanen, the only man to build an ocean-going ship in the middle of the prairies. His acclaimed western musical, *Cruel Tears*, has been performed in many theatres across Canada. In 1985 an anthology of his collected works, *Ken Mitchell Country*, was published. He also published a critical study of Sinclair Ross (1981) and wrote the script for the film *The Hounds of Notre Dame* (1980). In 1987 he performed his Bethune play in China, and more recently he took the play to Bethune's birthplace in Gravenhurst. His most recent publication is *Rebels in Time* (NeWest Press), a collection of three plays, including *Gone the Burning Sun*.

.

Part 3

Biographer and Subject: Liaisons Dangereuses

Chapter 5

Aimee Semple McPherson: Fantasizing the Fantasizer? Telling the Tale of a Tale-Teller

Janice Dickin McGinnis

It's very dangerous to believe what people say. I haven't for years.

– Jane Marple

Problem

The task of the biographer is very much like that of the detective. You know that something has occurred; your job is to straighten out exactly who did what and, more importantly, why. Sometimes there are only a few clues and you must construct scenarios that both accommodate them and utilize them in building your case. Sometimes there are a lot of clues and that can be a bigger challenge.

Whatever the situation, any biographer looking for "truth" would be well-served by possession of the quiet qualities of Agatha Christie's spinster, Jane Marple: nosiness, patience, shrewdness, and absolute ruthlessness when it comes to the final judgment. You have to get inside your subject's life but you must also be able to get out. In the end you must have the strength of character to abandon her to fate a second time.

I cannot imagine that any biographer can manage to remain neutral about her subject. That would be like managing to remain neutral about a room-mate. Attracted to her or not, you still care where she hangs out her stockings. Most of the time I like my subject. Always I find her fascinating. Sometimes I want to give her a good smack. And she has moved me to anger as well as to tears.

If I have a prayer in all this, it is that I be granted Miss Marple's ruthlessness. I need this because I am faced with a woman who had little understanding of herself and who told tales when she meant to tell truth. I have cause to believe that, in the telling, these tales turned to truth for her. To challenge her, then, is to challenge the basis of the life's work she sacrificed herself for, a life's work backed by a belief that what she did was always for the good of others, although, in fact, it sometimes was for the good of nobody, least of all herself.

I offer the following as an example of the type of problem I face as the biographer of a woman about whom so much has been said by so many. I deal here with only a few weeks, but certainly the most famous few weeks, of her life. None of the accounts, official or unofficial, is to be taken at face value, and in the final analysis, neither is my own.

A Tale

In the late afternoon of 18 May 1926, Sister Aimee Semple McPherson, pastor of the Angelus Temple in Los Angeles and founder of what was developing into the world-wide Foursquare Gospel Movement, struck out to sea off Ocean Park Beach with her customary strong crawl and disappeared. Despite around-the-clock water-side vigils by members of her flock and despite the offer of a reward, which spurred two men to risk unto death their own lives, no body was recovered. Aimee's mother and partner, Minnie Kennedy, speculated that God might have taken all of Aimee home, that no body would ever wash ashore.

Minnie was tough and strong and stolid. She continued to give interviews and preach sermons and pose for photographs but she was as close to the breaking-point as women like Minnie ever get. Rolf Kennedy McPherson, age thirteen, Aimee's son by her second husband, was brought into town from the Winters, California, ranch where he usually boarded to take his role in the family pageant of grief. His sixteen-year-old sister, Roberta Star Semple, the posthumous child of Aimee's first husband, looked wanly from the front pages as she felt the mantle of succession enfolding her shoulders. She would later say she spent this period of her life sitting on the cellar stairs, seeking peace.

Aimee's body did eventually reappear, walking in off the desert to Agua Prieta, Mexico, at 1 a.m. on the morning of 23 June. She said that she had escaped from kidnappers. She said that she had, that day, walked twenty miles across the desert. She collapsed but exhibited no marked thirst. She was not sunburnt. Her shoes were not scuffed, "New Era" still clearly visible on the heel. Soon tire tracks would be discovered stopping and then turning around just past Agua Prieta. At that point appeared shoe prints with "New Era" clearly visible on the heel.

Minnie, stunned but as stolid as ever, brought the children to Douglas, Arizona, where Aimee lay in a hospital bed. The Los Angeles chief of detectives and a district attorney officer came with them. Minnie leaned over to whisper in Aimee's ear. The press would later report that her words were "Don't say anything!" Roberta says her grandmother asked that ageless maternal question, "Did they rape you?"

The press noted that there was no outpouring of familial emotion. The news photos show poses much like the countless other poses members of the family had struck and would continue to strike before the flash cameras over the years. Minnie, Rolf, Roberta – all smile thinly and politely, accepting this as part of their jobs. It is Aimee who usually sparkles before the camera, but somewhere between Ocean Park and Agua Prieta, the sparkle had smouldered down deep and left behind it a haunted, feral stare. It would not be the last photo in which Aimee would be caught looking like she was not living inside her body.

Aimee returned to the City of the Angels, on 26 June, exactly forty days after her disappearance. Thirty thousand people came to the railway station to greet her. "I am so happy!" she said, just before being placed in a flower-bedecked chair and carried above a bouquet-bearing crowd to a bloom-covered motorcar. Her explanation of her absence was a highly romantic tale of abduction and escape – complete with chloroform, white slavers, threats of violence, ransom notes, and, in the end, a personal test in which good triumphed over evil. The only thing missing to make this into the quintessential princess story was Prince Charming. Aimee, as always, depended upon herself to find a way through the flames.

Briefly, Aimee described her ordeal as follows. She was called out of the water to bless a sick child. As she leaned into the car to see the babe supposedly held in its mother's arms, Aimee was drugged, pushed, and covered with a blanket. She was provided with clothes: a simple sun dress and her own expensive brand of lingerie. She was tortured until she provided convincing details for the ransom notes being sent to Minnie. She was moved from one unknown location to another. And finally, late that last morning, left alone even by "Rose" (her female keeper), Aimee wriggled her body from the cot and across the floor to a discarded tin can. She later would demonstrate for the press how she had managed to cut the bonds which held her hands behind her back, freeing her for her ordeal in the wilderness, sans guide, sans water, sans shelter. It was a miracle she survived.

Doubts

There are, however, at least two problems with accepting Aimee's tale as the truth. One problem has to do with lack of corroboration of and very real flaws in her account of her whereabouts, and the other with evidence pointing to quite another tale altogether.

At the very least, corroboration of Aimee's story required the location of her last holding-place. Despite her clear description, searches involving herself and others over an extensive expanse of desert failed to locate the shack in question. It is true that there was some hard evidence in terms of the ransom notes in Minnie's possession, but they would soon find a more comfortable niche in an alternate theory.

And what of the kidnappers? A little later there would be phone calls and visits and identifications but this would all turn out to be part of a shakedown organized through a blind lawyer soon to die mysteriously in

Aimee Semple McPherson, 26 June 1926, upon her triumphant return to Los Angeles after forty days in the desert. (Courtesy United Press International and L. Thomas, The Vanishing Evangelist *[New York: Viking, 1959].)*

a motor accident. Other people, without fraudulent intentions, would report having seen suspicious characters in Aimee's vicinity at relevant times but nothing ever came of this information. It seemed that the abductors had appeared, failed in their fearful business, and disappeared, without a trace.

The same could not be said for the "New Era" tracks in the desert sand. They had, in fact, been mapped and published on the front pages of the nation's newspapers. There were also various and several reports that a woman in dark glasses and cloche hat had been seen in a blue Chrysler coupe at various California locations during Aimee's absence. The car was driven by a man police thought to be Kenneth Ormiston, formerly radio engineer for KFSG, Kalling Four Square Gospel, the Temple's radio station.

Faced with a scandal that could destroy their life's work, Aimee and Minnie expressed their desire for a criminal investigation to uncover more clues, to find the kidnappers, and to put to rest the rising accusations against Aimee's character that threatened to drag the Temple to doom. Instead, the official investigation would uncover more witnesses and even some "hard" evidence – a "little blue trunk" full of Aimee's clothes and a grocery list in Aimee's writing found outside what the press termed "the Love Nest in Carmel," California, where Ormiston had stayed for several days with a woman who took care not to be seen – that pointed to willing participation on Aimee's part in her own disappearance.

For a variety of reasons, not the least of which was the fact that a grand juror took the grocery list with her to the washroom and apparently flushed it out to sea, charges of corruption of public morals, obstruction of justice, and conspiracy to manufacture evidence were dismissed against Aimee and Minnie and Ormiston. Aimee collapsed in the courtroom but the next day left town on a Vindication Tour, joking as she bid farewell to the reporters at the station about her luggage, a "little blue trunk."

Difficulties

There are two obvious difficulties with the way I have laid out the tale above, and there is no way I can correct either without making the other worse. The first is that there are too many details; the second is that I leave too many details out. For example, there is the fact that Ormiston turns himself in to the police, who let him go and then want him back. After Ormiston does show up again to swear an affidavit more notable for chivalry than truthfulness, he is once again allowed to disappear without a

trace; he does not even turn up for the divorce proceedings brought against
him by his wife, who seems, all in all, a thoroughly nice person, if we are
to believe her press.

There is also Lorraine Wiseman, who says she is the woman who was
with Ormiston at Carmel (or maybe it was her sister, Miss X?), with whom
Aimee spends time comparing hairstyles and handwriting and who in the
end turns out to be an ex-inmate of an insane asylum with a history of
attention-getting behaviours. I have also left out Minnie's growing suspicion that Aimee has not told her all, and have not mentioned Aimee's
(psychosomatic?) illnesses and uncharacteristic anti-Catholic accusations
from the pulpit against representatives of the police department and district attorney's office. I have not even tried to explain how it is that the
prosecutor goes to jail. (Aimee visits him in San Quentin in 1931 while on
honeymoon with her third husband.) Oh yes, and did I mention the judge
who faced an impeachment trial for things he allegedly did for Aimee?

And there is much, much more. This is the most thoroughly documented period of Aimee's life. The story was on the front pages of the
world's newspapers; articles and tracts and books appeared at the time
and would continue to appear over the years; there exist over 2,000 pages
of court documents; and there are newsreels and interviews and sermons.
And no one made much pretense to neutrality on this one: you were on
one side or you were on the other. Either she was kidnapped or she
disappeared. On a hot afternoon, more than sixty years later, in an apartment across from Central Park, New York, her daughter and I found
ourselves reduced to the same choices. Roberta referred to Aimee's "kidnapping"; I replied using the term "disappearance." Neither of us challenged the other.

Roberta is, despite her very public differences with Aimee, very protective of her mother. People who were protective – or at least understanding – of Aimee in 1926 chose the "kidnapping" side. Not to do so was to
play into the hands of enemies. The clear alternative was that she had run
off with her lover. Accusations of illicit sex are still capable of bringing
evangelists down. In Aimee's era, the danger was even more present. She
was a woman in a man's job, something she herself frequently referred to.
Moreover, she was a sexually attractive woman and had taken measures,
for whatever reasons, over the preceding couple of years to make herself
even more sexually attractive. Intentionally or not, she used that sexual
power to spread the word of the Lord. But in doing so, she directly challenged stereotypes of more than one kind.

She may not have been the only woman in the 1920s whose activities came into conflict with the Mary/Eve dichotomy of female life-plan opportunities but her situation must surely have been one of the most complex. This is because everything – her temple, her family, her self-definition, her work – depended upon her being a "virgin"; there was no way she could admit to any activities, or even thoughts, that might win for her the appellation of whore. Furthermore, I believe she personally needed belief in her own "virginity" in order to go on; I believe she believed the kidnapping tale the instant she made it up.

Explanations

Aimee Semple McPherson had not been raised in circumstances favouring adherence to twentieth-century liberal and/or feminist definitions of truth. Hers was a world where women lived one life while professing another, where explanations did more to prescribe than to explain. Sense was made up of something other than facts. In addition to the schizophrenia inspired by her era's approach to the female condition, two other influences would have an impact on Aimee's standards of "proof": she was raised in a religious setting that stressed faith over observation and she had a power of intuition so phenomenal that it must have made use of the intellect seem both poky and unproductive and the hand of God seem near.

The last decade or so has seen a considerable increase in scholarship on the lives of women and a fundamental shift in how our foremothers are perceived. Despite the sense of power and release this may give us, we are not allowed to read backwards, to say they must really, somehow, have known what was going on. I have no doubt that some did. I have no doubt that many more were inflicted by a feeling of dis-ease, a dissatisfaction with the way things seemed to turn out for them. I also have no doubt that there were ways to manoeuvre and to achieve personal success within the prevailing belief structure and that Aimee's life provides a blueprint for such manoeuvring.

Aimee was born near the end of the Victorian era, on the threshold of the 1890s, a decade celebrated for its gaiety elsewhere but surely not in Salford, Ontario. She was the fourth child of a prosperous farmer of fifty-nine and the only child of a Salvation Army girl of nineteen. According to Aimee, she was born in answer to Minnie's prayer for a girl child who would grow up to be a preacher. Aimee describes herself as beginning to preach by age four, to the farm's animals, a milk pail her pulpit. Surely she did not expect to make conversions of dumb animals. That would have been blasphemous. Clearly, consciously or not (probably not), Aimee's agenda had other underpinnings. An ability to read and hold an audience would stay with her all her life. That she recognized this much about herself is apparent from her admission that she felt dolls too tame an audience.

By her own description, Aimee was vital, athletic, flirtatious, highly intelligent and arrogant about the fact, mildly rebellious, and spoilt. One writer, Nancy Barr Mavity, has described Aimee's childhood as that of a "flamingo in a chicken coop." Roberta agrees with this but I think it is wrong. Aimee was always an exotic, but one of her strengths lay in knowing how to push to the edges of things, how to take charge but not make change, how to stand out but not be different.

Indications are that she did well within the social structure in Salford and Ingersoll. Her wedding at age seventeen to itinerant evangelist Robert Semple seems to have been well attended. It was only later that the community found itself unable to accommodate with grace the success of its local gal made good. For her own part, Aimee would continue to sentimentalize her childhood "back there on the little Canadian farm" right up to and including the night she succumbed to an overdose of sleeping pills in Oakland, California, in September 1944.

Aimee's strength would lie, always, in grasping quickly what was going on and figuring out how best to turn things to her advantage. Roberta names as Aimee's childhood heroine Grace Darling, the daughter of a lighthouse keeper on the Farne Islands off the coast of England, who, according to the several tellings of the tale, talked her reluctant father into joining her in a lifeboat during a particularly vicious North Sea storm to evacuate survivors from the wreck of the *Forfarshire*. Grace, who surely must have been a strapping country girl with considerable grasp of boat lore (else her father must have been foolhardy to the point of idiocy), is generally presented as a gentle (though "well-made") Victorian maiden with more sympathy than skill, more heart than sense. No wonder Aimee came so easily to terms with double-talk.

Ambivalence about the true basis of female success also lay closer to home. In her teens Aimee won a popularity contest, but one that really involved selling the most newspaper subscriptions in a given area in a given time. No doubt "popularity" had something to do with it, but I would guess that the exercise gave Aimee an opportunity to hone her fine gift of salesmanship and that, had the contest been for young men rather than women, it would have been called something else.

Fundamental acceptance of faith as more important than facts in the formulation of truth also must have had an early and effective influence on

Aimee. She was raised in a world where the Red Sea literally parted, where God was in Heaven and He had put us on earth and that was that. This did not mean that she did not challenge church doctrine. At age sixteen, she wrote letters to the Montreal *Family Herald* expressing troubled thoughts spurred by the teaching of evolution by her high school science teacher. Throughout her life, she would cite this struggle as one of the great turning-points in her youth. The other was her conversion to pentecostalism by Robert Semple. She was not the first young girl, nor will she be the last, to be confused about the source of her ecstasy. Semple died within two years of their marriage, leaving her alone and pregnant in China. He was the love of her life but she thought of him as her saviour. Going home to God always, always, involved going home to Robert.

If fundamentalist teaching makes it kosher to believe in miracles, an intuitive mind makes it easy. Roberta gave as one reason why Harold McPherson left and eventually divorced Aimee the fact that he, solid and successful green grocer that he would become, could no longer stand her miracles. When a problem presented itself, Minnie would counsel, "Let's pray on it," and sure enough these two kneeling, concentrating, resourceful women would come up with something. Hard work, phenomenal strength, native ability, considerable thought concealed as prayer, and intuition identified as divine revelation would see these women through many trials together.

Tale-Telling

How does a biographer see her way through all this? Or, to go ahead and put a fine point on it, how do I see my way through all this? I must admit that on occasion I am tempted to turn to prayer. However, on sober second thought (not entirely unrelated to the fact that I am unclear as to what my course should be were I to receive indications of divine guidance), I have decided instead to settle on confession.

The text of the confession involves first an assessment of myself (a late twentieth-century feminist, agnostic from a religious background, brainwashed into standards of proof by the legal profession and standards of academic respectability by the historical profession) and then an admission that any retelling of Aimee's tale by me cannot escape either the faults or the strengths of the person just described. Anything she writes will bear the mark of her era, of her upbringing, of her personality, just as much as did anything Aimee ever wrote.

I became acutely aware of this one day as I was musing over an image I had of Roberta sitting on the cellar stairs during her mother's disappearance. I realized I had a very clear picture of a little girl, her back against a closed door, her knees drawn up, her dress tucked modestly under. Not only could I see her but I could see what she saw: sloped green ceiling, narrow black treads, the bottom three steps in darkness. I knew why they were dark: that is where they angled left and ended in another closed door.

I have not yet seen the inside of the parsonage of the Angelus Temple. The stairwell in my mind is one that ran between the back kitchen and the upstairs hall in a rectory I lived in as a child. As a matter of fact, I have a lot of stairwell memories, fantasies, and fears that might be of some interest should someone want to plunder my life for copy someday. But the point is that I have to fight like hell to be able to bring my own understanding and my own power of criticism to Aimee's and Roberta's and Minnie's stories, all the while keeping in check an urge to empathize.

I think I can do this and I think this is what I have over Aimee. I understand better than she did where one thing ends and another begins. Maybe all this means is that, for whatever reason, I have assimilated traditional taxonomy better than she did or could. I am certainly better educated than she was, although Roberta says her mother read tirelessly and her sermons indicate an exceptional grasp of popular culture as well as an ability to confront some fairly difficult philosophical arguments. I am also fundamentally more intellectual than was Aimee – not smarter, just more intellectual.

Hers was an intelligence that leapt from association to association and, I think, was not one that easily accommodated intellectual standards of truth. Truth was what made sense within the tale you were telling, and tales were about something other than truth – they were about lessons, lessons that gave you insight into how the world worked, how things fit together. If little truths did not fit under the big "real" truth, then they had to be cut or dropped to satisfy the need at hand.

This is of course precisely the process I am currently following in "writing Aimee." It is not possible, nor would it be desirable, to record every known detail of her phrenetically pursued existence. Telling everything known means that you will also have to leave out everything "not known." I have used the disappearance here as an extreme example of something I will probably never know the whole truth about but something I must nevertheless address. Just because the truth was not part of

Aimee's tale does not mean I can leave it out of mine. I must, like Miss Marple, pursue the truth as ruthlessly as I can.

I end with a story: Roberta took me out to lunch on the same hot day that we had avoided trading thoughts on the disappearance/kidnapping (or kidnapping/disappearance?). We walked back to her apartment, following a large black woman who was wearing a white dress with red polka dots. Roberta asked, "Do you remember in *This Is That* when my mother talks about the bull chasing her when she is wearing a dress with red moons on it? It took me years to realize those moons were polka dots. That's my mother, polka dots were always moons!"

I want to celebrate Aimee's moons but I want to write about her polka dots, too.

Janice Dickin McGinnis, a lawyer and historian by training, was granted a Canada Research Fellowship by the Social Sciences and Humanities Research Council of Canada in 1988, partly to pursue work on the legal aspects of the life and works of the Canadian-American evangelist Aimee Semple McPherson. This work has since expanded into a full-scale biography, now being written. Although the piece in this publication is the first work she has published on the topic, she has made a number of presentations, in part to help her consider how to attack this complex subject. In order to take the time necessary to get to know her subject fully, McGinnis has continued in the interim to publish and speak in the area of socio-legal problems, often working from a historical basis. Such work has included a recent comparison of venereal disease and AIDS, as well as a criticism of the feminist anti-pornography position. In addition to her work on Sister McPherson, Professor McGinnis is currently working to republish three "lost" works by women: letters home by the first doctor in Alberta's Peace River district; a selection from the memoirs and novels of a Norwegian pioneer; and a series of letters sent to a psychologist by an educated woman forced to support herself and her son through menial labour. She is also engaged in collaboration with other scholars, notably in a project to use legal case reports as sources for the history of women. Professor McGinnis teaches in both the Canadian Studies and the Law and Society programs in the Faculty of General Studies at the University of Calgary.

Note

There exist thousands of words written by Aimee Semple McPherson and millions written about her. The best general biography is Lately Thomas, *Storming Heaven: The Lives and Turmoils of Minnie Kennedy and Aimee Semple McPherson* (New York: William Morrow and Co., 1970). The two most reliable sources for the forty lost days are Lately Thomas, *The Vanishing Evangelist* (New York: Viking Press, 1959), and Nancy Barr Mavity, *Sister Aimee* (New York: Doubleday, 1931). By and large, the other few available "non-political" accounts use these biographies as their sources. There are also available accounts of Aimee's life that have a distinctly political edge. Representative of the anti-Aimee faction is Rev. John D. Goben, *Aimee: The Gospel Gold Digger* (New York: Peoples' Publishing Co., 1932). Representative of the pro-Aimee side is Raymond L. Cox, *The Verdict Is In* (Los Angeles: Research Publishers, 1983). The place to start with Aimee's own writings is *This Is That, Personal Experiences, Sermons and Worship* (Los Angeles: Echo Park Evangelistic Association, 1923). Copies of her newsletter, *The Bridal Call*, reside in several libraries, and notes from her sermons as well as other materials are in the Billy Graham Archives in Wheaton, Illinois. Newspapers offer a vast amount of material. Not only did the Los Angeles papers follow her slavishly throughout her career but she was reported in the press in the locales where she held her numerous missions: in the United States, Canada, Australia, and England. Since she frequently travelled the world, there no doubt exist other references I will never be able to track down. Contemporary periodicals as well as memoirs of contemporaries are useful for establishing her reputation if not always for establishing fact. Aside from the material in Wheaton, there is material at the Temple that I may or may not be able to get into. There is also some material on her early life in repositories in the Salford area. It seems likely that Roberta Salter will donate her own personal papers to Radcliffe College. Since so many people had contact with Aimee in her busy life, there are no doubt numerous references to her in numerous private papers that I may or may not find it possible to track down and go through. There are thousands of pages of court documents. The majority of these pertain to the disappearance and its aftermath and to Roberta's successful slander suit (really aimed at her mother) against a Temple official. There are other personal suits of this nature plus legal fights over wills, breach of promise, breach of contract, and an assortment of other matters. As for interview candidates, Roberta Salter is the best living witness with regard to her mother's earlier years in Los Angeles and even before. She has set limits on what she will answer. I have yet to get an interview with Aimee's son, Rolf McPherson, but I expect this would tell me more about the Temple than about Aimee. Many people came into contact with Aimee, but so far I have little confidence that any will be able to give me a better view into her soul than Roberta has. It could not have been easy to get behind Aimee's glittering presence. I am not sure that I will in the end, either, but it won't be for lack of available material.

Chapter 6

Galt versus Byron:
"I" and "Other" in Biography

Anna Makolkin

> Again, consider the whole class of Fictitious Narratives; from the highest
> category of epic or dramatic Poetry, in Shakespeare and Homer, down to
> the lowest of froth – Prose in the fashionable novel. What are all these but
> so many mimic Biographies?
>
> – Thomas Carlyle, "Biography," 68

> Men are guided in their conduct above all by their beliefs and by the
> customs that are the consequence of those beliefs. These beliefs and cus-
> toms regulate the smallest acts of our existence and the most independent
> spirit cannot escape their influence.
>
> – Gustave Le Bon, *The Crowd*, 146

The Victorian era was not only the epoch of romantic idealism, fervent
nationalism, and the rise of poetry. It was also the time when the cult of a
poet became a turning-point in the history of Victorian biography and in
the history of biographical discourse. One such landmark of biography
was John Galt's *The Life of Lord Byron*, written in 1830, shortly after the
publication of Thomas Moore's famous *Letters and Journals of Lord Byron*.[1]
Despite the fact that John Galt had an established literary and public reputation when he embarked on the interpretation of Byron's life, his biography and his name are at the periphery of history and of Byron scholarship.

John Galt's biographer, Ian Gordon, shed some light on this literary
and historical paradox: "Two of Byron's old associates – Thomas Moore
and J.C. Hobhouse – had already published a great deal of Byron's memo-

rabilia, and, almost considering they had exclusive rights on him, openly resented Galt's intrusion.[2]

Galt's "intrusion" was the work of a mature author who had already been on the literary stage for eighteen years, having published, among numerous works, the two-volume biography of Benjamin West (1820); *Annals of the Parish* (1821); *Sir Andrew Wylie*, three volumes (1822); and *The Entail*, three volumes (1822). *The Life of Lord Byron* was well received in his time. After its publication, Galt was asked to write a series of short biographies of actors, which won the approval of even the belligerent *Monthly Review*.

Galt's biography of Byron is an interesting psychological document, for it shows the two famous Victorians in conflict. In his biography, Galt calls himself "a builder of a monument" to a poet. Galt was intrigued by Byron, the poet and person against whom "the spirit of the times ran strong" and who provoked "vehement and continual controversy."[3] Byron, the rebel and "revolutionary romantic," intrigued Galt, who himself was no less

John Galt (1779–1839), friend, confidant, and envious biographer of Lord Byron; also founder of Guelph, Ontario (1827). (Reproduced in John Galt, The Autobiography *[London: Henry Cochrane & McCrone, 1833].)*

controversial and torn between his multiple loyalties, and who, as Lord Byron used to tell him in the old days, "had not deference enough."[4]

Galt's biography of Byron created a sensation in his time. Three editions were published and 10,000 copies sold promptly in 1830. It was bitterly attacked and enthusiastically praised.[5] According to Ian Gordon, Christopher North called Galt's view of Byron "ludicrous" and expressed the then predominant indignant opinion of the British aristocracy that "people in the humble condition of Mr. Galt" should not dare to write about an aristocrat, even one like Byron so disliked by his fellow artistocrats.

Galt was aware of his Victorian trespassings, and he also knew how to win the "disposition of the world," as he called the influential Victorians and reading public of his day. Exercising his pen in a popular genre, he had to address first the most popular myths cherished by the popular reader, namely nationalistic mythology. Addressing his reader, Galt tried to appeal simultaneously to the two national groups, the English and the Scots, engaged in a centuries-old rivalry about the stature of their respective heroes: "To those who are acquainted with the Scottish character, it is unnecessary to suggest how very probable it is that Mrs. Byron [poet's mother] and her associates were addicted to the oral legends of the district and of her ancestors, and that the early fancy of the poet was nourished with the shadowy descriptions of the tales o' the olden time."[6]

The semantic scheme of the passage is the following:

```
Scottish  ← ← ← ←  oral legends  → → → →  Mrs. Byron
character              ↓                   Scottish
   ↓                   ↓                      ↓
   ↓ → → → → → → → →  poet  ← ← ← ← ← ← ← ←   ↓
```

"Mrs. Byron" and "Scottish character" mark the communication line between Galt and the Scottish national group. Galt cultivates ties between Byron, who was part Scottish, and the Scots. "Oral legends" accomplished what "Mrs. Byron" and "Scottish" could not, providing the complete bond between the poet, as a property of the group, and the group as a whole. Galt later acknowledges that there was little in Byron's poetry of the "melancholy and mourning of Ossian." Yet the biographer stresses that Byron, as well as Ossian, might have been "evidently influenced by some strong bias and congeniality of taste, to brood and cogitate on topics of the same character as those of that bard."[7] While "Ossian" and "oral legends" add to the set of nationalist allusions, Byron remains primarily an English national symbol.

The Scottish part of Byron's pedigree is a convenient point of transition from Galt's communication with one national group, the Scots, to his communication with the other, the English. While addressing the English, the biographer states that Byron's Scottish ancestry accounts for his negative personal traits:

> Descended of a distinguished family, counting among its ancestors the fated line of the Scottish kings, and reduced almost to extreme poverty, it

Lord Byron (1788-1824), poet and object of John Galt's biography. (Reproduced in John Galt, The Life of Lord Byron *[London: Henry Colburn and Richard Bentley, 1830].)*

> is highly probable, both from the violence of her temper, and the pride of blood, that Mrs. Byron would complain of the most mendicant condition to which she was reduced, especially so long as there was reason to fear that her son was not likely to succeed to the family estates and dignity.[8]

Byron's mother, with her "violent temper" and "distinguished ancestry," presents a unique opportunity both to please and to attack the Scots while simultaneously delighting the English. The dark side in Byron is presented as the quality of the "Other": "But still it is to his mother's traditions of her ancestors that I would ascribe the conception of the dark and guilty beings which he delighted to describe."[9]

In contrast, allusions to the English side of Byron's ancestry embody his positive qualities. The motif – Byron and the Scots – serves as a preamble to placing Byron among the English national heroes, such as Shakespeare and Milton:

> In his short career he has entitled himself to be ranked in the first class of the British poets for quantity alone.

> In the power, the originality, and the genius combined of that unexampled performance, Lord Byron has placed himself on an equality with Milton.[10]

Thus, Galt first places Byron between two national groups, Scots and English, and then gradually introduces Byron to his own group. The image of the poet undergoes a transformation, from descendant of Scottish kings to English national poet:

Scottish → → → Mrs. Byron   British → → → British poets
↓   Milton
↓   ↓
↓   ↓
↓   ↓
poet   Lord Byron

Byron's heroic image gradually evolves from a son of a Scottish woman with a violent temper to "Lord Byron," a member of the British aristocracy. Referring to Byron as "Lord," Galt appeals to the traditional societal respect for nobility and thus indirectly flatters the group ego. Galt does not distort but rather displaces the information freely. This displacement establishes contact between the biographer and his zero-degree biographee, the most unsophisticated reader whose spiritual livelihood is sustained by nationalistic mythology.[11]

The Victorian biographer also exploits the religious nostalgia of his contemporaries, who regard themselves as Christians. To please them Galt makes Byron a believer: "... for his Lordship again expressed how much the belief of the real appearance of Satan, to hear and obey the commands of God, added to his views of the grandeur and majesty of the Creator."[12] Galt places his subject within the Christian context, thereby returning the hero to an inimical environment.

In his efforts to "convert" Byron, Galt relies on sources that cannot be verified: "His Lordship said, 'I do not reject the doctrines of Christianity; I want only sufficient proofs of it, to take up the profession in earnest; and I do not believe myself to be so bad a Christian as many of them who preach against me with the greatest fury – many of whom I have never seen nor injured.' "[13]

To unite his hero with the group's Christian mythology, Galt introduces a different dichotomy. In place of the mythic structure known as Christian versus atheist, he suggests a degree of distinction within the Christian group and places Byron there:

$$
\begin{array}{lll}
& \rightarrow \rightarrow \rightarrow \rightarrow \rightarrow \rightarrow \rightarrow \rightarrow & \text{Christians devout} \\
& \uparrow \qquad\qquad\qquad \downarrow & \\
\text{Christian group} \rightarrow \rightarrow & & \text{Byron} \\
\downarrow & \qquad\qquad\qquad \downarrow & \\
& \rightarrow \rightarrow \rightarrow \rightarrow \rightarrow \rightarrow \rightarrow \rightarrow & \text{Christians non-devout}
\end{array}
$$

This new classification does not place Byron outside the mythic boundaries; the poet is no longer an atheist but rather a non-devout Christian among other Christians. Galt's strategy unites Byron and his group via the expected Christian mythology.

Further, the non-devout Christian is described as a hard-working individual whose "constant employment was writing, for which he used to sit up as late as two or three o'clock in the morning."[14] The biographer reconciles the national hero and the group through the Puritan work ethic and the common perception of Christianity. Galt ends the biography by stating that his subject's life was written "in order to determine how to organize the evidence to produce in their minds the effect he wants to produce."[15]

The preface is often the first moment of encounter with such a "preferred audience," and a biographer indirectly communicates to the readers his or her misgivings and narrative strategies, and implicitly establishes a safe discursive atmosphere. The dialogue between biographer and biographee reveals a censorial presence. The preface is the place where readers may be reminded of the complexity of biographical writing, as exemplified by Galt's preface to his *Life of Lord Byron*:

> My present task is one of *considerable difficulty*; but I have long had a notion that sometime or another it would fall to my lot to perform it. I approach it, therefore, *without apprehension*, entirely in consequence of having determined, to *my own satisfaction*, the manner in which the biography of so singular and so richly endowed a character as that of the late Lord Byron should be treated, but still with no small degree of diffidence; for there is a wide difference between determining a *rule* for oneself and producing, according to that rule, a work which shall *please the public*.[16]

The sign "please the public" is a direct appeal to the audience. With phrases such as "apprehension," "considerable difficulty," and "fallen lot," the passage is an example of a preliminary dialogue between biographer and biographee in which the author explores the reader's response. Among the audience that Galt wishes to please with his portrait of Byron there may be individuals who will not like Galt's description. The precautionary self-censorship or a dialogue with the unknown biographee provides the necessary comfort to a biographer who does not conceal his desire to "please the public."

Galt resumes direct communication with his imaginary opponent 195 pages later when he asks for approval of his description:

> The task just concluded may disappoint the expectations of some of my readers, but I would rather have said less than so much, could so little have been allowed; for I have never been able to reconcile to my notions of propriety, the exposure of domestic concerns which the world has no right claim to know, and can only urge the place of curiosity for desiring to see explained.[17]

Those readers whose approval Galt seeks and to whom he confides his difficulties in presenting Byron appear twice in the discourse: on pages 1 and 196. These moments provide evidence about the existence of a reader whose opinion Galt values and to whom he finds it necessary to apologize. Who is this unknown addressee? Galt explains to him or her his position on propriety, and this opinion seems to echo the style of the familiar obscenity acts. Perhaps the unidentified addressee is the imaginary censor, who assists the author in protecting the discourse against the real censor's arraignment.

The "victorious Other" is always a threat, a source of competing desire.[18] The biographical subject, a famous poet, presents no exception, for he is no less an enigma to a biographer than is a legendary hero. Like a fairy tale giant or mythical character, a biographical subject – a luminary – emanates such excessive forcefulness that it may impart to the biographer an inferiority complex. A biographer of a genius who was his personal friend may find himself in an even more difficult position. He may eventually ask, "What transforms a human being into a genius?"

Galt is in a situation similar to that of Moore – he enjoyed Byron's personal acquaintance. Galt defines a genius as a man "of particular quality, inborn and particular to the individual."[19] He considers genius of every kind a quality belonging to some "inner temperament," and that his subject possesses it. He accentuates the fact that his subject is a genius, but this does not prevent him from placing his own poetic efforts next to Byron's:

> On leaving England I began to write a poem in the Spenserian measure. It was called *The Unknown,* and was intended to describe, in narrating the voyages and adventures of a pilgrim, who had embarked for the Holy Land, the scenes I expected to visit. I was occasionally engaged in this composition during the passage with Lord Byron from Gibraltar to Malta, and he knew what I was about.[20]

Galt creates a suggestive semantic structure:

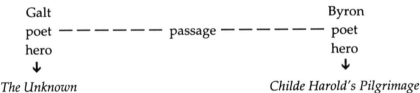

The biographees may come to daring conclusions, and Galt immediately corrects himself:

> In stating this, I beg to be distinctly understood, as in no way whatever intending to insinuate that this work had any influence on the composition of *Childe Harold's Pilgrimage,* which Lord Byron began to write in Albania; but it must be considered as something extraordinary, that the

two works should have been so similar in plan and in the structure of the verse. His lordship never saw my attempt that I know of nor did I his poem until it was printed.[21]

Following Strauss's decoding formula, the secret biographee may notice that the first statement is "corrected," in fact, by the statement that represents the continuation of the previous one.[22] Although Galt is begging "to be distinctly understood," he gives the impression of being willing to be misread. Placing *The Unknown* next to *Childe Harold's Pilgrimage,* Galt creates a new motif inside the familiar biographical motif, that is, his role in Byron's creative work.

Claiming that the two works were created independently, the biographer insinuates that he may possess the same "inner temperament" as his subject. The motif appeals to the biographer who may, thus, satisfy his own *exegi-monumentum syndrome*[23] or his desire to be remembered through the "Other," which is modestly checked in another statement: "It is needless to add, that beyond the plan and verse there was no other similarity between the two works; I wish there had been."[24]

The comparison between the two poets suggested by the signal "two works" reinforces the two previous passages and allusions. The hidden "Mozart-Salieri complex" may be detected between the lines, the wish of an unrecognized individual.

The coincidence of the two works symbolizes the encounter of two creative individuals – a biographer, a writer and poet, and his subject, a poet. The discursive conflict of interest alludes to the fragile barrier of objectivity when the known and the unknown poets face each other. The victorious "Other" and a lesser "I" – the two selves – confront each other in a genre that encourages exposure of the true self, and the attentive reader cannot fail to notice the biographer's "desire to be another." Biographers are torn between two opposite feelings towards their subject – "the most submissive reverence and the most intense malice," as Girard describes the conflict between self and other. The duty of biographers saves them from themselves and from embarrassment in front of the reading audience. After all, the readers may compare *The Unknown* with *Childe Harold's Pilgrimage* and pass their own judgment. Galt's corrective statements are signs of his acknowledgment of the readers' capacity to distinguish between the unknown poet and the known "scribbler."

This subtle conflict of the two "I"s would be brought into the open three years later when Galt would undermine the very monument to Byron that he himself had built. In his autobiography, published in 1833, Galt would write the following:

> When the Life of Byron was written, I entertained a higher opinion of his originality than I do now, for I am reduced to the alternative of considering him as one of the most extra-ordinary plagiarists in literature, unless it can be shown that he is the author of a four volume novel, from which the incidents, colouring, names, and characters, of his most renowned productions are derived.[25]

The readers may or may not be convinced that Galt is right, but they definitely sense the agony of the less famous "I" trying to cast a shadow upon the "victorious 'Other,'" an icon of the English and Scots.

Dr. Anna Makolkin obtained her Ph.D. in comparative literature at the University of Toronto in 1987. She is adjunct professor at York University and University of Toronto and a research fellow at the Centre of Russian and East European Studies at the University of Toronto. In 1989–90 she was Northrop Frye fellow at the University of Toronto, and she is a member of eight learned societies. Author of numerous scholarly publications, she pursues research interests in the area of theory of biography, discourse analysis, philosophy, and semiotics. Her most recent publications are *Name, Hero, Icon: Semiotics of Nationalism through Biography* (Berlin: Mouton de Gruyter, 1992); and *Semiotics of Misogyny: Chekhov's and Maugham's Short Stories* (New York: Edwin Mellen Press, 1992). Her current research project is *Expanding the Heroic Paradigm*. She plans to write a biography entitled *John Galt, the Intruder*.

Notes

1 John Galt, *The Life of Lord Byron* (London: Henry Colburn and Richard Bentley, 1830).
2 Ian Gordon, *John Galt* (Edinburgh, Oliver & Boyd, 1972), 95.
3 Galt, *The Life of Lord Byron*, 1.
4 Gordon, *John Galt*, 86.
5 Ibid., 95.
6 Galt, *The Life of Lord Byron*, 20.
7 Ibid., 20.
8 Ibid., 21.

9 Ibid., 21.

10 Ibid., 327.

11 The term "zero-degree biographee" was first used by Anna Makolkin in "On Poetics of Biography: Transformations in Some Biographies of Byron and Pushkin" (Ph.D. diss., University of Toronto, 1987).

12 Galt, *The Life of Lord Byron*, 289.

13 Ibid., 289.

14 Ibid., 361.

15 Ibid., 135.

16 Ibid., 1.

17 Ibid., 196.

18 René Girard, *Deceit, Desire and the Novel* (Baltimore: Johns Hopkins University Press, 1965), 87.

19 Galt, *The Life of Lord Byron*, 15.

20 Ibid., 182.

21 Ibid., 182.

22 Leo Strauss, *Persecution and the Art of Writing* (Westport, Conn.: Greenwood Press Publishers, 1973), 25.

23 Anna Makolkin, *Name, Hero, Icon* (Berlin: Mouton de Gruyter, 1992).

24 Galt, *The Life of Lord Byron*, 183.

25 Galt, *Autobiography*, vol. 2 (London: Cochrane McCrone, 1833), 179.

Chapter 7

La famille O'Leary de Québec, l'épiscopat catholique romain d'origine irlandaise en Amérique du Nord au XIXᵉ siècle: Deux attitudes

Georges Henri Dagneau

James O'Leary came to Canada from Ireland in 1826, having participated in the uprising of 1798. One of his children, Maurice, was married in Quebec City in 1836, and among his children, three managed to write extensively on their home town. James Manus (1839–1902) published a booklet about the history of St. Patrick's church, and four pieces about the quarantine at Grosse-Île, where many Irish immigrants died during the mass immigrations of the 1830s and 1840s. Thomas (1843–1925) published historical studies in a Quebec daily newspaper, and afterwards became warden of the Château de Ramezay, Montreal, in 1895 and supervised the museum of the Antiquarian and Numismatic Society of Montreal. The third son was Peter Michael (1850–1929), who became a priest, served in the diocese of Quebec City, taught at the Séminaire de Quebec, and enlisted as Roman Catholic chaplain with the first Canadian contingent sent to South Africa in 1899–1900. He enlisted again with the Canadian Expeditionary Force during the First World War and was discharged in 1917. An archivist with the Dominion Archives, he was posted to Quebec City. When Georges Henri Dagneau was seven, he first encountered Father O'Leary, at a military exposition in 1918 in Quebec where "la maquette Duberger" was on display. Measuring more than fifty square metres, this model of Quebec City had been made by Jean-Baptiste Duberger and John By between 1806 and 1808 for the Royal Engineers. In 1918 Father O'Leary was in charge of the model, having restored it, at the request of Sir Arthur

Doughty, dominion archivist, after its return from England in 1908. The model of his native city, together with old cannon balls, some from 1759, and stories told by his grandfather and elderly aunt, became Georges Henri Dagneau's Proustian madeleines, the point of departure for this memoir of a family whose sympathetic attitude to their home city and to French Canadians in general was in sharp contrast to the francophobia of Roman Catholic archbishops and bishops of Irish extraction. Outside the province, it was often Irish bishops – Fallon being the best known – who were in charge of separate schools. The O'Learys were different, and Dagneau concludes that this old Quebec City family deserves as much recognition in their home city as families with names like Vézina, Charest, and Plamondon.

Mon père était un fonctionnaire du ministère des Postes à Québec. En 1914, on fit d'importants travaux d'agrandissement au bureau principal, rue du Fort, là où forcément les bombardements durent être les plus intenses, pendant les guerres du XVIIᵉ et du XVIIIᵉ siècle. En creusant, les ouvriers mirent à jour bon nombre de boulets, probablement ceux de 1759. Un midi, mon père arriva à la maison avec un de ces trophées: s'ensuivit naturellement une première leçon d'histoire. J'avais trois ans.

Par la suite, ma famille compléta le tableau de l'histoire de la ville à l'aide de récits et d'images mais surtout de visites aux endroits les plus intéressants. Finalement, en 1918, ma mère m'amena à l'Exposition provinciale où l'on avait monté la maquette Duberger – ce fameux modèle qui représente la ville de Québec vers 1810, et réalisé par Jean-Baptiste Duberger, du corps des ingénieurs royaux à Québec, qui a été expédié en Angleterre en 1810. Cet après-midi là, l'abbé Peter Michael O'Leary, lieutenant-colonel honoraire à titre d'aumônier catholique romain, en uniforme kaki, baguette à la main, expliquait la maquette aux visiteurs. En apercevant ma mère, il la salua, lui dit quelques mots en français, me jeta un coup d'oeil et, après une légère inclination de la tête, reprit ses commentaires en anglais.

Cet immense jouet, repeint à neuf, illustrait soudain tous les lieux dont on m'avait parlé. Tout pouvait y revivre, à ma mesure, presque à ma taille: ma vieille ville rajeunissait comme pour venir à ma rencontre! On eut beau l'exiler à Ottawa pendant plus de soixante ans, elle ne sortit jamais de ma mémoire. Je pris part, dans la mesure du possible et de mes moyens, aux luttes des Québécois pour récupérer leur bien, ramené d'Angleterre au Canada en 1908, grâce au gouverneur général du temps, Lord Grey. Destinée

The controversial Quebec Model (la maquette Duberger), constructed 1806–1808 by Jean-Baptiste Duberger and John (later "Colonel") By as a "plan-relief" of the city in preparation for the construction of a number of defensive fortifications. In 1810, the model travelled to England and became part of a collection at the Royal Military Museum, Woolwich, England. It returned to Canada in 1908 for the 300th anniversary of the founding of Quebec City. In Ottawa, Father O'Leary made repairs on behalf of the Sir Arthur Doughty, dominion archivist. Since the mid-1970s, the model has resided in Artillery Park, Quebec City. (Courtesy Environnement Canada, Service des Parcs, Québec.)

à rehausser les fêtes du troisième centenaire de Québec, elle y arriva trop tard et fut remisée à Ottawa. Arthur George Doughty, l'archiviste du "Dominion," qui avait été l'un des artisans de son retour, en confia la restauration à l'abbé O'Leary entre 1909 et 1910. Il y travaillait à Québec en réparant et repeignant chaque pièce qu'il retournait ensuite à Ottawa.

Pendant la première guerre, l'abbé O'Leary fut de nouveau aumônier militaire – il l'avait été en 1899–1900, lors de la guerre des Boers – mais dut revenir au pays en 1917. Vers la fin des hostilités, le gouvernement fédéral décida, pour fins de propagande, de mettre sur pied une exposition des trophées de guerre recueillis sur les champs de bataille européens. À la suggestion de Doughty, on décida d'y inclure la maquette Duberger. C'est ainsi qu'elle fut montrée au public à Québec en fin août 1918, première étape de l'itinéraire pan-canadien.

"Obsédante maquette," écrivait Jean-Paul Desjardins, de Parcs-Canada, en 1976. En 1978, Bernard Pothier, historien au Musée de l'homme à Ottawa, publiait une brochure sur la maquette, son auteur et leur histoire. Enfin, en 1981, le modèle fut rapatrié et installé dans un merveilleux site avec tout le secours que la muséologie peut accorder à une pièce semblable. À Québec!

Pourquoi y revenir? Parce que, en fouillant dans les papiers des O'Leary conservés à Ottawa, j'ai découvert des détails non seulement intéressants et inédits mais qui sont aussi en rapport avec mon expérience d'adulte parcourant le continent nord-américain pendant au delà de dix ans!

Le rôle de l'abbé O'Leary en ce qui concerne la maquette Duberger est déjà connu. Ce qui l'est moins, c'est que ses deux frères, comme lui, épris de leur ville natale, Québec, aient écrit de façon importante sur elle sans obtenir le crédit qui leur est dû.

Les trois frères O'Leary, James Manus (1837–1902), Thomas (1843–1925) et l'abbé Peter Michael (1850–1929) étaient les fils de Maurice O'Leary (1810–1890) et de Rose O'Donnell (1805–1895). Tous deux étaient nés en Irlande. Maurice vint au Canada avec sa famille en 1826; les O'Leary étaient originaires du comté Wexford en Irlande du sud-est. On ignore la date d'arrivée de Rose O'Donnell, mais on sait que leur mariage eut lieu à Québec en 1836 et que Maurice O'Leary s'y donnait comme tailleur. Par la suite, il devint inspecteur des marchés de la haute-ville et, finalement, cotiseur. La famille a presque toujours habité le faubourg Saint-Jean-Baptiste, tout comme la mienne, dont le grand-père maternel était également cotiseur: j'ai vu sa signature au bas de l'acte de décès de Maurice O'Leary. De 1879 à 1897, la famille O'Leary vivait au 33 de la rue Artillerie. L'abbé O'Leary demeurait au 33 de la côte Scott de 1907 à 1929.

Ma rencontre avec les archevêques et évêques catholiques romains de souche irlandaise a été beaucoup plus compliquée et plus lente. Dans ma famille, dont une partie avait émigré à Manchester, New Hampshire, on ne les aimait pas. En 1932, à la mort de mon père, je découvris sa carte de membre de l'Ordre de Jacques-Cartier: nombre de ses propos s'expliquaient d'eux-mêmes. L'épiscopat irlandais en faisait les frais.

Devenu journaliste en 1936, je fus très tôt chargé de m'occuper, à la rédaction, de "nos minorités canadiennes-françaises": c'était pénétrer dans l'intimité des luttes des francophones en dehors du Québec pour l'obtention d'écoles séparées bilingues.

En 1937, c'était le deuxième congrès de la langue française et la fondation de ce qui est devenu le Conseil de la vie française en Amérique. De 1948 à 1952, je travaillai comme journaliste au *Droit*, d'Ottawa, et y ai connu les survivants des grandes luttes d'avant la première guerre. Enfin, de 1963 à 1973, comme responsable des relations culturelles du Québec avec les francophones du reste du continent, je traversai celui-ci de Victoria jusqu'à St. John's et de la Rivière-la-Paix en Alberta, jusqu'à Lafayette en Louisiane. Je connaissais déjà l'hostilité des archevêques et évêques irlandais à l'égard du français: elle devint une réalité dont je pouvais désormais identifier les acteurs. On accuse à tort les Québécois de racisme alors qu'ils se méritent tout au plus le reproche de xénophobes. Je ne verserai pas dans le travers d'accuser ces prélats de racisme, alors qu'ils n'étaient, eux, que francophobes.

L'opposition entre Québécois catholiques et Irlandais catholiques a tout de même existé. Comment se pose la question alors? En partant du cas de la ville de Québec et en s'en tenant à la période qui précède la première guerre, on distinguera entre, d'une part, les conflits sérieux, violents, sanglants même entre "gangs" rivales de débardeurs, qui se déroulèrent sur les quais surtout en 1870 et en 1879–80, aux prises avec le déclin du port de Québec, qui réduisait sans cesse le volume de travail disponible pour ces pères de familles! Dans le faubourg Saint-Jean-Baptiste et aux alentours, c'est-à-dire au Cap-Blanc mais pas à Saint-Sauveur, il n'y eut jamais de conflits impliquant des adultes. C'étaient des batailles d'enfants avec échanges verbaux et pugilistiques exagérés à loisir lorsqu'on en parle quarante ans plus tard! Évidemment, on reprochait aux Irlandais de lancer des cailloux.

Est-il sûr que la francophobie se concentrait chez les archevêques et évêques irlandais, ne descendant pas dans le bas-clergé? Non, ce n'est pas sûr. Toutefois, un facteur place les premiers dans une position privilégiée en vue de nuire aux francophones tandis que, par définition, elle exclut les simples prêtres. La même explication vaut pour les laïcs qui s'impliquaient dans la vie paroissiale.

Au Québec, en vertu des traités de 1759, 1760 et 1763, le droit civil français fut non seulement reconnu mais entériné par l'autorité britannique. C'est ce droit qui donna lieu par la suite au droit paroissial en vertu duquel les propriétaires fonciers d'une localité déterminée érigée en paroisse au point de vue canonique, pouvaient l'être au point de vue civil aussi, former ainsi une corporation et obtenir le droit de percevoir des taxes pour l'érection et l'entretien des lieux du culte de la religion de la corporation. C'était la "fabrique de paroisse" telle que nous la connaissons encore.

Évidemment, un problème de droit se pose ici à savoir si ce qui était légal, à ce sujet, dans l'ancienne Nouvelle-France et en Acadie, l'était toujours dans le Canada et les Maritimes de 1774, dans le Bas-Canada de 1791, dans le Canada-Uni de 1841 et dans le Canada confédéré de 1867, dans l'ensemble du territoire dans chaque cas.

Sauf que la même question se pose à l'égard de la *"sole corporation,"* formule juridique d'origine britannique en vertu de laquelle seul l'évêque du diocèse est propriétaire et administrateur de tous les biens fonciers de la congrégation religieuse en cause, quelle qu'en soit la dénomination. De toute façon, c'était la seule que le clergé et le laïcat irlandais connaissaient. Ils y recoururent en s'installant au Canada et aux États-Unis, en dehors du Québec. Les Canadiens français, en s'implantant, par émigration, en Ontario, en Acadie, dans l'Ouest et même en Nouvelle-Angleterre y importèrent le seul système qu'ils connussent: la formation d'une paroisse avec élection de marguilliers parmi les propriétaires fonciers! Scandale chez le haut clergé irlandais qui y voyait une de ces tendances révolutionnaires propres aux *"Frenchmen"*: des laïcs dire à des prêtres où, comment et quand construire une église? *"Preposterous!"*

Dans la mesure même où, selon la formule britannique, seul l'évêque était propriétaire des immeubles, les simples curés et vicaires passaient au second plan. Il ne s'agit pas de dire qu'il n'y eut aucune francophobie chez les prêtres irlandais. Mais lorsqu'il y en eut, elle fut moins importante dans ses conséquences, le premier plan étant occupé par l'épiscopat.

C'est d'autant plus vrai que, très tôt, se posa la question des écoles. Dans les provinces autres que Québec, à majorité protestante au XIXe siècle, on imagina la formule des écoles séparées, pouvant bénéficier des subventions gouvernementales, à quelle que confession qu'appartint l'institution en cause.

"L'école séparée" ne l'est que sur le plan religieux. Sur le plan linguistique, il n'y a jamais eu d'"écoles séparées." Il y a eu avant 1949 des "écoles bilingues" où l'anglais était enseigné d'abord et le français ensuite, dans une mesure limitée qui a fait l'objet de luttes juridiques à n'en plus finir, aboutissant même au comité judiciaire du Conseil privé d'Angleterre à Londres. Dans une école séparée, on voulait en plus y introduire le bilinguisme pour le bénéfice des enfants des Canadiens français, les parents devaient en assumer tous les frais, c'est-à-dire payer des taxes supplémentaires.

C'est vis-à-vis de cette situation que la francophobie de l'épiscopat irlandais, là où elle exista – et ce fut dans la majorité des cas – s'exerça en ne faisant rien pour alléger le fardeau de leurs diocésains francophones. Pourquoi? L'analyse de cet aspect de l'histoire n'a pas été faite de fond en comble.

Si certains de nos intellectuels avaient bien lu Karl Marx, ils auraient constaté qu'en exil en Angleterre, il étudia en profondeur l'histoire de l'Irlande. Il en avait conclu qu'il ne se passerait rien dans les îles britanniques tant que Londres n'aurait pas réglé "la question irlandaise." Il ne s'est rien passé dans le Royaume-Uni sauf la fin de l'empire et le déclin du pays tandis que l'Irlande devenait une république souveraine. L'application de l'analyse marxiste dans la verte Erin comme au Québec, voire au Canada, donne des résultats dont aucun ne se pose comme la preuve d'une avance marquante.

Car on ne comprend rien à l'histoire du continent nord-américain si on n'introduit pas de façon importante l'histoire des îles britanniques, en particulier de l'Irlande, ce que l'historiographie française de France néglige toujours. De ce fait, on minimise un facteur souverainement important, celui de la religion, dans toute l'étendue du continent.

De 1659 à 1949 au Canada, 270 prêtres catholiques romains ont été nommés évêques, dont 193 étaient nés au Canada, 30 en France, 27 en Irlande et 22 dans d'autres pays. Aux 27 Irlandais d'Irlande, il faut ajouter ceux qui sont nés au Canada de parents immigrés d'Irlande: c'était le cas de Michael Francis Fallon, le type du francophobe!

Quelle a été la conséquence de cette francophobie? Au Canada, elle a visé à remplacer, sur le siège archiépiscopal de chaque province, sauf le Québec, l'archevêque francophone par un Irlandais et à empêcher le francophone d'accéder à celui que détenait un Irlandais. Résultat: Saint-Boniface au Manitoba a un archevêque et vient d'être annexé à Winnipeg qui a aussi un archevêque, pas francophone évidemment. Et dans les Maritimes, les Acadiens ont dû se battre *"unguibus et rostris"* – il n'est pas difficile d'imaginer pourquoi j'utilise une locution latine! – pour obtenir qu'un des leurs soit nommé archevêque!

Un vieux débat encore sans solution partage ceux qui croient qu'en dehors du Québec, les enfants doivent apprendre l'anglais tôt pour gagner leur vie, le domicile paternel et l'église suffisant à la maîtrise du français, et ceux qui pensent, au contraire, qu'il faut insister sur la priorité chronologique, en quantité et en qualité, de l'usage et de l'apprentissage de la langue française. La maîtrise de l'anglais viendra bien toute seule, par la suite, et par la force des choses, ce qui n'exclut pas son enseignement, bien entendu, mais le situe à un moment de la croissance de l'enfant où il évitera les confusions.

Je parle en connaissance de cause: combien j'en ai vu et entendu de ces Canadiens français qui, les larmes aux yeux, baragouinaient une sorte de français ... bilingue! Comme j'en ai connu d'autres qui se tiraient très bien d'affaires. Question de famille, de milieu, d'aptitude, de circonstances, d'époques? Oui, sans doute, mais surtout, pour une partie d'entre eux, question de différences entre ceux qui avaient dû se contenter du *"high school"* et du *"college"* et ceux qui avaient bénéficié du cours classique. Celui-ci se donnait dans un collège, lequel, à son tour, dépendait de la présence d'un archevêque ou évêque francophone.

Cette discussion du problème n'est pas exhaustif, je le sais. Il y a aussi l'endogamie et l'exogamie, les recensements décennaux et la façon dont les questions, dans la section démographique et dans celle des langues, ont été conçues et posées. Il y a également les conséquences de la dispersion des effectifs. (Ce seul facteur couvre de ridicule ceux qui accusent les Canadiens-français de racisme: pourquoi se seraient-ils dispersés s'ils voulaient faire triompher leur *"race"*?) On fera entrer en ligne de compte nombre de facteurs, y compris le fait que les Canadiens français soient toujours minoritaires à la Cour suprême! On passe alors à la politique.

Pour rester dans le domaine de l'histoire, on s'attèlera plutôt à l'étude d'une notion particulière, l'*"ascendency,"* que je n'ai découverte que dans un des livres de Donald H. Akenson, qui a fort bien analysé tout le problème irlandais au Canada. On ne trouve pas ce mot dans les encyclopédies. En revanche on le rencontre chez bon nombre d'historiens. Comment les catholiques ont-ils pu s'introduire dans ce qui était un château-fort anglo-protestant? Il y a là un phénomène politique, originellement relié à l'Angleterre protestante et à l'Irlande catholique, par la suite transporté au Canada et finalement oublié au profit d'autres analyses dont la pertinence et l'utilité sont, à mon avis, fort relatives.

Revenons à nos archevêques et évêques irlandais. L'épiscopat irlandais a favorisé l'apprentissage de l'anglais très tôt avec des conséquences terribles. L'une d'elles a été l'impossibilité où se sont trouvés les groupes francophones, en dehors du Québec, de se constituer en communautés plus ou moins importantes, viables et identifiables. Les Mennonites le pouvaient; les Canadiens français, non. Pourquoi? Parce qu'on savait que jamais les Mennonites ne formeraient une province de leur langue. Les

Canadiens français? Oui. À cause du Québec. Et cela, il ne le fallait à aucun prix. Ceux qui croient qu'il y a eu un Canada se trompent, volontairement ou non. L'épiscopat irlandais n'est pas étranger à ce phénomène!

Pourquoi les archevêques et évêques irlandais ont-ils joué ce rôle? Leur attribuer une volonté machiavélique coupable de tout serait ridicule. Que beaucoup d'entre eux aient été ce qu'on appelle en anglais des *"martinets,"* c'est-à-dire des autoritaires facilement violents, c'est certain.

Au contraire, il faut insister sur plusieurs facteurs. Tout d'abord, l'histoire de l'Église en Angleterre, en Écosse et en Irlande est indispensable à la compréhension du phénomène: ainsi en 1798, lors de la grande rébellion irlandaise, il n'y avait pas d'évêques pour guider les fidèles. Il y avait, en revanche, des prêtres qui marchèrent à la mitraille, à poitrine découverte. La répression de la même rébellion permit à l'Angleterre d'exterminer *manu militari* tous les aristocrates irlandais issus des vieilles familles gaéliques, celles qui transmettaient la langue des Irlandais. Jamais le clergé n'a joué de rôle dans la perpétuation du gaélique. Aussi, lorsqu'après le *"disestablishment"* et la montée du catholicisme en Angleterre, l'Irlande put compter enfin sur un épiscopat en place, celui-ci passa du côté anglais, surtout qu'il n'y avait plus de nobles pour justifier et légitimer l'usage du gaélique. Les Irlandais perdirent leur langue.

Deuxièmement, les évêques irlandais durent étudier en dehors de l'Irlande. Des collèges irlandais, il y en eut dans presque toutes les capitales de l'Europe continentale. La plupart des évêques irlandais savaient au moins une langue étrangère et beaucoup connaissaient le français pour l'avoir appris à Paris.

En contre-partie, notre clergé ne put pas, au XIXe siècle, voyager facilement à l'étranger. De même n'y eut-il jamais séparation entre bas et haut clergé ici. En outre, ils savaient à quoi s'en tenir sur les distances à parcourir pour "missionner" en Canada! Les clercs irlandais en arrivant de leur petite île devant l'immensité continentale nord-américaine en eurent le souffle coupé!

Simultanément – c'est-à-dire entre 1850 et 1900 – il y eut, aux États-Unis, une vague de *"nativism"* et d'anticatholicisme. Dans cette foulée, toute langue étrangère, que ce fut le français, l'italien, l'espagnol ou l'allemand, devenait un obstacle à l'évangélisation des non-catholiques. Naturellement, les Franco-Américains et les Acadiens de la Nouvelle-Angleterre et de la Louisiane ne pesèrent pas lourd dans cette vague zélatrice, qui s'accompagnait de richesses et d'organismes nouveaux comme les Chevaliers de Colomb.

Finalement, il ne faut pas oublier que le rétablissement de la hiérarchie catholique en Irlande, au XIXe siècle, fut le fruit de négociations politiques. Pour les évêques irlandais, faire de la politique, c'était normal. Chez les Irlandais, tout se passait au plus haut niveau. Le bas clergé et le laïcat n'avaient qu'à suivre. Dans le cas des Canadiens français, c'était plutôt vers "la base" que se dirigeaient les tentatives d'influence politique – situation tout à fait différent!

Ce ne sont là que quelques-uns des facteurs qu'il faut étudier pour tenter de comprendre la francophobie de l'épiscopat irlandais, dans sa majorité. Le fait que la plupart d'entre eux parlaient le français leur permettait non pas de dissimuler leur francophobie mais de la laisser aller son petit bonhomme de chemin, sans trop d'esclandre et à l'abri de lois et de règlements que la même attitude inspirait chez les laïcs de langue anglaise dans la politique.

Revenons à la famille O'Leary. Le nationalisme irlandais n'est pas basé sur la langue, tandis que celui du Québec et des minorités repose essentiellement sur la maîtrise du français. Dans la mesure où l'église et l'école n'y contribuaient pas, nos gens de langue française perdaient les deux points d'appui traditionnels qu'ils avaient toujours utilisés. C'est pour cette raison que l'attitude des archevêques et évêques a joué un rôle important. N'oublions pas qu'en Irlande, en 1991, il ne reste plus que 10 000 personnes capables de parler et d'utiliser couramment le gaélique, sur une population de plus de 3 537 643 habitants (recensement de 1986).

James O'Leary, l'ancêtre, et sa femme, Mary Berrigan (je n'ai aucune certitude sur l'orthographe de son nom), parlaient-ils le gaélique? Pour les gens nés au XVIIIe siècle, c'est plus que probable. Et Maurice O'Leary et sa femme, Rose O'Donnell, tous deux nés en Irlande au début du XIXe siècle? C'est possible, mais je n'irais pas plus loin. Les trois frères, nés au Canada? J'en douterais fort. Rien dans les documents que j'ai trouvés n'autorise à l'affirmer.

D'ailleurs dans un fort bon anglais, James Manus O'Leary (1837–1902) publia sa brochure sur l'histoire de l'église Saint Patrick de Québec, en 1895. Elle parut d'abord dans le Daily *Telegraph* et Frank Carrel, qui venait de prendre la direction du journal de son père, la publia en brochure qui se vendait 15 sous.

L'intérêt de cet opuscule de 48 pages ne découle pas seulement de son contenu historique, mais surtout du fait que le premier paragraphe reconnaît la légitimité et la légalité du fait français:

The difficulties encountered by the Irish Catholics of Quebec, in the erection of a place of worship were similar, in many respects, to those which presented themselves to their fellow countrymen, engaged in like undertaking, in other parts of North America and arose chiefly from want of means. There were other difficulties, however, of a more unsurmountable nature, which, strange as it may appear, were caused by the legal and independent position enjoyed by the Catholic church in Canada. To understand this, it may be necessary to state that the capitulation of Quebec, in 1759, made no change in ecclesiastical affairs, and the immunities and rights, which the Catholic church possessed under the French regime, were guaranteed by the treaty of Paris in 1763.

On ne saurait être plus clair. Or, ce texte est de la main même de Maurice O'Leary et se trouve dans les papiers de l'abbé O'Leary, conservés aux Archives nationales du Canada. L'un des trois fils, sans doute James Manus, dont l'écriture se retrouve dans les lettres qu'il a écrites et signées et qui sont aux archives de l'archevêché de Québec, en a fait une copie au propre. C'est ce même texte, mot à mot, qu'il reproduit dans le premier paragraphe de la brochure qu'il a consacrée à l'histoire des Irlandais à Québec. En somme, Maurice O'Leary, débarqué d'Irlande à Québec, se mit à l'oeuvre pour connaître le nouveau milieu dans lequel il allait vivre. Il a jugé bon d'en faire part à ses fils. L'un d'eux crut qu'il n'avait rien de mieux à faire que d'utiliser textuellement les paroles de son père.

James Manus O'Leary se signala dès 1872 en publiant dans *The Catholic Record* de London, Ontario, quatre articles dans autant de livraisons consécutives de cet hebdomadaire sur la Grosse-Île et le tragique épisode de l'arrivée massive d'immigrants irlandais malades d'une fièvre épidémique qui en emporta des milliers, voire des dizaines de milliers dans la tombe. Les articles furent, par la suite, reproduits en 1894 dans le *Daily Telegraph* de Québec et utilisés largement par J.-A. Jordan dans son livre de 1909 à la suite du dévoilement de la croix de granit érigée à la Grosse-Île même lors du 75e anniversaire de l'ouverture de la quarantaine.

En 1875, il publia dans *The Canadian Antiquarian and Numismatic Jounal* de Montréal un article sur l'écusson aux armes du roi de France que le général Murray avait fait enlever d'audessus d'une des portes de Québec pour le donner, en guise de trophée, à la ville de Hastings en Angleterre. Le fait avait été signalé dans une revue anglaise, *The Gentleman's Magazine* de Londres, en 1886 et James Manus O'Leary pigea la revue et l'article, vraisemblablement à la jeune bibliothèque du non moins jeune parlement de la nouvelle capitale fédérale, Ottawa, où il travaillait comme commis de la Poste. En 1925, les démarches de P.C. Larkin, haut-commissaire de Grande-Bretagne au Canada, ramenèrent l'écusson à Québec: il trône depuis lors dans la salle du conseil de ville. Pas une fois, le nom de James Manus O'Leary, auteur de la découverte de l'écusson, ne fut mentionné et pourtant son rôle dans l'affaire était connu depuis 1920, grâce à Ernest Myrand. Pourquoi ce silence?

À la bibliothèque MacLennan de McGill à Montréal, il y a un livre classé au nom de Thomas O'Leary, mais au début duquel celui-ci dit qu'il ne fait que publier une correspondance qui a été découverte par son frère, James Manus O'Leary. *Canadian Letters* reproduit les lettres d'un Anglais en voyage au Canada en 1792 et 1793. Comme on ne connaît ni le nom de l'auteur de ces lettres, ni leur destinataire, l'historiographie canadienne n'en a pas tenu compte, ce qui n'a rien d'étonnant. Toutefois, Sir Arthur George Doughty encouragea Thomas O'Leary à les publier. On n'a jamais su quand, où et comment James Manus O'Leary avait découvert ces papiers!

Quant à Thomas O'Leary, il collabora au *Daily Telegraph,* y publiant au moins trois articles, dont un devait atteindre la célébrité près d'un siècle plus tard, un peu grâce à moi. En effet, le 21 mars 1894, il faisait paraître dans ce journal un article intitulé *Champlain's Tomb.* C'est ce texte, découvert en préparant mon livre sur les O'Leary, que je photocopiai et distribuai à cinq de mes amis, chercheurs en histoire et en archéologie. L'un d'eux y attacha de l'importance, se livra à des fouilles sous la basilique selon les indications de Thomas O'Leary et aboutit à un échec dont je ne me désolidarise pas.

Thomas O'Leary a aussi fabriqué de ses mains cinq miniatures représentant les cinq portes des remparts de Québec. Il les a données à un marchand de Montréal du nom de Carsley, qui les a données à son tour à McGill, qui les a finalement passées au Musée McCord où elles sont soigneusement conservées ... à l'abri des regards du public!

En 1895, Thomas devint le conservateur-gardien-bibliothécaire-factotum de la Numismatic and Antiquarian Society of Montreal et, par le fait même, du musée du château de Ramezay, où il logeait. Il est, à ma connaissance du moins, le seul gardien ou conservateur de musée qui, dans l'exercice de ses fonctions, reçut une blessure physique qui lui valut, peu après, la perte d'un oeil. En effet, selon le compte rendu de *The Gazette* du 28 janvier 1913 – l'événement eut donc lieu le 27 – vers 1 h de l'après-midi, au moment où Thomas O'Leary voulut fermer le musée pour pouvoir prendre son repas, il vit à l'étage un visiteur dont les gestes étaient étranges.

En s'approchant, Thomas O'Leary se trouva soudain en face d'un revolver. Puis, le voleur attaqua manuellement le gardien à l'aide d'un marteau, le frappant violemment à la tête. Les cris et la bousculade attirèrent l'attention, la police intervint mais le voleur eut le temps de fuir. Conduit à l'hôpital, Thomas reçut les premiers soins, mais il n'en perdit pas moins l'usage d'un oeil.

Thomas mourut au musée en 1925. Son épouse, Mary Ann O'Hare, lui survécut et mourut à Montréal en 1948.

Le dernier des trois frères, l'abbé Peter Michael O'Leary, retiendra maintenant notre attention. Mais il faut expliquer auparavant que, sur les huit enfants qu'elle eut, Rose O'Donnell n'en vit que quatre se rendre à l'âge adulte. La quatrième était une fille, Mary Ann. Elle naquit le 31 mai 1841 et mourut accidentellement le premier février 1891. En revenant de la messe, à St. Patrick, alors rue MacMahon, en passant sur la rue St-Jean, près de la rue des Glacis, un énorme glaçon se détacha d'un toit et la tua instantanément.

L'abbé O'Leary naquit le 28 juin 1850 et mourut le 23 décembre 1929. Peter Michael O'Leary fit ses études au collège de Sainte-Anne de la Pocatière et fut ordonné prêtre en 1879 à l'âge de 29 ans.

Dans sa monographie sur la maquette Duberger, Bernard Pothier a très bien jaugé l'abbé O'Leary. Tout ce que je peux ajouter, c'est qu'à mon avis, il fut ce qu'on appelle "une vocation forcée": il est devenu prêtre pour faire plaisir à sa mère. Pendant longtemps, il se sentit mal à l'aise dans le célibat. Il compensa par de grands besoins d'argent, source d'une saga qui exige tout un chapitre du livre que je consacre à la famille, en ce qui concerne les emprunts et les hypothèques. Il fut toujours honnête et respecta toujours la légalité. Mais il exigeait sans cesse de nouvelles liquidités.

Il occupa un très grand nombre de postes, se permit une escapade qui finit plutôt bien que mal, s'enrôla comme aumônier militaire en 1899 et fit la campagne de l'Afrique du sud. Il revint en après avoir montré un véritable courage et s'être mérité l'admiration de tous par la façon dont il administra les derniers sacrements à tous les soldats blessés sur le champ de bataille, quelle que fût leur religion. Sans l'ombre d'un doute, il fut très courageux.

À son arrivée à Québec, le 4 novembre 1900, fut-il l'objet d'un accueil triomphal. À Montréal le chapitre métropolitain du Imperial Order of the Daughters of the Empire lui donna un calice en reconnaissance de sa bravoure et de sa charité exercée sans distinction de religion. La nouvelle s'en répandit dans la presse au grand dam de l'archevêque de Montréal, Paul Bruchési, qui en

Father Peter Michael O'Leary, Chaplain 2nd Battalion, Royal Constabulary, Boer War. Photograph by Pittaway, Ottawa, 1899. (Courtesy Archives du Séminaire de Québec, Québec, #90.0342.)

demanda compte à son collègue de Québec, Louis Nazaire Bégin, qui négligea de laisser, dans les archives, la trace de sa réaction!

En 1905, l'abbé O'Leary devint archiviste en poste à Québec, sur la recommandation directe de Arthur George Doughty et avec le concours de Mgr O.-E. Mathieu alors recteur de l'Université Laval. À partir de ce moment, les Archives nationales du Canada ont conservé toutes les lettres de l'abbé O'Leary à son chef, Doughty. Il y a là neuf ans de correspondance: on n'y relève rien, absolument rien, contre les Canadiens français.

En 1910, il reconnaît que c'est Doughty qui a repéré la maquette Duberger à Woolwich et qui est l'un des artisans de son retour à Québec. L'abbé O'Leary restaura la maquette, pièce à pièce, entre 1910 et 1914. Il s'enrôla une seconde fois comme aumônier militaire en 1914: il avait 64 ans. Il alla au front en France, dut revenir en Angleterre, fit un voyage au

Canada, retourna en Angleterre et fut finalement démobilisé en 1917. Il reprit son travail, organisa à Québec en 1918, la première exposition de la maquette Duberger, et en 1924–25 se livra à une véritable bataille d'arrière-garde au sujet de sa pension de retraite. Il avait maintenant 75 ans. Il demeurait alors chez madame Arthur Marquis, au 33 de la côte Scott (aujourd'hui le 945 – la maison est encore là). Il la légua à la fille de madame Marquis, Flora, qui la vendit le 3 avril 1930 à Gédéon Paré. La maison était encore hypothéquée.

Au cimetière Saint-Patrick, le lot de la famille O'Leary où l'abbé a été inhumé le dernier en 1929, a été revendu. Il ne reste aucune trace de la famille O'Leary du faubourg Saint-Jean-Baptiste dans notre ville. C'est trop peu. Le présent travail se veut une sorte de compensation. Les O'Leary du faubourg Saint-Jean-Baptiste méritent autant de reconnaissance que les Châteauvert, les Charest, les Desroches, les Dorval, les Grenier, les Plamondon, et les Vézina.

Né le 6 août 1911 à Québec, **Georges Henri Dagneau** a fait ses études au Séminaire de Québec et à l'Université Laval ainsi qu'aux Facultés libres de Lille en France. Bachelier en arts, licencié en droit et diplômé de l'Ecole supérieure de journalisme de Lille, il était journaliste de 1936 à 1963 à Québec, Ottawa, Chicoutimi et Montréal pour des quotidiens, des hebdomadaires et des institutions de relations industrielles et publiques. De 1963 à 1976 il était fonctionnaire au Ministère des Affaires culturelles du Québec à titre de Responsable des relations culturelles avec les groupes francophones hors-Québec et aux États-Unis. Retraité depuis 1976, il se livre à la recherche historique au sujet des Irlandais et des minorités francophones d'Amérique, en se concentrant sur la ville de Québec. Il a déjà collaboré à de nombreuses revues ainsi qu'à la publication du quatrième tome de l'*Histoire municipale de Québec de 1867 à 1929*, publiée par la Société historique de Québec. Ancien président de la Fédération des Sociétés d'histoire du Québec, il a été membre de plusieurs autres associations du même domaine.

Note

Les sources pour ce texte sont comme suit:

Les divers écrits des trois fils O'Leary.

À Québec, les archives de l'Archevêché, du Séminaire, de Notre-Dame de Québec, de St. Patrick's, de la "Literary & Historical Society", et les livres de Mme Marianna O'Gallagher.

À Sainte-Anne de la Pocatière, les archives du collège.

À Montréal, les archives de la ville, de l'Archevêché, du Château de Ramezay, de l' "Antiquarian & Numismatic Society" de St. Patrick's.

À Ottawa, les archives de la ville, de Notre Dame d'Ottawa, de St. Patrick's, et surtout les archives nationale du Canada: recensement agricole de la paroisse Sainte-Catherine de Portneuf, dist. no 7, Canada-est, 1851, bobine 1132, 77–8, ligne 38; les papiers O'Leary, MG 30 D 16, vol. 2, livre 15; Milice et Défence, RG 9, S III, vol. 4637; RG 37, vol. 270; RG 37, vol. 189 à 200.

Témoignages oraux de Mme Marjorie O'Dowd, veuve de John Lindsay, de Montréal (1910-1987) et de M. Sainte-Foy Lockwell, de Québec, (1905–), qui a servi la messe de l'abbé O'Leary.

À Dublin, Hibernian Research Co. Ltd.

La presse des deux langues de Québec, Montréal et Ottawa.

Part 4

On the Edge of History

Chapter 8

Strive On! James, Son of William Lyon Mackenzie

Chris Raible

The child was barely two weeks old when his parents came before the kirk session of the parish of Alyth. For the Sabbath, the 31st day of July in the year of our Lord one thousand eight hundred and fourteen, it is recorded:

> Compeared Isabel Reid, late servant to Andrew Mustard in Newton of Balhary, and declared, That she had lately brought forth a child in forni-cation – being interrogated who was the father of her child, declares, That it was Wm. Lyon McKenzie Merchant in Alyth, and that the child was begotten in this Parish ... Compeared next said W.L. McKenzie, who hav-ing heard the above declaration read over to him, declared, That the above was the truth.[1]

A week later, the father was fined 13 shilling, 4 pence, and the Kirk Session authorized the baptism of the child. The scandal was purged.

There was nothing unusual about this stern church judicial procedure – it was common throughout Scotland. The church elders had acted under powers conferred by statute.[2] It had been defined more than 250 years earlier by the *First Book of Discipline* of the Church of Scotland, authored by John Knox himself.[3] By 1814, like most parishes in Scotland, Alyth had somewhat modified (and mollified) the strictures of the *Book of Discipline*, but kirk sessions were conducted regularly to deal with whatever sins disrupted the community. That summer in Alyth, there had already been eight cases of fornication.

Such was the world into which the child, baptized James Mackenzie, was born. He was early given to the care of Elizabeth Mackenzie, his paternal grandmother. By then sixty-five years of age, Elizabeth was a profoundly pious Presbyterian who no doubt fully approved of the dark process that purged the sin of her nineteen-year-old son (and only child), William Lyon Mackenzie.

Elizabeth's principles were permanently imprinted on the conscience and character of young James. Again and again James's adult letters testify to the profound influence on him of that extraordinary woman. Eleven days after her death at the age of ninety, he wrote to his father: "I think often of my grandmother ... she gave to me as to you the first impulses and what is good I owe to her. In looking back I thank Heaven that no instance of unkindness rises against me to her ... Kind good noble hearted being – I feel she was in her quiet unobtrusive goodness superior to your Statesman and the mockery of great men."[4]

In 1820 William Lyon Mackenzie emigrated to Canada, following the failure of his general store in Alyth, employment in England, and a visit to France. In 1822 James, his grandmother Elizabeth, and Isabel Baxter, the young woman whom Elizabeth had selected to become her son's wife, followed. In June they arrived in Quebec; in July Isabel and William were married in Montreal; and in August they were settled in Dundas, where Mackenzie operated a general store. But "settled" is hardly correct. The family soon moved to Queenston, and in November 1824, to York, the centre of political action.[5]

These transitions can not have been easy for young James. Once the only charge of an elderly, devoted grandmother, in Canada he found himself living with a barely remembered father and a stepmother but twelve years his senior. His home life can hardly have been happy. An infant half-sister died; a second baby succumbed to smallpox; a third sister died in 1825. And Mackenzie soon suffered the financial problems that were to follow him throughout his life.[6]

By the spring of 1826, eleven-year-old James was working in his father's printing office, where he was eyewitness to the "types riot," when a band of Tories, led by Samuel Peter Jarvis, attempted to silence the *Colonial Advocate* by trashing its printshop.[7] His father was away when the raiders struck, and it is not difficult to imagine the young apprentice's feelings of guilt and his fear of parental reprisal, of what he referred to years later as harsh opprobrium and "the dominion of fear."[8]

In time, James became a skilled journeyman printer, and like many in the trade, he began drinking, which caused constant friction with his father.[9] While working for the *Advocate*, James joined the Typographical Society and chaired the "Committee of Vigilance," but the "union" was too weak to enforce any of its rules about hours and pay. By 1836 James was in business for himself, accepting printing contracts with the Legislative Assembly. He was also "printer" for his father's new paper, the *Constitution*.[10]

A dozen years in Canada had made the boy a man, outwardly confident but inwardly troubled. He fell from his father's grace, perhaps over a remark made by James about his natural mother, Isabel Reid. He left York, found jobs as a journeyman printer,[11] and eventually reached Ohio.

When the rebellion erupted in December 1837, James started back to Canada, walking 400 to 500 miles and then travelling by stage from Erie, Pennsylvania, to Navy Island, which he reached two days after the *Caroline*, the "Patriot" supply ship, was burnt on 29 December.[12] Following the evacuation of Navy Island, he joined the Patriot army heading westward, serving as a commissary officer – "Beg General," the men called him – responsible for supplying food and other needs by scrounging help from local inhabitants as the force moved through the American countryside. At Toledo, James held meetings, made speeches, and collected $1,200 in clothing and provisions.[13]

The Patriot mission was another Canadian invasion, a landing on Fighting Island in the Detroit River. During the abortive attempt, James was commended by his superior officer. He was almost killed, owing his life to Benjamin Lett, who was later infamous for blowing up the Brock monument.[14] Following the Fighting Island failure, the force moved across the Lake Erie ice in a futile attempt to support the Patriots on Pelee Island. Arriving too late, they were compelled to continue to American territory, "travelling on ice all night after a march the longest and severest" that James had ever experienced.[15] Ohio, however, was no sanctuary, for a federal warrant had been issued for James's arrest. He was forced to flee to New York state.[16] In Buffalo, James reconnected with Navy Island companions and conspired in another incursion, the "Short Hills" raid,[17] which failed. Threatened with arrest, James fled back to American territory.

Soon he was in Lockport, New York, editing the *Freeman's Advocate*, a newspaper of the Patriot Hunters,[18] an American secret society pledged to rid Canada of British rule. When the paper was abandoned the following spring, James found work elsewhere as a printer.

Between July 1838 and August 1840, James sent his father more than forty letters, which are marked with discouragement for Canada and disillusionment with Americans, whose only God, James claimed, was "the Almighty dollar." He wrote of his struggles, and his father served as father

James Mackenzie (1814–1901), illegitimate son of William Lyon Mackenzie. (Courtesy the Allen County Historical Society, Lima, Ohio.)

confessor. Mackenzie Sr. was the "only correspondent" to whom James could write "naturally" and "without premeditation."[19] To no one else did he dare let loose such an unedited flow of opinions, frustrations, passions, and fears. James asked for guidance, but at the same time, he was ever eager to give advice to his father. There was a reciprocity between father and son.

For James, those were unsettled, even lost, years. Filled with regret and repentance, he desperately wanted to remake himself. In New York state, he assured his father he had embarked on a course of self-improvement, boasting of "industry and sobriety," of giving up tobacco and bad company, and of feeling "much better so doing." Nevertheless, he felt tossed about, unable to chart his own way. "This being kicked through the world like the wandering Jew is rather unpleasant," he told his father.[20]

Hesitatingly, he took the first steps towards a different future. He began the study of law, which appealed to his passion for the written word and offered him an entrée into the classical education he had always sought. Law appealed to his need for order in a disordered society and in his own disrupted life. Law gave him a passage into a world, thus far denied him, where he could make his own decisions and determine his own future. He loved the study of law for itself, but more he pursued it as a way to free himself from the wiles and whims of employers. Law was also to lead him into the political arena and his future career as a prosecutor and judge.

The situation changed dramatically in 1840. In Rochester, in spite of being jailed for violating American neutrality laws, William Lyon Macken-zie had been publishing a newspaper called *Mackenzie's Gazette*. Following his release in May, he lured James to Rochester to assist with the publica-tion. Whatever their old differences, the two had politics in common and a genuine mutual admiration. However, interest in the Canadian cause was waning, and the newspaper failed to pay its operating costs.

James found work in other Rochester newspapers and became active in the printers' union. But he found little opportunity in journalism or in law. In late October 1841, he went west, first to Cleveland, then to rural Ohio, where he took up teaching in a one-room school. As it happened, he liked his new vocation, for it stimulated his love of reading and his con-tinuing course in self-education. And his salary allowed him to continue the study of law.[21] At one point, he was forced to borrow money, but he quickly paid it back. His pride even made him resist a temptation to marry. The young lady in question was wealthy, and "it would have been unequal," James told his father.[22] All this time, he seems never to have forgotten his biological mother in Scotland, and he corresponded with her from time to time.[23] Her eventual fate, alas, is unknown.

After passing the bar in 1843, James left Cleveland for Damascus, a village in sparsely settled northwest Ohio. There was little legal business there, so he returned to teaching. He also began to make political speeches for the Democratic Party, and by November 1844 he was elected county prosecuting attorney, not an important, powerful, or lucrative position, but one that combined his two loves, law and politics.[24] In years to come, James was elected prosecutor in Putnam and Allen counties. Ultimately he was elected a judge.

In the confusing climate of ante-bellum America, with its passionate debates over slavery and western expansion, James began his political career. Like his father, he had strong personal convictions, but no great vision for the nation and state and no great personal aspirations. He was young, flexible, and realistic. His expectations were not very high. His experience with Canadian authorities had convinced him of the evils of colonial monarchy, but his experience with the Patriots had shown him the deficiencies of popular democracy. He thus never again allowed his political passions to cause him to make costly personal sacrifices. Although he continued to believe in American democratic principles, he was ever sceptical of American democratic practices.[25]

At the same time, he was losing interest in Canada, coming to believe that responsible government there was only an ephemeral hope. And though he won elections as a prosecutor, a member of the Ohio legislature, and a judge, he felt victimized by American "nativism," the political movement that sought to restrict rights and privileges of immigrants.[26]

James did not stay long in Damascus. He moved on to Kalida, in neighbouring Putnam County, where he united legal practice, politics, and his old interest, journalism. He may have hated "picking types" as a journeyman compositor, but printing ink was in his blood. He became owner and editor of the *Kalida Venture*, and despite economic and political setbacks, he owned the paper some ten years, a longer unbroken publishing period than his father ever managed. Like his father, he preached with the printed word. One of his favourite devils was the banking system, which he accused of issuing notes and then defaulting on them, thus robbing people of millions of dollars.[27]

James also had other matters to occupy his thoughts. He began "paying attentions to a young woman." His decision to marry Lucina Polly Leonard, twenty-four years old, of Kalida, was carefully premeditated. "Certainly she ... appears well," he told his father, "and is I believe a woman of well cultivated and high moral sense." In May 1846 the couple married. On 21 September 1847 a child was born and named Elizabeth for two of her great-grandmothers. James was devoted to his daughter, who was a constant reminder of his father and his grandmother. A second girl, Lucina Augusta, was born two years later. In all, there were to be seven children, three more born in Kalida and the two youngest in Lima, where the family moved in 1859. James had found his place. "I know nowhere that I can do better," he wrote to his father, "and that gives the sanction of necessity to my repose of feeling."[28]

The "repose" was broken in September 1850 when three-year-old Elizabeth died. Mackenzie tried to console his son with reminders of the early deaths of his own three daughters in the 1820s and of how the family had managed to survive. He also sent James a lock of hair belonging to his deceased grandmother, Elizabeth, as well as an obituary published at the time of her death ten years earlier.[29]

Ever since James's marriage in 1846, almost every letter from his father expressed the hope or plan for a visit. Finally in 1854, Mackenzie did get to Columbus, where James was in session with the Ohio legislature. After more than a dozen years of separation, James was much pleased. "I was glad to find your health so much better than I expected," he told his father in a post-visit letter, "and to find the general agreement of views which exists after so long a separation between us." James also noted with surprise and delight how much alike were their voices, gestures, and expressions.[30]

That summer of 1854, James was "more content with my wilderness house than would have been expected." But it was clear that he should not remain in Kalida. "Improvement is going on around us & I shall be required to move as my business will be affected," he told his father. "How that will be I cannot determine."[31] The following January, somewhat discouraged but not totally dispirited, he sold his printing business. The newspaper no longer paid its way "in influence nor in money."[32]

It would be three more years before James and his family finally moved from Kalida to the larger and soon more prosperous community of Lima. The move was prompted by his strong feelings that his children would receive a sound education in Lima and that his wife would be "happier and more at home" there. In spite of suggestions that he had sacrificed his own ambitions in the move, in actual fact he gave up very little. In 1858, shortly after moving to Lima, and coincidentally the year that his father resigned from the Canadian Legislative Assembly, James bought *The Allen County Democrat*. Although he kept the paper less than three years, he had clearly found his political home. In 1861 he was elected prosecuting attorney for the county, and, four years later, judge of the Court of Common Pleas 3rd District. He was twice re-elected, in 1869 and in 1873.

In 1879, at the age of nearly sixty-five, he retired.[33]

Through his father, James kept abreast of Canadian politics, and he was often dismayed at the failure of Canada to follow, or even appreciate, his father's wisdom. The two men maintained a running commentary on questions concerning Canada's future, including the persistent issue of annexation. Although the senior Mackenzie never endorsed the idea – his own sad years in New York had left him disillusioned about the United States – he was not entirely opposed to it either. In 1859, a year before his *Weekly Message* closed, he invited James to contribute a column advocating annexation. James did so, writing with strength and conviction, laying out geographic, economic, and political arguments. The piece was published in September.[34]

To James's profound distress, for many months following the publication of his piece, he heard nothing. Several times he wrote his father, but to no avail. Rather than assuming some illness, lack of energy, or shame for having no money for postage, James blamed himself. "I would like to know in what I have justified your action," he wrote, "as it has occasioned me surprise and regret." He assumed something he had written had given offence. "If it is my political opinions that offend you, let me remind you that I came to this country in earlier life than you did – and therefore was more facile to catch the impression of American opinions, fluctuating, changing, & far less earnest than you have even esteemed it." Perhaps, James feared, his father thought James had not condemned slavery enough and had praised the United States too much. "America is the last home of freedom," he wrote. "True slavery exists here, but is it wise by political convulsion & violence to force it out hastily & without awaiting a reasonable time?" James wondered if perhaps his father thought that he had sold out his principles in order to advance his political aspirations.

Had he, once again, after all these years, somehow failed to live up to his father's expectations? He admitted that the people among whom he lived were "narrow, unintelligent, greedy & grasping." Nevertheless, he remained because he hoped that his children, all American born, would succeed where he as a foreigner had failed.[35]

Finally his father sent a hastily written reply whose contents are unknown.[36] Whatever the reason for the senior Mackenzie's silence – it may have been only an aging man's forgetfulness – it was broken, and the two stayed in touch for another year. Mackenzie's last known letter, before he died in August 1861, was to James: "Life, James is an uncertain boon," he wrote. "I'm sorry that you yourself are finding the maintenance of a young and interesting family such a heavy load. All may come right yet. I may have news for you ere long, in which I'll come and tell it to you."[37]

Whether James attended his father's funeral is uncertain, but he kept up some connection with his Canadian family. When his half-brother William enlisted in and then deserted from the Union Army during the American Civil War, James attempted to use his political connections to help him. In 1871, when his other half-brother, George, was killed in an Indiana railway accident, James accompanied the body back to Toronto. As late as 1886, James was writing to his Toronto relatives, sharing memories of his father.[38]

In the years following his father's death, James became one of the more prominent citizens of Lima. He helped to found the town library. He and Lucina in time had several grandchildren. The family built a grand house on Market Street, on the "golden mile" of fine houses in Lima. In 1881, forty-four years after their marriage, Lucina died.[39]

With few surviving letters and no diaries, little can be known of James's inner life during the years before and after his wife's death. From the external evidence, it seems clear that he felt at last truly settled. Raising and educating his family, doing his duty and more for his community, paying his taxes, and criticizing his government, he had become typically American. Unlike his father, James Mackenzie made no dramatic impact on his world, but he made his contribution and he had his influence. He found his place and his restlessness was gone. On 9 May 1901, at almost eighty-seven years of age, James died. His obituary made the front page of the Lima *Times Democrat*.

Some fifteen years earlier, he was roused to the defence of his father's place in history. In 1885 John Charles Dent wrote *The Story of the Upper Canadian Rebellion*, which was highly critical of Mackenzie. James was outraged. His father's "ability, eminence and unselfishness," he argued, had been "fearfully & designedly misrepresented & falsified."[40]

Throughout his life, James Mackenzie remained emotionally dependent on his father. And yet he had his own personal strength. The sustaining influence of his grandmother's teaching never left him. The closing lines of that 1860 letter in which he worried about his father's long silence reveal a great deal about him:

> This, however, is but a letter of enquiry. If there are matters that too severely occupy your time, or if your silence is your preference, I may regret it, but shall no further complain or urge in the matter. Acting, as for twenty years I have done, substantially alone & for myself, & as I expect to do for the balance of my life, in the discharge of the duties I owe to my family. I shall expect to find the earnest of my life motto, to "strive on" & discharge as heretofore my humble duties, as I shall expect frankly to answer [for] them here & hereafter.[41]

Chris Raible is a writer, broadcaster, and historical interpreter. His articles and reviews appear regularly in *The Beaver*, the *York Pioneer*, and *Ontario History*, and he has written for the *Globe and Mail*, the *Toronto Star*, and *Canadian Forum*. He was educated at the University of Chicago, the University of Manchester, and the Unitarian theological seminary associated with the University of California. As a minister (he retired from active church duties in 1986), he served churches in New York, Wisconsin, Massachusetts, and Toronto. He has taught and lectured at various American universities and colleges. In Toronto, he has taught at Ryerson Polytechnical Institute, and he served for a season as resident historian for CBC radio's "Later the Same Day." He currently works for the Toronto Historical Board, volunteers for the Ontario Historical Society, and is a member of the board of the Town of York Historical Society. He is engaged in continued research into the life and influence of William Lyon Mackenzie. Raible's *Muddy York Mud*, an anecdotal history of York in the 1820s, was published in November 1992.

Notes

Author's Note: A version of the paper appeared in *The Beaver*, October/November 1991.

1 Scottish Records Office, Edinburgh, intra CH.2/912/4, *Kirk Session Records for the Parish of Alyth*, 1814. ("Compear" was a Scottish legal term meaning "to appear before a court of law.")

2 See Leah Leneman and Rosalind Mitchison, "Scottish Illegitimacy Ratios in the Early Modern Period," *Economic History Review*, series 2, 40, no. 1 (February 1987): 41–63.

3 See Geoffrey Parker, "The 'Kirk Law Established' and the Origins of the Taming of Scotland: St. Andrews 1559–1600," in Lea Leneman, ed., *Perspectives in Scottish Social History, Essays in Honour of Rosalind Mitchison* (Aberdeen: Aberdeen University Press, 1988).

4 Archives of Ontario (AO), Mackenzie-Lindsey Papers (MLP), James Mackenzie to William Lyon Mackenzie, 4 January 1840.

5 Charles Lindsey, *The Life and Times of William Lyon Mackenzie* (Toronto: P.R. Randall, 1862), chaps. 3, 4; and AO, MLP, Lindsey Correspondence (LC), James Mackenzie to J. Lindsey [his half-sister Janet], 22 November 1885.

6 Toronto Historical Board (THB), handwritten inscriptions in the Mackenzie Family Bible; and Nancy Luno, *A Genteel Exterior: The Domestic Life of William Lyon Mackenzie and His Family* (Toronto: THB, 1990).

7 Testimony of James Mackenzie in William Lyon Mackenzie, *The Destruction of the Colonial Advocate Press* (York: Colonial Advocate Office, 1827), 13–14.

8 AO, MLP, James Mackenzie to William Lyon Mackenzie, 4 January 1840.

9 See Sally F. Zerker, *The Rise and Fall of the Toronto Typographical Union, 1832–1972* (Toronto: University of Toronto Press, 1982), 22–23; and AO, MLP, James Mackenzie to William Lyon Mackenzie, 1839–40; and National Archives of Canada (NA), William Lyon Mackenzie King Papers (WLMKP), James Mackenzie to William Lyon Mackenzie, 1839–1840.

10 AO, MLP, Prospectus for the *Constitution*, 18 April 1836.

11 See, for example *Globe*, Cobourg, Ont., 4 July 1837, where James is listed as "printer."

12 Metro Toronto Reference Library, Baldwin Room (MTLBR), Henderson Papers (HP), James Mackenzie to W. Henderson, 6 April 1873.

13 MTLBR, HP, James Mackenzie to W. Henderson, 6 April 1873.

14 Edwin C. Guillet, *The Lives and Times of the Patriots* (Toronto: Thomas Nelson & Sons, 1938; repub. University of Toronto Press, 1968), chap. 9; Allan J. MacDonald, "Benjamin Lett," *Dictionary of Canadian Biography*, vol. 8, *1851–1860*, edited by Francess G. Halpenny (Toronto: University of Toronto Press, 1985), 501–2; James Mackenzie, "Benjamin Lett," *Allen County Democrat*, 5 January 1859; AO, MLP, LC, James Mackenzie to Charles Lindsey, 2 November 1862 and 23 January 1863; AO, MLP, LC, James Mackenzie to George Lindsey, 28 May 1886; NA, WLMKP, R.W. Ashley Jr. to James Mackenzie.

15 MTLBR, HP, James Mackenzie to W. Henderson, 6 April 1873.

16 Donald McLeod, *A Brief Review of the Settlement of Upper Canada* (Cleveland: F.B. Lenniman, 1841; Belleville: Mika Publishing, 1972), 228–29; and AO, MLP, clipping #3396.

17 Guillet, *Life and Times*, chap. 11; and Colin Read, "The Short Hills Raid of June, 1838," *Ontario History*, vol. 68, no. 2 (1976).

18 *Mackenzie's Gazette*, 13 October 1838; MTLBR, HP, James Mackenzie to J. Henderson, 6 April 1873; AO, MLP, LC, James Mackenzie to George Lindsey, 28 May 1886.

19 AO, MLP, James Mackenzie to William Lyon Mackenzie, 14 March 1846.

20 Ibid., 29 January 1840.

21 MTLBR, HP, James Mackenzie to W. Henderson, 6 April 1873; and AO, MLP, James Mackenzie to William Lyon Mackenzie, 26 October 1841, 16 December 1841, 10 April 1842, 9 May 1842, 22 May 1842, 21 January 1843, 22 March 1844, and 21 December 1846.

22 AO, MLP, James Mackenzie to William Lyon Mackenzie, 22 May 1841 and 4 July 1844.

23 Ibid., 15 June 1838, 23 August 1840, 10 October 1842 and 29 September 1847; and NA, WLMKP, William Lyon Mackenzie to James Mackenzie, 2 October 1845.

24 AO, MLP, James Mackenzie to William Lyon Mackenzie, 23 October 1843, 11 January 1844, 22 March 1844, 23 August 1844, and 8 November 1844.

25 Ibid., 8 November 1844.

26 Ibid., 20 November 1844, 8 June 1855; and MTLBR, HP, James Mackenzie to W. Henderson, 6 Apr 1873.

27 AO, MLP, James Mackenzie to William Lyon Mackenzie, 23 August 1844 and 20 August 1845; and *Kalida Venture*, 23 May 1845 and 5 June 1846.

28 AO, MLP, James Mackenzie to William Lyon Mackenzie, 6 May 1846, 26 July 1846, 24 September 1847, and 3 February 1850, and William Lyon Mackenzie to James Mackenzie, 14 August 1849; *Kalida Venture*, 28 May 1846; and *Historical Files*, Allen County Historical Society, with special thanks to Jeanne Porreca.

29 NA, WLMKP, William Lyon Mackenzie to James Mackenzie, 3 October 1850, which refers to a letter, not preserved, from James, 16 September 1850.

30 AO, MLP, James Mackenzie to William Lyon Mackenzie, 27 June 1854.

31 Ibid., 27 June.

32 Ibid., 17 January 1855.

33 Elliot Howard Gilkey, *The Ohio Hundred Year Book: A Hand-Book of the Public Men and Public Institutions of Ohio* (Columbus: Fred J. Hier, State Printer, 1901), 554; Charles C. Miller, ed., *History of Allen County, Ohio and Representative Citizens* (Chicago: Richmond & Arnold, 1906), 34; W.M. Rusler, ed., *A Standard History of Allen County, Ohio*, vol. 2 (Chicago and New York: American Historical Society, 1921), 195; *A Portrait and Biographical Record of Allen and Putnam Counties, Ohio* (Chicago: A.W. Bowen, 1896), 562; and AO, MLP, James Mackenzie to William Lyon Mackenzie, 15 September 1858 and 23 May 1860.

34 *Mackenzie's Weekly Message*, 13 September 1859.

35 AO, MLP, James Mackenzie to William Lyon Mackenzie, 23 May 1860.

36 James's letter of 23 May 1860 has a notation in William Lyon Mackenzie's handwriting: "ansd. 30 May '60."

37 AO, MLP, William Lyon Mackenzie to James Mackenzie, 22 June 1861.

38 AO, MLP, LC, James Mackenzie to C. Lindsey, 14 November 1861; James Mackenzie to George Lindsey, 28 May 1886 and 31 May 1886; and MTLBR, HP, James Mackenzie to W Henderson, 6 April 1873.

39 See John R., ed. Carnes, *The 1976 History of Allen County, Ohio* (Evansville, Ind.: Unigraphic, 1976); Gilkey, *The Ohio Hundred Year Book*; Miller, *History of Allen County*; Rusler, *A Standard History*; *Historical Files*, Allen County Historical Society; *A Portrait and Biographical Record*; and *History of Allen County, Ohio* (Chicago: Warner, Beers & Co., 1885).

40 AO, MLP, LC, James Mackenzie to George Lindsey, 28 May 1886.

41 AO, MLP, James Mackenzie to William Lyon Mackenzie, 23 May 1860.

Chapter 9

William Patrick: Ecumenical and Economical Presbyterian

David Rollo

> As the individual man has "trusteeship" for a time on this earth over
> created things, in like manner the Church in its "ecumenical" compulsion
> to achieve the units of the visible Church and to fulfil its mission ... has a
> "trusteeship" which makes wastage of resources a sin. Herein lies the
> basic interlocking of "ecumenical" and "economical." To separate this is
> to drive a wedge into the very "Economy of God."[1]

Although William Patrick helped to found the United Church of Canada,
he has been neglected by most historians of the movement that in 1925
united Congregationalists, Methodists, and some Presbyterians in one
church. Historians who sought the church's nineteenth-century Canadian
roots found them in men such as George M. Grant and William Caven.
Patrick was a Scot who was accused of introducing the issue of union
improperly, of handling it illegally, and of justifying his actions in terms
verging on blasphemy.[2] This often difficult and dour man with a mission
and a strong belief in the "Economy of God" found his support for union
not in the more populous eastern regions of Canada but in Winnipeg and
the Prairies. For these reasons, he has been largely neglected.

William Patrick, the son of a draughtsman, was born in Glasgow on 8
September 1852, the second of four children. He attended Gorbals Youths'
School prior to enrolling in Glasgow University, where he was a committee member of the student Liberal club and also a member of the Dialectic
Society, the university debating society. In 1875 Patrick graduated with
first class honours in mental philosophy. From 1874 to 1878 he studied at
the Free Church College in Glasgow. Scholarships and prizes afforded him

study in Heidelberg in 1876. He was apparently conversant in several European languages.[3]

Ordination into the ministry came in December 1878 at Free St. David's Kirkintilloch, near Glasgow, where Patrick served as minister until the spring of 1892. In 1882 he was first elected to Kirkintilloch School Board, and in 1885 he became board chairman, a position he held until 1891. During his time as chairman, he was involved in two major controversies. Patrick's support of the amalgamation of educational endowments and bequests and his support of a proposal to amalgamate the higher classes of the two burgh schools[4] drew public criticism, some of which took the form of cartoons suggesting, interalia, that the rationalization of the patchwork quilt of endowments was a conspiracy by Patrick to deprive needy children of free school meals in order to finance his educational theories. Nevertheless, he was successful in bids for re-election. Later in Canada, he showed this same strong interest in schemes of amalgamation, despite criticism and controversy.

A life-long abstainer (and a life-long bachelor), Patrick helped to institute the Kirkintilloch Temperance Union, a precursor of similar concerns in Canada. In the 1885 parliamentary general election, Reverend Patrick spoke in favour of the Liberal candidate for Dunbartonshire, R.T. Reid, a Scottish Home Ruler, but he was defeated by his Conservative opponent. Another Liberal Home Ruler with whom Patrick was identified, albeit briefly, was the illustrious politician, writer, and world traveller Robert Bontine Cunninghame Graham. From 1886 to 1892 Graham was the member of Parliament for the neighbouring constituency of North West Lanarkshire. On one occasion, at the request of local coal miners, Patrick provided hospitality for Graham, then accompanied him to the platform where he was a speaker. Graham shared the platform on that occasion with the then lesser known Keir Hardie.[5]

In June 1892 Patrick left Kirkintilloch and was inducted into Free St. Paul's Church, Dundee. He was awarded the honorary degree of doctor of divinity by Glasgow University in March 1893. From 1892 to 1900 he edited the monthly religious journal *Youth*. In March 1894 Dr. Patrick became seriously and painfully ill with disgestive problems, which he bore "heroically" throughout the remainder of his life. One of his contemporaries observed that he allowed himself no indulgences and few relaxations.[6]

While in Dundee, Patrick was vice-convenor of the Free Church Committee on the Welfare of Youth and, together with a United Presbyterian minister, was joint convenor of the committee responsible for the training of ministers for those two churches prior to their union in 1900.

Rev. James Robertson, superintendent of Home Missions for the Presbyterian Church in Canada from 1881 to 1902 and member of the Board of Manitoba College, visited Scotland in late 1896 until early 1897.[7] Robertson spent part of this time as the guest of Patrick, who subsequently recalled that he had learned from Robertson "the nature and magnitude of the Home Mission task to which the Churches of Canada were summoned."[8]

Following the death of the eminent principal of Manitoba College, John Mark King, in 1899, Patrick was offered, and accepted, the post of principal in early 1900. *The Westminster*, a Toronto-based religious journal, commented on 17 February 1900:

> This appointment is of exceptional importance to the Church and to Canada
> ... The Principal of Manitoba College holds an office more important to
> the better life of that vast empire west of the Great Lakes than the Premier
> of the Province or the Governor of the Territories ... Experience has proved
> how unlikely it is that a man transplanted from Scotland to Canada after
> he has reached middle life will become thoroughly Canadianized, or will
> enter with enthusiasm into new and strange work and become a real force
> in the life of the church.[9]

Despite these reservations the article conceded that on grounds of scholarship and administrative experience Patrick was a first-rate choice.

Church and theological college associates gathered in Edinburgh to bid farewell to Dr. Patrick. The names of those attending would suggest that Patrick was highly regarded by the liberal evangelical wing, which included Professor George Adam Smith, who spoke in his praise. Both Smith and Patrick had been students of the famous Professor Edward Caird, professor of moral philosophy at Glasgow University. Smith was a pioneer of the new Higher Biblical Criticism.[10] Patrick's induction as principal of Manitoba College took place at Knox (Presbyterian) Church, Winnipeg, on 12 April 1900. He also assumed the chair of Old and New Testament exegesis.[11]

His adopted city of about 40,000 population exhibited characteristics associated with rapid growth. Journalist James Gray claimed that the Winnipeg of his youth, which was the Winnpeg Patrick found on his arrival, was a "lusty, gutsy, bawdy, frontier boom-town roaring through an un-

Rev. William Patrick, DD, principal, Manitoba College, 1900–11. A dour Scot, he was an early advocate of church union in Canada. (Courtesy Western Canada Pictorial Index, University of Winnipeg, Winnipeg, #A0672-20608.)

equalled debauch."[12] In private correspondence, Patrick appeared to agree with Gray's assessment, but publicly, and especially when home in Scotland, he claimed that the standard of morality in Winnipeg was high, that poverty scarcely existed, and that intemperance was slight.[13] He was no doubt aware that remarks publicly expressed in Scotland would be read by potential recruits to the ministry and to mission work in western Canada. Also, like many immigrants he may have felt the need to avoid negative remarks about his adopted country when addressing an audience in the old country.

In Winnipeg, however, Patrick expressed concern about issues such as the sale of alcohol. As president of the interdenominational Manitoba Moral and Social Reform Council, Patrick sought to eliminate hotel bars, which he considered an important link in the chain of alcohol distribution. He also supported local control of liquor licensing.[14]

Patrick's considerable administrative skills were recognized by the provincial government when it appointed him chairman of a nine-man Agricultural Commission set up to enquire into the advisability of establishing an agricultural college in Manitoba. The commission reported in late 1902, the final report being published in early 1903. Among its recommendations was the establishment of a Department of Domestic Science at the proposed college, in order to make "girls and young women ... more expert and competent helpmates for agriculturalists, and indeed for anybody of whatever occupation."[15] The language was typically patriarchal.

Patrick was also active in solving labour-management disputes. In April 1906 he helped to settle a violent street railway strike in Winnipeg, receiving thanks from grateful employees, who claimed that Patrick had worked "faithfully and untiringly to obtain conditions acceptable to our membership and ... [is] entitled to all credit for bringing about a satisfactory settlement." Along with Principal Sparling of Wesley College, Patrick received from the union a copy of an illuminated address that echoed similar sentiments.[16]

The theme of consolidation of resources runs through Patrick's career, from his time on the Kirkintilloch School Board to his chairmanship of the Agricultural Commission, but Patrick's greatest attempt at consolidation was in the ecclesiastical sphere, namely, the proposed creation of the United Church of Canada.

Patrick left Scotland when two of the Presbyterian churches that had seceded from the established Church of Scotland, as a result of the 1843 Disruption, were about to merge. But in Canada, any union would have to be across denominational boundaries, since consolidation had already taken place, in the case of Presbyterians in 1875, and in the case of the Methodists in 1884. There had been attempts at interdenominational union, the most serious initiative coming from the Anglican Church. But this possibility had receded when the Lambeth Conference of 1888 had approved the

Quadrilateral, one point of which was acceptance of the "historic episco-
pate" as a condition of union.[17]

Patrick had arrived in Canada at a time when Presbyterian liberals
were looking for leadership on the issues that confronted their church. He
seized the opportunity to provide this leadership.[18] During the opening
session of the Presbyterian General Assembly meeting in Winnipeg in
1902, a committee, which included Patrick, was appointed to convey greet-
ings to the Methodist General Conference also meeting in Winnipeg. In the
words of E. Lloyd Morrow, an anti-unionist commentator, Patrick abruptly
and fortuitously launched "the frail bark of organic union on the calm sea
of ecclesiastical politics – a sea destined to become rough with waves of
opposition to the proposed merger."[19]

Patrick's dramatic plea was well received by the Methodist Conference, for it immediately carried a resolution favouring such union. This
was followed by the appointment of a committee to consult similar "union
committees" that might be set up by other church bodies. In 1903 the
Congregationalists appointed a similar committee.

Patrick had not been authorized to make anything other than a few
fraternal remarks to the Methodist Conference. He added to the controversy when he justified his actions during the Presbyterian General Assembly held in Saint John, New Brunswick, in 1904. It was his western
Canadian experience, he claimed in Saint John, that convinced him of the
benefits of church union. In the West, he added, "people had virtually
stepped over the barriers of denominational distinction and worked hand
in hand in the furtherance of the Christian cause."[20] Patrick was undoubtedly aware before he made this speech that throughout rural Canada,
particularly in the West, local union churches had sprung up. The futility
of competition among apparently similar Protestant denominations was
becoming obvious to residents of such areas.[21] Patrick's first published
article on church union, in September 1904, reflected this feeling:

> The polity and administration of the church are matters of expediency to
> be determined in the light of reason and experience. The institutions of
> the church should be altered and removed like those of the state ... The
> word of God no more prescribes Episcopacy, Independency or Presbyteri-
> anism than it prescribes a monarchy or a republic.

He had a similarly pragmatic view of doctrine: "The number of essential
doctrines is small. It is idle to expect agreements in details of doctrine

anymore than in ethics or politics ... These truths felt rather than confessed have modified our attitudes towards statements of doctrine."[22]

Such sentiments would obviously be criticized by rigid adherents to one of the essential canons of the Presbyterian faith – the Westminster Confession of Faith, which had its roots in Calvinist traditions. Union with a non-Calvinist church would involve compromise or even abandonment of the confession, which acknowledged Scripture as the supreme standard of faith. Although not hostile to the Confession, Patrick placed greater emphasis on union. Among his critics was the Reverend Dr. McLaren of Knox College, Toronto, who argued that it was unsafe for Patrick and other advocates of union to claim that they were led by the spirit. (Patrick had claimed that he was led by a "voice" to speak about church union in Winnipeg.)[23]

More imaginative opposition came from the Reverend Dr. John Mackay, a Canadian who had studied at the Free Church College in Glasgow from 1899 to 1902. He pointed out that the union between the United Presbyterian Church and the Free Church of Scotland in 1900 had resulted in a legal imbroglio over church property. On his return Mackay became minister of a Presbyterian church in Montreal. In 1906 two Presbyterian churches in the United States were united, with a resulting row over property. Mackay concluded that denominational restructuring was a matter of expediency rather than divine will.

At the 1906 Presbyterian Church of Canada General Assembly, Mackay proposed an amendment to the first draft of the "Basis of Union" advocating that future union have a federal or cooperative structure as opposed to being a complete organic union. Patrick poured scorn not only on Mackay's amendment but also on Mackay. Despite the amendment's defeat by 179 votes to 22, there were enough abstentions to support the belief that Patrick had alienated potential supporters, particularly those of Mackay's generation.[24] One observer noted that although Patrick's scholarship might be admired, his withering scorn for those who did not share his views added little to the peace of Zion![25]

In 1908 Mackay became principal of Westminster Hall, a new Presbyterian College in Vancouver. In 1909, in the course of a series of articles advocating a federal alternative, he touched on a widely held, but mostly unstated, assumption that the proposed church union would be a bastion of British Protestantism against the religions of newer immigrant groups such as the Ruthenians.[26] Mackay preferred a more multicultural approach, which became known as "the Ruthenian experiment"[27] by which "a number of Churches [were] organized from within and federated with some of the stronger denominations," a loose union that Mackay preferred to "the same deadening uniformity upon all the peoples."[28]

Mackay marshalled intelligent and constructive arguments against Patrick's definition of a more uniform union, and Mackay represented the East, especially Montreal and Ontario, and to some extent the Maritimes, where church union was never as strong among Presbyterians as it was in Winnipeg and the West, the source of Patrick's support. At the 1910 General Assembly, Mackay pleaded for the presbyteries, sessions, and congregations to be consulted on the "Basis of Union" without being influenced by a prior vote of the General Assembly. He also suggested that "congregations be invited to consider at the same time the feasibility of some scheme of co-operation of federation of the Protestant Churches in ... Canada." But Mackay's motion was defeated. The Presbyterian Church's Barrier Act "required the approval of a majority of presbyteries for any change in church law relating to doctrine, discipline, government or worship,"[29] and the Union Committee referred to that act in order to send the Basis of Union to the presbyteries (and not to congregations, as advocated by Mackay). The motion was carried carried by 180 votes to 73.[30]

Although the assembly's action was legal and "entirely presbyterian,"[31] the dissidents felt that hope of meaningful consultation had disappeared, and organized themselves outside established church structures to debate the "right of the General Assembly to legislate the Church out of existence." The dissidents were able to tap support from the many uncommitted commissioners (delegates). Although from 1906 to 1910 the unionist vote at assemblies was around 180 and the non-unionist ranged from 25 to 75, there were on average about 500 to 550 commissioners. Thus, there were many abstentions on the union question.[32]

In addition to his various public roles, Patrick was constantly dedicated to scholarship. In 1906 Patrick's major work, *James, the Lord's Brother*, was published. That year he contributed to the encyclopaedic *Dictionary of Christ and the Gospels*. Of more than one hundred contributors, five, including Patrick, were resident in Canada.[33]

At the same time, his life in Winnipeg was busy with visitors and committee meetings. In a letter to his brother, David, in Kirkintilloch, on 26 January 1908, Patrick gives an insight into the many pressures:

> When I was writing to you on Friday last I was anticipating and longing
> for a quiet afternoon and evening but I was disappointed. From four till

ten there were visitors in my house. The last two hours were given to a Home Mission Committee meeting held in my dining room.

Saturday proved no exception to the other days of the week for I was summoned to a meeting of our Indian Committee and thereafter I had a long interview with our Home Mission superintendent regarding work among the Ruthenians. The late contention among them has not been wholly allayed.[34] The embers are still smouldering.

On Sunday afternoon I addressed the Bible Class of Westminster church on Christianity and Poverty. This is a subject on which I have read extensively and thought much. I am lecturing this year to my students on Sociology and in this connection happened to be dealing at this very time with the many questions suggested by the existence of poverty. I spoke to a body of listeners who regarded me with the utmost attention.[35]

Despite many public commitments, Patrick, partly because of health problems, partly overwork, did not build personal links with church and community as much as he would have liked. His familiarity with western Canada gave him confidence to risk an initiative on church union. His lack of familiarity with Toronto and Montreal caused him to underestimate opposition from those quarters. His west of Scotland background helps to explain both his vigorous skill in debate[36] and his intolerance towards opponents, which in a Canadian context was very divisive.

Nevertheless he retained his ideals and could write in May 1910:

It is the right of the people to have leaders to whom the common Christianity of Canada is of more account than the success of any single church, for the common Christianity of Canada is the salvation of Canada ... Canada has led the Christian world already in the path of Church union. A still greater and more distinguished opportunity presents itself.[37]

Patrick died in Scotland on 18 September 1911. Almost three years later came the outbreak of the Great War – an event that would cause several European liberal theologians to radically reappraise their idealism. But a practical commitment to what was then a uniquely Canadian institution, merging Calvinist and Arminian traditions, justifies Professor Clifford's view that Patrick should be assigned a central role in Canadian church history.

David Rollo is a graduate of St. Andrew's University (Queen's College, Dundee), with an M.A. honours degree in political science and economics. His thesis, "Comparative Aspects of Irish Politics in Boston, New York and Glasgow" during the late nineteenth and early twentieth centuries, was written in partial fulfilment of a graduate degree in North American studies at Edinburgh University. He has been a librarian in Canada and Scotland, where he is in charge of Ayr College Library. He has written articles on Canada for the Scottish press, and has spoken on comparative Scottish-Canadian topics. Since childhood, he has been interested in William Patrick, for whom the public library in Rollo's home town in Scotland is named. At Dalhousie University, Halifax, Rollo followed the career of Patrick in a course on Canadian religious history. And upon his return to Scotland, he came across an illuminated scroll and other documents relating to Patrick. Thanks to David Rollo, those documents are now in the University of Winnipeg library.

Notes

1 George Morrison, "The United Church of Canada, Ecumenical or Economical Necessity" (B.D. diss., Emmanuel College, University of Toronto, 1956), 83.

2 N. Keith Clifford, "The Origins of the Church Union Controversy," *Journal of the Canadian Church Historical Society* 18, nos. 2–3 (June–September 1976), 34–52

3 Scottish Record Office (SRO), Extract from Register of Barony Parish, Glasgow, 4 January 1879; and obits in the *Kirkintilloch Herald*, 4 October 1911, and in the Montreal *Gazette*, 30 September 1911.

4 A.D. Morrison, *The Story of Free St. David's now St. David's United Free Church, Kirkintilloch, 1843–1926* (Kirkintilloch: Kirkintilloch Herald, 1926), 94–95.

5 *Kirkintilloch Herald*, 4 October 1911, 8.

6 Morrison, *Story of Free St. David's*, 96; T.B. Kilpatrick, "William Patrick: 1852–1911, an appreciation," *The Presbyterian* (Toronto), 5 October 1911, 359–60; and Rev. Henry Henderson, "Principal Patrick, D.D. a sketch," *Youth* (Edinburgh), June 1900, 102–5.

7 G. Morrison, "The Canadian North-West: An Interview with Rev. James Robertson, D.D.," *Youth* (Edinburgh), May 1897, 101–4.

8 William Patrick, "The Case for Church Union: How the Movement Began," *The Presbyterian* (Toronto), 12 May 1910, 583–84.

9 "Dr. Patrick is Principal-Elect of Manitoba," *The Westminster* (Toronto), 17 February 1900, 188–89.

10 "Principal Patrick Dies in Scotland," *Manitoba Free Press* (Winnipeg), 17 February 1900, 188–89; and B.J. Fraser, *The Social Uplifters: Presbyterian Progressives and the Social Gospel in Canada, 1875–1915* (Waterloo: Wilfrid Laurier University Press, 1988), 9.

11 A.G. Bedford, *The University of Winnipeg: A History of the Founding Colleges* (Toronto: University of Toronto Press, 1976), 77.

12 J.H. Gray, *Red Lights on the Prairies* (Toronto: Macmillan, 1971), 35.

13 *British Weekly* (Scotch Edition), 2 July 1903, 294, 297.

14 *Manitoba Free Press*, 20 February 1908; and *Free Press*, 21 October 1911.

15 Manitoba, Legislative Assembly, *Journals* and *Sessional Papers, 1903 Sessional Papers*, no. 17, *Report of the Agricultural College Commission, 1902*, 491–502.

16 D.J. Bercuson, *Confrontation at Winnipeg: Labour Industrial Relations and the General Strike* (Montreal/Kingston: McGill-Queen's University Press, 1980), 11–15; R.B. Fleming, *The Railway King of Canada* (Vancouver: University of British Columbia Press, 1991), 120–21; *The Voice* (Winnipeg), 30 March 1906, 1, and 13 April 1906, 1; Morrison, *Story of Free St. David's*, 118–19; United Church Archives, University of Winnipeg, "Blessed are the Peacemakers," illuminated scroll presented to Rev. William Patrick by the Amalgamated Association of Street and Electric Railway Employees of America, Division 99, Winnipeg, April 1906.

17 J.W. Grant, *The Canadian Experience of Church Union* (London: Lutterworth, 1967), 83.

18 N.K. Clifford, *The Resistance to Church Union in Canada, 1904–1939* (Vancouver: University of British Columbia Press, 1985), 20.

19 E.L. Morrow, *Church Union in Canada* (Toronto: Thomas Allen, 1923), 14–15.

20 *Saint John Daily Sun*, 7 June 1904, 1.

21 C. Macdonald, "James Robertson and Presbyterian Church Extension in Manitoba and the North-West, 1866–1902," in D.L. Butcher et al., eds., *Prairie Spirit: Perspectives on the Heritage of the United Church of the Canadian West* (Winnipeg: University of Manitoba Press, 1985), 85–99; and S.W. Dyde, "Church Union in Canada, From a Presbyterian Standpoint," *Journal of Religion* (Chicago), 2 March 1922, 147–58.

22 *The Westminster*, September 1904, 190–94.

23 *The Presbyterian*, 12 May 1910.

24 Clifford, *Resistance to Church Union*, 45.

25 C.E. Silcox, *Church Union in Canada* (New York: Institute of Social and Religious Research, 1933), 189.

26 Bedford, *The University of Winnipeg*, 78–79; Macdonald, "James Robertson," 95–99; and Mary Vipond, "Canadian National Consciousness and the Formation of the United Church of Canada," *United Church Archives Committee Bulletin* 24 (1975): 5–27.

27 Clifford, *Resistance*, 45–46, 248; R.R. Smith, "A Heritage of Healing, Church Hospital and Medical Work in Manitoba, 1900–1977," *Prairie Spirit*, 265–82; and P. Yuzyk, *The Ukrainians in Manitoba: A Social History* (Toronto: University of Toronto Press, 1953), 73, 141.

28 J. Mackay, "The Case against Church Union, Article II," *The Presbyterian*, 26 November 1910, 584–85.

29 J.S. Moir, *Enduring Witness: A History of the Presbyterian Church in Canada* (Toronto: Presbyterian Church in Canada, 1987), 203.

30 Clifford, *Resistance*, 48.

31 Moir, *Enduring Witness*, 203.

32 Clifford, *Resistance*, 48, 54.

33 Patrick, *James, The Lord's Brother* (Edinburgh: T&T Clark, 1906); and J. Hastings, ed., *A Dictionary of Christ and the Gospels* (New York: Scribners, 1906).

34 Patrick seems to be referring to the fear held by "Ruthenians" or Ukrainians in 1907–1908 that Presbyterian support for the Independent Greek (Orthodox) Church was really an attempt to assimilate Orthodox Christians rather than a means of providing spiritual help for Ukrainian immigrants. (See Yuzyk, *The Ukrainians in Manitoba*, 73.)

35 William Patrick Private Collection, letter from William Patrick, Winnipeg, to David Patrick, Kirkintilloch, 26 January 1908.

36 G.C. Pidgeon, *The United Church of Canada: The Story of Union* (Toronto: Ryerson, 1950), 31–33.

37 Patrick, "The Case for Church Union, Parts V and VI," *The Presbyterian*, 26 May 1910, 652–54.

Chapter 10

Jesse Lloyd and Silas Fletcher: Two Well-Known Unknowns

Ronald J. Stagg

Biography is both science and art. While the scientific approach, the methodical search for and examination of evidence, is critical to the process, so are the evaluation and interpolation of the result. If too little evidence exists, a biography can be more art that science, approaching or even crossing the border between history and historical fiction. Conversely, a biography based on limited evidence can become an antiquarian's dream, a collection of facts revealing little or nothing about the personality of the subject, a mere recitation of what happened when.

This paper is, in part, a discussion of the problem of constructing biographies from limited evidence. Men such as Sir George-Étienne Cartier and Sir Francis Hincks left few personal papers, but with such major figures, public papers and private papers of contemporaries fill many gaps. This problem is compounded when dealing with minor figures, for such additional sources are relatively unavailable. A further complication, which forms the basis of the discussion in this paper, arises when a minor figure, about whom little documentation seems to exist, has been the subject of a biographical sketch, one with significant imperfections. Is it possible to go beyond the existing flawed biographies, which assume a life of their own, once published, to create a sound biography? Both Jesse Lloyd and Silas Fletcher are the subjects of older biographies, Lloyd's published in 1951 and Fletcher's in 1949. In the first case, the information is incomplete and incorrect; in the second, it is incomplete and derived from dubious sources. Though "known," both men remain unknown.[1]

Jesse Lloyd's biographers were really the biographers of his wife. A brief account of his life appears in *The Bridging of Three Centuries: The Life and Times of Pheobe Crossley Lloyd – A Girl Bride of a Rebel of 1837* by J.H. Walton and E.G. Lloyd. There are problems, not the least of which is that Jesse Lloyd's place and date of death are incorrectly identified. With Fletcher, the problem is more with questionable sources. John Barnett's "Silas Fletcher, Instigator of the Upper Canadian Rebellion" relies too much on family stories or legends. In each man's case, the issue is whether enough information can be obtained about a minor person to verify or correct the printed account.

Lloyd is undisputably the more important of the two men. While he attained notoriety, or fame, depending on which side of the political fence one sat, as a second-rank leader of the Home District rebellion of 1837, he deserves greater recognition for his role in founding Lloydtown. In the 1830s Lloydtown was the largest urban centre north of the capital Toronto, and it remained a major regional centre until the last quarter of the nineteenth century, when the railway shifted trade and population to Schomberg, a short distance to the east.

Land petitions show that Jesse Lloyd arrived in 1808, not 1788 as suggested in the biographical sketch. Land records also reveal much about Lloyd's business sense. What emerges is a picture of a shrewd businessman who, like his father and uncles, dealt in clergy reserve lots, a fact that must not have pleased his fellow Quakers, since they believed in separating church and state. Among his dealings was a legal contest with an impoverished local widow over who had the right to lease a particular reserve lot. This case suggests that Lloyd was a tough-minded businessman. Township records, another useful source for biography in early Ontario, show him active in township politics, holding various municipal offices between 1829 and 1836. He also acted as a spokesperson for local landowners, of which, of course, he was one. From this it is easier to understand why he became involved in provincial politics, on the reform side, in the early 1830s. Anyone involved in communication and land settlement in the 1830s tended to be either rewarded or frustrated by provincial regulations and the people who oversaw them.

Quaker meeting records reveal that Lloyd was ejected from the Society of Friends in 1831, not 1837, and for non-attendance, not for political activities, as his biographic sketch maintains. One gets the impression of a very busy entrepreneur, hampered by the lack of a good road to the Yonge Street meeting, putting business before religion.

Luck plays a part in doing the biographies of early minor figures. Douglas Lloyd, a descendant of one of Jesse's cousins, happened to be working on family genealogy. He corrected some facts about the family, shared some of his assumptions, and gave a hint or two about the family's (including Jesse's) mill-owning activities. A casual conversation with someone else provided information that a will existed for Jesse Lloyd, a document previous researchers had overlooked. This will provided valuable insight into the state of Lloyd's affairs at his death. He owned almost no property. Because he had sold off lots to form Lloydtown, most of his holdings were in the form of claims on clergy reserve lots.

Lloyd's part in the Rebellion of 1837 is well recorded in the testimony of participants. He led the largest and best-trained unit of the rebels down to Montgomery's Tavern, the unit that formed much of the front ranks in the advance on Toronto on 5 December. Less obvious was Lloyd's probable role in precipitating the uprising. A reading of William Lyon Mackenzie's papers led to the reminiscences of Thomas Storrow Brown, one of the rebel leaders in Lower Canada. By comparing dates in the two men's accounts, one can determine that Lloyd knew about plans for a rising at Toronto when he paid a visit to Lower Canada in mid-November, when plans for the rebellion in Upper Canada were known only to a select few. Lloyd, William Lyon Mackenzie, and perhaps Silas Fletcher planned the rebellion before any of the other leading figures, such as Samuel Lount and Peter Matthews, had been persuaded, or even approached, to take part.

What emerges from the research is a well-rounded picture of a hard-driving local entrepreneur, anxious to see his area develop, prepared to go to whatever lengths necessary to see that the welfare of his fellow inhabitants, and of course his own, improved in the face of an exploitive, seemingly uncaring provincial oligarchy. Lloyd might well have returned to King Township after the rebellion to become a dominant force in the township had not fever ended his life while he was in exile in Tippecanoe County, Indiana, in 1838. If it is not possible to get inside the head of Lloyd to understand his motivation, it is possible from the extensive documentation available to make some informed guesses.

Silas Fletcher is a more difficult study. Aside from his role as a third-rank leader of the uprising, Fletcher is of no great significance as a historical figure. A fair bit is known about Fletcher's life. A Fletcher genealogy provides information on the family's past: his birth at Chesterfield, Massachusetts, in 1780, his marriage in 1809 to Isabella Sutherland, his fathering of fifteen children, and his death in Chautauqua County, New York, in 1847. The arrival of Silas and his younger brother, John, in Whitchurch Township in 1806 is also a matter of record, as is his first land dealing.

Although granted 200 acres in Toronto Township, Fletcher purchased 200 acres in East Gwillimbury in early 1807. In 1808 and 1809 he sold off both halves, continuing to live on the half he had sold to his brother. His desertion during the War of 1812 and his statements made after the Rebellion of 1837 seem to confirm the family story that he never liked British government and preferred American democracy. His later extensive land trading can be traced in land records. His part in founding the Farmer's Storehouse Company in 1824 and his role as director are documented. Newspapers show a great deal about his reform activities in the 1830s and also tie him to William Lyon Mackenzie. As early as 1830 Fletcher helped to organize a meeting at Newmarket to endorse Mackenzie and Jesse Ketchum as candidates for election. Several times in succeeding years he supported reform schemes organized by Mackenzie, including the establishment of a Committee of Vigilance at Hope (Sharon) in 1833 to press for reform. He supported other reform causes as well, including the establishment of a mutual fire insurance company for the Home District.

Even Fletcher's career in the United States, subsequent to the rebellion, is known in some detail. After participating in early attempts by Canadians to retake their colony, he became disillusioned with the lack of response within Upper Canada, as did many other exiles, and abandoned the movement. In 1838 he purchased a dairy farm in Chautaugua County and devoted the rest of his life to it. His only other business venture was as an apparently silent partner in a woollen mill he purchased in 1839 for his son Daniel and a fellow exile, Nelson Gorham. Silas never returned to his adopted homeland of Upper Canada.

Some parts of Fletcher's life are, however, only available through family stories, a notoriously unreliable source. His career as a horse trader across Upper Canada is such example. More importantly, his role in the rebellion is another, for without this Fletcher is of small consequence in history. John Barnett claims that Fletcher actually pressured Mackenzie to start a rebellion and that Fletcher was one of the chief organizers in the northern townships. His proof is family stories, local tradition, the fact that Fletcher led a contingent of rebels to Toronto, and the fact that in the months prior to the uprising he sold off or gave to other family members much of his land. A check of land records does show that Fletcher sold off some of his land before the rising, though not perhaps as large a proportion as Barnett claims. And records from the rebellion period show that Fletcher did encourage some men to join the rebellion and that a large number of men from his area participated in the rising. However, this is not sufficient evidence to prove that Fletcher was urging Mackenzie to action or that he alone persuaded many of his neighbours to join the rebellion. There is in fact no way to prove this, although it can be confirmed that Fletcher was a local organizer and that he carried messages to Toronto during the rebellion.

It is thus possible only to say that Fletcher preferred the American to the British style of government. As to the events of his life, a little can be said about his business activities, something about his support for reform, and something more about his activities during the rebellion. His biography remains a hazy outline. Using the art of biography, Barnett created for key areas of Fletcher's life more a series of possibilities than a series of probabilities or certainties.

As a result of the additional information available, Lloyd can and will be seen in a new light, but Barnett's image of Fletcher is likely to prevail until such time as more material is discovered. One might naturally wonder whether it is worth the effort to try to redo the biography of such minor figures. One might also ask whether any attempt should be made to write biographies of even less important figures, given the difficulty in finding sources. The answer to these questions has to be a very strong affirmative.

If we have biographies only of major historical figures, it will not be possible to fully understand the society of a given period. Nor can statistical studies, or quantitative history, reveal everything about why society reacted as it did to various events, influences, movements. The sum of the actions of minor figures helped to determine the course of our development. The sum total of the biographies of numerous minor figures of the rebellion period, even partial biographies, may show us that a large proportion preferred American institutions or that a large number were involved with and frustrated by the development process in their townships. As research turns to the lives of these figures, it may be that other individuals, like Jesse Lloyd, will become "known" again.

Ronald Stagg is interested in the history of Ontario between the late eighteenth and early twentieth centuries, and much of his writing has to do with the early nineteenth century. He co-edited with Colin Read a book for the Champlain Society, *The Rebellion of 1837 in Upper Canada,* and has published articles on the rebellion and on other subjects relating to the period, such as the "Children of Peace." One of his articles appeared in the Ontario Historical Society's collection *1837 Rebellion Remembered*. In nineteen biographical sketches for the *Dictionary of Canadian Biography*, including one on William Lyon Mackenzie, co-authored with Fred Armstrong, and three for the *Canadian Encyclopedia*, his subjects' lives covered the period from the last half of the eighteenth century to the beginning of the twentieth. In a similar vein, papers he has presented at conferences and to historical societies and museum audiences have ranged over the nineteenth century. While a sizeable portion dealt with the period leading up to and including the Rebellion of 1837, his subjects have included such diverse ones as Goldwin Smith's Toronto, the politics of Upper Canada/Canada West 1837–67, and the history of the town/city of west Toronto. For over a year, Professor Stagg wrote a historical column for a regional magazine dealing with York Region. Two of his articles have appeared in *Horizon Canada*. He has also given lectures and written in a popular vein on architectural details of Toronto houses. For variety, he sometimes gives lectures to wine societies on wine-related topics.

Note

1 A biographical sketch of Lloyd, with bibliography, by this author appears in *Dictionary of Canadian Biography*, vol. 7, *1836–1850*, edited by Francess G. Halpenny (Toronto: University of Toronto Press, 1988). Fletcher appears in two articles by John Barnett: "Silas Fletcher, Instigator of the Upper Canadian Rebellion," *Ontario History*, vol. 41 (1949); and "John Button of Buttonville," *Ontario Historical Society Papers and Records*, vol. 39 (1947). Genealogical data is found in E.H. Fletcher, *Fletcher Geneology: an account of the descendants of Robert Fletcher of Concord, Mass.* (Boston, 1871). Fletcher's reform activities can be found in *Colonial Advocate*, 18 July 1833; Archives of Ontario (AO), C.R. Dent Collection; *The Patriot*, Toronto, 11 November 1836; *Constitution*, Toronto, 9 August 1837. His land activities are found in AO, Land Index, and AO, Abstract Index to Deeds for various townships, including Toronto, East Gwillimbury, Reach, and Vespra. His activities in the rebellion are mentioned in National Archives of Canada, Rolph Papers, RG5 A1, vol. 180; AO, Mackenzie-Lindsey Collection, Mackenzie Clippings, Box 29, #4687; AO, Rebellion Papers, no. 9; and in J.C. Dent, *The Story of the Upper Canadian Rebellion*, 2 vols. (Toronto, 1885). A physical description appears in *Upper Canada Herald* (Toronto), 12 December 1837.

Chapter 11

Henry Caesar Childers, 1868–1963: A Biographical Sketch

John Connor

Arma virumque cano ...[1]

Henry Caesar Childers was born in Mount Street, Mayfair, London, on the 23rd of November 1868, the first child of Robert Caesar Childers and Anna Barton of Glendalough, Wicklow, Ireland. In the course of the next eight years, the family was augmented by another son, Robert Erskine, and three daughters, Sybil Rose, Dulcibella, and Constance.

In many respects this was a family "to the manor born." The father held the first chair in Oriental languages at the University of London, and the mother came from a family of substantial estate in Ireland and had interests in the Bordeaux wine shippers, Barton and Gestier. Robert Caesar had worked for the East India Company but had been invalided home in the mid-1860s. As a result of his interest in the Orient, he compiled a dictionary of the Pali language, peculiar to Sri Lanka (then Ceylon). In 1876 he died of tuberculosis. After his death, Anna cared for the family, and at her death, the five children were dispatched to the Bartons at Glendalough, where their uncle, Robert Barton, and his wife, Agnes, who was a sister of Robert Childers, cared for them.[2]

Glendalough was an extensive and well-appointed estate. Nannies cared for the children, and a governess tutored them. Henry and Erskine learned to handle horses, and enjoyed riding to hounds, shooting, and fishing. Henry was a "whipper in"[3] with the Carlow Hunt, an exclusive club in County Wicklow, fifty miles southwest of Dublin. At the same time, he was a gentleman jockey, riding in pink silks. He once entered a cross-country race and was in the lead when he became careless and allowed his mount to take a wrong turn, thus losing the race. In addition, the brothers acquired substantial skills as mariners and became accomplished sailors. In short, their upbringing was typically landed gentry.

About 1880 Henry was sent to C.W. Goodhart's school in Highbury, a recently developed suburb of London, in preparation for Harrow, where he spent two years. In September 1888 he entered Royal Military College, Sandhurst, but from February to August 1889, he was on sick leave. Although his conduct was reported to be "very good," his marks were low, he failed the course, and he was "too ill to attend for re-examination."[4] Unlike his brother Erskine, Henry appears never to have gained renown in scholarship. In eight terms at Harrow, his name appears most frequently in the lower echelons of the class lists except in terms when he was forced to repeat his program. On one such occasion, he qualified for a prize in classics but his interest in the classics lapsed until years later in Nova Scotia. When his children began to study Latin and Greek, he memorized an entire book of Virgil's *Aeneid*, which he sometimes recited while milking cows.[5]

Little evidence remains of Henry's activities during the early 1890s. He came into an inheritance, described as "moderate," and may have spent it rather quickly, for he seems never to have learned good money management. He climbed mountains in Austria where he struck up a lifetime friendship with Leo Amery, later famous in 1940 for his House of Commons speech that led to the fall of the Chamberlain ministry. Henry also fished for salmon in Scotland, rode to hounds, and sailed. In Ireland, his great friend was "Pip" Booth, whose sister he contemplated marrying but for various reasons, most apparently involving a lack of sufficient income, did not.

By the second half of the 1890s, Henry was at loose ends. In his late twenties, he was still unprepared for the rude realities of earning a living, and he had no family estate or business to fall back on. His brother, by contrast, had already established himself. Following graduation from Cambridge, Erskine became a clerk in the House of Commons. During the summer of 1897, Henry joined his brother on a cruise in Erskine's thirty-six-foot cutter, *Vixen*, in the waters around the German Friesan Islands and into the Baltic through the Kiel Canal. The cruise lasted until early December, Henry taking a two-week break in October. The log for these marine wanderings provided the structural framework for Erskine Childers's *Riddle of the Sands*, first published in 1903, and it is not hard to discern the models for the sophisticated civil servant and the rough and ready sailor in Erskine and Henry respectively.

Soon after the completion of the cruise, Henry sailed for New York and set out for the Klondike, perhaps to pan for gold, but more likely to observe the gold fever and to talk to miners and trappers. He bet $10 in the famous Soapy Smith's Tavern, lost the money, and never gambled again. He had learned to snowshoe only after reaching the North, but on hearing of the Boer War, he and a postman took turns breaking a trail through the hip-deep snow and managed to snowshoe out of the Klondike. Henry sailed down to Vancouver and took the train to Winnipeg. The recruiting sergeant for the Lord Strathcona's Horse questioned whether a cavalry regiment could accommodate someone so small, but Henry argued and demonstrated that he could handle horses. He mustered at the Fort Garry barracks north of Winnipeg, travelled to Ottawa, where he had his photograph taken, and on Saint Patrick's Day, 1900, sailed as trooper 494 on the *Monterey* out of Halifax.[6] He survived the war with only a minor wound and a bout with typhoid.

Henry Caesar Childers (1868–1963), in dress uniform of Strathcona Horse. Photograph by S.J. Jarvis, Ottawa, 1900. (Courtesy Anna Childers, Thornhill, Ontario.)

Henry returned to Canada by way of London, where he received a campaign medal from King Edward VII honouring engagements in the Orange Free State, Belfast, and Natal. He took up farming with the Johnson brothers at Vaseux Lake in British Columbia, then for $35, through the Soldiers' Resettlement Board, he bought land at Bear Creek near Kelowna, where he bred and schooled polo ponies. He built his own forge, and in order to irrigate the dry land, he paid $6,000 for the construction of a dam and flume. At Kelowna in June 1910, Henry married Sybil Christobel Allen of the County of Cork, daughter of an Indian Army captain, born in Pietermaritzburg, South Africa. During the First World War, he rented his farm at Bear Creek and moved his wife and young family, Anna and Walter, to Kelowna, four miles away, where they rented a house. Henry succeeded in convincing the recruiting officer of his old regiment, Lord Strathcona's Horse, that he was a shade under forty rather than his actual age, a shade under fifty. In Winnipeg, the comfortable Fort Garry barracks were unavailable to the Stathcona Horse, and the replacement barracks proved cold and drafty. Henry contracted diphtheria, which prevented him from going overseas.

He returned to the farm near Kelowna, where he determined to take up market gardening, which he had learned through a correspondence course offered by the International Correspondence School, Chicago. He produced a successful crop of fruits and vegetables but soon discovered that the only market was in the Prairies, since the local market was satiated with produce. Sybil Childers made money on a flock of hens and small fruit (raspberries, strawberries, and rhubarb), and in one season, thanks to Sybil's management skills, the farm cleared $1,500. Unfortunately, the large farm of 450 acres proved too lonely for Sybil, who saw too little of distant neighbours. On the advice of the family doctor, Dr. Knox, the farm was put up for sale. It was purchased by a religious order of teaching brothers who wanted to establish a residential school.

Henry was now flush with cash. The family had already moved to Nova Scotia, where they joined Sybil's cousin, Oswald Brown, on an apple farm, called "Brampton," at Chipman Corner in the Annapolis Valley. Henry was persuaded to invest in farm operations. Prudent husbandry yielded a bumper crop of Russets, McIntoshes, Goldens, and Gravensteins, which in normal times would have sold locally or in the United Kingdom, via an agent for the Dominion Atlantic Railway. The postwar recession reduced their income, and Oswald Brown absconded with the proceeds of sales in England. The farm was sold at a sheriff's sale to Dr. Fullerton of

Port Williams, a close friend, and the Childers vacated the property. Henry sued Brown and won a settlement of $1,700, thanks to his careful accounting of farm operations. (When managing for others, Henry was a good accountant; the opposite was true when he managed his own affairs.) By the onset of winter, 1922, the family had moved to a fifty-acre farm at Avonport, about five miles from Wolfville. The farm, which the family named "Avon," after a nearby river, fronted the Gaspereau River near where it entered the Minas Basin. Before the Expulsion of 1755, the land had belonged to Acadian farmers.

Henry was about to embark upon yet another commercial endeavour. He obtained some Jersey cows and aspired to become a cream shipper. One of his purebreds, Lily of Avon, daughter of a cow he had bought to start the herd, produced such a quantity of milk in her best year that she qualified to be officially registered for her ROP (Record of Performance). Henry was naturally proud, but his wife's careful accounting showed that Lily's income from the Halifax Creamery was less than the cost of feeding and maintaining her. As the recession of the mid-1920s spread, butterfat sank to fifteen cents a pound, and the farm failed to generate sufficient funds to service the mortgage, which was paid only with the financial assistance of a relative by marriage, Flora Priestley, who resided in Florence, Italy.[7]

Somehow the household survived. Daughter Anna found employment as a teacher in a nearby rural school before moving to Ontario, and Walter studied agriculture and became an expert on grasses with Agriculture Canada. Henry's wife suffered the most. It was difficult being married to a man who appeared to value his animals above his wife and children and whose annual income was always unpredictable. Sybil suffered from manic depression, and in 1933 she succumbed to a nervous breakdown, from which she never recovered. She died after a protracted period of hospitalization. Nevertheless, Henry met every difficulty with a sense of stoic imperturbability and a stiff upper lip. In other words, his stubbornness prevented him from admitting that the farm drove him deeper into debt each year.

There are a number of anecdotal memories of Henry's doings in Nova Scotia. He is credited with introducing soya beans to the province, and with enthusiasm he entered into correspondence with Henry Ford on the prospects for using the bean in construction of horn assemblies. One year Henry was short of hay, so at low tide one day, he took his scythe and began to cut tall sedge grass that was growing on a high point in the Gaspereau River. As the tide returned, he continued to cut the grass, unaware of impending danger. Since he was deaf in one ear, he did not at first hear the shouts of concerned neighbours, the Coldwells, who could see that the incoming tide had completely surrounded the small piece of high ground. Finally Henry heard the shouts, and quickly set down his scythe and swam ashore. The neighbours took him in and dried man and clothing. Henry placed his soaked wrist watch in the oven, and it continued to work for years. He returned the next day to collect the hay, which the incoming tide had brought to shore.

When grass seed could be bought for under a dollar a pound, Henry read an account of canary grass, which grew in wet places. In the middle of a cow pasture was a small, wet, and otherwise unproductive area. He obtained government literature and decided to experiment, undeterred by the fact that canary seed cost over $10 a pound.[8] As he had in British Columbia, Henry built himself a forge to shoe his horses and to fashion wrought-iron equipment for the farm. Clearly Henry had an enquiring mind and was ready to take on any challenge. At the same time, he seems to have lacked the moderation and caution of training and experience. His greatest problem was his inability to manage money. Had he been willing to take a salaried job, he might have indulged his impractical, experimental nature with impunity.

When the Second World War began, Henry had entered his seventies. Nevertheless, he sought to enlist in the Canadian Army, but his services were politely refused. Undaunted, he obtained a job in the Halifax Naval Dockyard, gaining satisfaction in the knowledge that he was contributing to the nation's cause. In 1922 the Avonport farm was sold to a neighbour, Edward Haliburton, for $5,000, $1,500 more than Henry had paid for it. Henry spent about five years in London close to his sisters. It can only be assumed that his means were limited – two trusts yielding, perhaps, £200 per annum. He then went to live with his son in Ottawa before taking up residence at the Veterans' Health Centre. In the last decades of his life, he engaged in playing chess at the Military Club, reading, and occasionally writing letters to the editor of the *Ottawa Citizen*. Articulate to the end, he died at the age of ninety-five in 1963.

The life and times of Henry Childers is of biographical interest on a number of counts. He was a survivor, whatever the vicissitudes, which included the early deaths of his parents; the experience of war; economic depressions coinciding with his attempts to pursue a livelihood in agriculture, for which he was ill prepared; and the ordeal of his wife's chronic illness and death. It must be stated, however, that without Sybil, his greatest asset, he might not have survived. When Henry married her, his sisters recognized Sybil's strength and stability and were greatly relieved. The children of Henry and Sybil also valued her fine qualities.

Henry was a man of considerable connections, most significantly his younger brother, Erskine, whose career ran the gamut from civil servant to artilleryman in the Boer War and the First World War, from author to political philosopher, military intelligence airman, and confidant and adviser to the leaders of the emerging Eire. While Henry's initiatives tended to end in minor disaster, most of Erskine's undertakings enjoyed substantial success, with one exception – as propagandist for those opposed to the Anglo-Irish Treaty of 1921, which resulted in his execution. Other members of the family enjoyed prominence. Henry's cousin, Sir Hugh Childers, served as Gladstone's chancellor of the Exchequer, following service in Australia. Sir Hugh was responsible for the imposition of unpopular excise duties on alcohol, thereby contributing to the fall of the government in 1885. The 1910 edition of the *Encyclopaedia Britannica* claimed he lost his own seat in the subsequent election for championing Irish Home Rule. A generation later, Henry's nephew, Erskine, son of Erskine, became an Irish cabinet minister, and later, president of Ireland from 1970 to 1973.

Henry's life, perhaps *in extremis*, reflects the experience of a cadre of British society that gravitated to the fringe provinces of Canada during the first forty years of this century. In 1900 the Annapolis Valley was prosperous, its economy based on apples, lumber, fish, and mixed farming; there were concentrations of thriving boat builders, and since the valley had been settled for over a century, social amenities were in place. Unlike their predecessors who had arrived before 1900 – the Acadians, demobilized garrisons, New England Planters, United Empire Loyalists, Highlanders, and Irish – the post-1900 settlers had very often been raised in relative affluence. Although short of capital, some received pensions, while others were children of members of the British administrative or military establishment who served out their careers in the Maritimes and came to regard Canada as home. Land with a house could be obtained cheaply, sometimes with the assistance of the Soldiers' Resettlement Board or the commutation of a pension. Mortgages were easily obtained, for there was much old money ready to be securely placed. Once the economic upheaval of the First World War had calmed down, £100 at an exchange rate of $5 per pound went much farther in Nova Scotia than in St. John's Wood, London, or Morningside, Edinburgh. The climate was more severe than Britain's, but the living was comfortable, especially if revenues from the farm were augmented by even a modest remittance. In the early 1920s, many settlers, like Henry Childers, looked forward to a comfortable semi-retirement based on ante-bellum conditions and peacetime stability and continuing prosperity. The Depression, however, brought despair and financial failure, especially for those with no external support.

Few of the post-1900 "remittance" families survive in the province today, and only a sprinkling of their children, mostly of retirement age, live in the Annapolis Valley. They were members of the last generation to believe in the rectitude of an empire on which the sun was not supposed to set. Henry Childers was an example of this type of settler, very self-effacing, stubborn, and innovative in his own way.

Biography affords an opportunity to observe the facts and circumstances of the past authenticated by the realities of human behaviour. Carlyle believed that heroes rise to meet circumstances, while Marx believed that circumstances and upbringing provide a person with the means to survive where others might have perished. The biographical record of Henry Childers suggests a Marxian interpretation of his life, though it must be added that he survived and prevailed only with the finanicial assistance and enduring patience of family members who always came to his rescue.

John Connor was born in Glasgow in 1934 and educated in Scotland and Ireland, reading business and economics at Trinity College, Dublin, before proceeding to post-doctoral studies at the Sorbonne. He has been professor of economics at Acadia University since 1959 and has held visiting appointments at the University of Rhode Island, Dublin University, and Green College, Oxford, where he was visiting scholar. From 1982 to 1984, he was chairman of the Nova Scotia Royal Commission on Forestry. The bulk of his research and publications has been in the fields of regional planning and development and, more recently, forestry development policy.

Notes

1 The opening words of Virgil's *Aeneid*: "I sing of arms and the man." Like Henry Childers, the "chocolate soldier" of G.B. Shaw's satire *Arms and the Man* charges off here and there to do battle.
2 Burke Wilkinson, *The Zeal of the Convert* (Gerrard Cross, Buck.: Colin Smythe, 1978); Andrew Boyle, *The Riddle of Erskine Childers* (London: Hutchison, 1977);

interview with Erskine Childers in *Irish Independent*, November 1922; and interview with Anna Childers, Thornhill, Ontario, August 1992.

3 The "whipper in" brings up the rear of the hunt and is responsible for keeping the hunt in order and making sure that a hound does not stray from the pack, in contrast to the master of foxhounds who screams tally-ho, blows his horn, and leads the melee. Henry Childers also had a hunting horn and knew how to use it.

4 Archives of the Royal Military College, Sandhurst.

5 Interviews with B.H. Gregg, Hantsport, N.S.; with E.D. Haliburton, Avonport, N.S.; and with Anna Childers; and notes made by Dr. Walter Childers. The memories of these observers do not always coincide.

6 The nominal roll, Lord Strathcona's Horse, in Ridpath, Ellis, Cooper, and Aiken, *The Story of South Africa* (Guelph: Jones Publishing Co., 1902).

7 Author interview with Lady Grizel Warner, a friend of Anna Childers's godmother.

8 Interviews with Mabel Holmes, Avonport, N.S.; B.H. Gregg; E.D. Haliburton; and Anna Childers.

Chapter 12

"Things Are Seldom What They Seem"

Donald Simpson

The first line of the song from *H.M.S. Pinafore*, in which Buttercup endeavours to warn the obtuse Captain Corcoran of his humble origin by reciting appropriate proverbs, is a suitable title for this paper on deception and legends. "Skim milk masquerades as cream," continues Buttercup, and there are many examples of the enhancement of humble origins, one of the best known being that of H.M. Stanley, who produced some highly misleading accounts of his own life, for many years denying his Welsh birth. Richard Hall shed a great deal of new light on his subject's early years both in Wales and in America, and he has been followed in recent years by Frank McLynn, with two massive volumes on Stanley.[1]

Lawrence of Arabia is another example of a heroic figure whose origins have been probed and achievements dissected,[2] but I am more concerned with lesser-known characters. I am also passing over debunking reappraisals by modern iconoclasts of the subjects of adulatory biographies and (sometimes ghosted) autobiographies, so I will do no more than refer to André Vachon's searching treatment of two noted figures from Canadian history, Adam Dollard des Ormeaux and Madeleine de Verchères, in the early volumes of the *Dictionary of Canadian Biography*.[3]

There have been many mendacious old soldiers, but Alexander Gardner, who died in 1877, occupies a special niche owing to the extraordinary photograph forming the frontispiece to his memoirs and often reproduced, in which the bewhiskered veteran wears a uniform made by an Indian tailor entirely of the tartan of the 79th Regiment, even to the turban. This biography, edited from his own memoirs by Major Hugh Pearce, was published under the title *Soldier and Traveller* in 1898. According to it,

Gardner was born in North America in the 1780s, the son of a Scottish emigrant; he travelled in Asia; and about 1820 he served Habibullah Khan in Afghanistan, where he married, but lost his wife in tragic circumstances. He entered the army of the Punjab in the 1830s, eventually becoming artillery commander to the Maharajah of Kashmir. Sir Henry Durand called him "one of the finest specimens ever known of the soldier of fortune." His story was investigated by C. Grey in *European Adventurers of Northern India*. Though this book is not free from some slipshod errors, it makes a convincing case – both by pointing out the contradictions in the various accounts Gardner gave of his life, and by tracing references to him in official records – that much of his autobiography is completely fictitious. He was probably an Irish deserter, born about 1801, and though he certainly served in the Kashmir Artillery, he was far from being a heroic figure, having committed a number of cruel and treacherous acts.[4]

"Breaker" Morant, the Australian rough-rider and balladeer who was shot during the Boer War and has achieved recent fame as the subject of a film, claimed to be the son of Admiral Sir George Digby Morant, but Margaret Carnegie and Frank Shields have revealed that his real name was Murrant and that his parents were master and matron of a workhouse.[5]

Another historical character, one who has been portrayed not only on screen but also on stage, with and without music, is Anna Leonowens, the English governess to the children of the King of Siam. The accuracy of her reminiscences has long been disputed, and A.B. Griswold's criticisms are outlined in A.L. Moffat's biography of Mongkut, the King of Siam. More recently her account of her own origins, as the daughter of an army officer and the widow of Major Leonowens, has been contradicted by W.S. Bristowe. In reality, she was the daughter of a sergeant, and her husband, Thomas Leon Owens, though briefly in a military pay office, was in the hotel business in Penang at the time of his death. However, to compensate for these deprivations, Mr. Bristowe has established that she was Boris Karloff's great-aunt and that she declined an offer of marriage from the brother of the Tichborne claimant.[6]

Was Tom Castro, the butcher from Wagga Wagga in New South Wales, really Roger Tichborne, heir to a baronetcy, thought to be lost at sea in 1854? The question was widely debated in England and Australia from his first claim in 1865 through the lengthy civil action of 1871–72, which ended with his withdrawal of his case, through his trial for perjury and forgery in 1872-73, and even after the claimant had been identified as Arthur Orton, originally from Wapping and sent to prison for fourteen years. The debate continues today: three accounts appeared in 1957, of which Douglas Woodruff's *The Tichborne Claimant* has become the standard work. After a detailed examination of the evidence, Woodruff expresses some doubts as to whether justice was indeed done – so perhaps Anna's unsuccessful suitor, Captain Orton, was not after all the claimant's brother. Among many other books on the subject, Michael Roe's *Kenealy and the Tichborne Cause* is particularly interesting on the Australian aspect.[7]

The Tichborne case was conducted in the full glare of publicity. On the other hand, the feature of the extraordinary deceptions of Sir Edmund Backhouse (1873–1944) was their secrecy. While never pretending to be anything other than himself, Backhouse is revealed in Hugh Trevor-Roper's brilliant *Hermit of Peking* as a man with at least three different images. The first was the superficial one recorded in *The Dictionary of National Biography*, the scholar and historian who spent most of his life in Peking and whose books and manuscripts have enriched the Bodleian and British Museum. Secondly there is the figure created in the two volumes of Backhouse's unpublished (and one gathers, unpublishable) memoirs, in which he is acquainted with Verlaine, Lord Rosebery, and Lord Kitchener, helps Beardsley to edit the *Yellow Book*, and travels widely before settling in Peking, where he becomes the lover of the Empress Dowager. Finally there is the man revealed by Trevor-Roper's assiduous researches, which create a fantasy world in which he becomes an influential figure in Chinese politics, a secret service agent – and indeed many senior British officials during the First World War were deceived by his long and completely imaginary saga regarding the supply of large quantities of arms from China. Ching-Shan's diaries and other documents emanating from him, which have been used as the basis of accounts of modern Chinese history, are now found to be forgeries masterminded by Backhouse, but the full flavour of his extraordinary skills in deceit, often apparently without material gain to himself, needs to be relished in Trevor-Roper's pages.[8]

Another autobiographer was Frederick Philip Grove. His novels and lectures, opposing contemporary materialism and upholding the quest for the unattainable, made an impact in Canada in the 1920s, and in 1947, the year before his death, he received the Governor General's Award for *In Search of Myself*. It told of how he was born in Russia in about 1872, the son of a wealthy Swedish family; of his studies in European cities and journeys further afield; of his emigration to America upon his father's bankruptcy in 1892; and of his nomadic existence in the following twenty years in the United States before settling in Manitoba in 1912. Growing critical attention to his work led some to question the accuracy of this account. The mixture of internal contradictions and an absence of external evidence to support it is summed up in Douglas Spettigue's *Frederick Philip Grove* (1969). Two years later, Spettigue identified Grove as a German, Felix Paul Greve, born in 1879 to a Hamburg streetcar conductor who served a prison sentence for fraud, published novels and other writings in Germany, and allegedly committed suicide in 1909. Critics on the whole regard Grove as a recorder of true experience, even if the external details are fictitious, and his literary reputation remains high.[9]

A few years after Spettigue's book, another German who achieved success in America and created a fictional origin – though in his case it involved at least twenty-seven aliases - was identified by Will Wyatt in *The Man Who Was B. Traven*, an absorbing book to which a summary can do scant justice. Traven, best known for the film made from his book, *The Treasure of the Sierra Madre*, comes marginally into our field by once being refused entry into Canada. Apart from one of his pseudonyms being "Croves," Traven has various points meriting comparison with Grove, and no doubt some alert Ph.D. aspirant is already working on a joint study.[10]

In contrast to these immigrants to North America are those who claimed to speak for its indigenous people. In 1935 Grey Owl (Wa-Sha-Quon-Asin), son of a Scot who had known Buffalo Bill and of an Apache woman, created a sensation on an English lecture tour. He was a romantic figure as author, orator, and trapper turned conservationist. He wrote four books, lectured widely, and greeted King George VI as "brother." Less than three years after his first visit to England, he died, aged forty-nine, and an outburst of newspaper stories denounced him as a fake, claiming that he had been an English boy born in Hastings who had run away, become a tough and quarrelsome figure in the Canadian West, and had several wives. Grey Owl's friend and publisher, Lovat Dickson, wrote a defensive biography, *Half-breed* (1939), in which he clung to the idea that although Grey Owl was indeed Archie Belaney, he might have had some Indian blood. Thirty-four years later, Dickson wrote a much more comprehensive and balanced biography, *Wilderness Man*, in which, without ignoring his subject's less attractive characteristics, he presented a man who had grown into the character he had adopted and whose work for the wildlife of Canada had given him a new stature in an age in which conservation (and indeed drop-outs!) had become fashionable. In 1990 Donald B. Smith (who had helped Lovat Dickson with *Wilderness Man*) presented the fruits of some twenty years of meticulous research on Grey Owl in *From the Land of*

Shadows. Pages of footnotes and sources testify to the breadth of his investigations, but even with all this, the inner life of a strange, basically insecure, and hence secretive man remains something of a mystery.[11]

In *Men of the Last Frontier*, Grey Owl listed some notable Indians, among them "Buffalo-Child Long Lance," whom Grey Owl never met, though his daughter Agnes did so briefly. Long Lance was a phenomenon in the 1920s. Chief of the Blackfoot, born in Montana, he joined the Canadian Army in the First World War, was promoted to captain, and was wounded and decorated for gallantry. A successful journalist for various Canadian papers, especially as a sports reporter (appropriately for the former light-heavyweight champion of the Canadian Army), he later became a lecturer and author, his autobiography, *Long Lance*, which began with his youthful recollections of tribal warfare, appearing in 1928. He was the highly acclaimed star of *The Silent Enemy*, a film recording the lifestyle of the vanishing Indian, and he showed skill and courage in learning to fly. However, some doubts began to be cast on his *bona fides*, and in March 1932 he shot himself. He had been virtually forgotten when in the mid-1970s Donald Smith began the investigations that resulted in *Long Lance, the True Story of an Imposter*. An immensely readable and scholarly book, it traces the story of a young man named Sylvester Long, born to a family of mixed blood in North Carolina, where they were classed as "colored." In part to escape the social implications of that category, Long began to exaggerate his Indian blood, a convincing exaggeration because his appearance strongly reflected the Indian element of his ancestry. He also falsified his birth date in order to gain educational advancement. His war service, during which he was twice wounded, brought him no higher rank than acting sergeant – and no boxing championship. But once he was launched on a career of spectacular lies in postwar Canada and the United States, his claims to all-round excellence became more and more inflated. He was a man of undoubted abilities, but his book combined fictitious reminiscences with accounts of Indian life derived from his reading and from conversations with a genuine Blackfoot. He is in many ways a tragic, rootless figure, and Smith not merely tells his story on the basis of far-reaching research, but sheds light on many aspects of race relations in Canada and the United States.[12]

In *A Native Heritage: Images of the Indian in English-Canadian Literature* (1981), Leslie Monkman links Pauline Johnson and Grey Owl as the most popular and widely recognized exponents of "authentic" Indian views. In *Pauline*, Betty Keller, Pauline Johnson's latest biographer, comments on the title of a previous biography, Ann Foster's *The Mohawk Princess, being some Account of the Life of Teka-Hion-Wake (E. Pauline Johnson)*: "It listed three falsehoods about the lady before the reader got past the cover of the book. Tekahionwake was a borrowed name, the lady was less than half Mohawk, and she was not a princess." However, Betty Keller's book is by no means a debunking of Pauline, who was certainly legally an Indian and who in her writing – and in the dramatic performances of her own works, often in costume – consciously emphasized her racial origins, even if in a less aggressive way than modern proponents for minorities usually affect. Pauline emerges from Keller's pages as a versatile, courageous, and like-able human being, though perhaps not a very distinguished poet.[13]

Charles Barrett, in *White Blackfellows*, has brought together stories of Europeans who have lived among indigenous peoples in the Pacific. On the whole, he and other writers on the subject have accepted the basic veracity of most of these accounts, though as their subjects were usually illiterate, editorial embellishments are prominent in published versions. In *Mrs. Fraser on the Fatal Shore*, Michael Alexander has appraised the story that is also the basis of Patrick White's novel *A Fringe of Leaves*, and J. Drummond examined the story of *John Rutherford, the White Chief* in the 1908 edition of this New Zealand story first published in 1830.[14]

Barrett is dubious about William Jackman (*The Australian Captive* [1853], edited by the Reverend I. Chamberlayne) and totally rejects, in a very brief chapter, the most famous of such characters, "Louis de Rougemont," whose story has been considered at length in Geoffrey Maslen's *The Most Amazing Story a Man Ever Lived to Tell*. De Rougement arrived in England in 1898, claiming to have lived with Australia's Aborigines for more than thirty years, and the serialization of his narrative in the *Wide World Magazine* was a sensation. Some geographers of repute expressed a belief in his veracity, and he was asked to lecture to scientific as well as to popular audiences. His fame was, however, short-lived, as a newspaper investigation identi-fied him as a Swiss named Grin or Grein who had indeed spent some time in Australia but certainly not in the circumstances he described. Oddly enough, some of the aspects of De Rougemont's story that were seized on to discredit him, such as his account of riding on turtles and certain abo-riginal customs, were later proved to be perfectly feasible, though this does not imply that they were part of his personal experience.[15]

The myth of the child reared by wolves has a pedigree extending at least as far back as Romulus and Remus, its most famous fictional embodi-ment being in Kipling's *Jungle Books*. Had Mowgli real-life prototypes?

There have been many stories of wolf children, but these generally fail to stand up to detailed investigation. Charles Carrington, Kipling's biographer, commented:

> Lord Hailey tells me he has come across dozens of alleged cases and doesn't believe in them. No more do I. They generally resolve themselves to accounts of neglected, half-witted, very low-caste children who have been pushed out into the jungle where they keep alive somehow, until some missionary or kind-hearted Englishman can be persuaded to provide for them by virtue of a fairy-story about wolves.

Charles Maclean's *The Wolf Children* investigates a particular case, that of Kamala and Amala, two girls claimed to have been found with wolves in 1920 by the Reverend J.A.L. Singh. This detailed account finds many unsatisfactory features about the records relating to the children, but its very sketchy epilogue offers vague evidence from an unnamed informant that is purported to establish the truth of the story, at least in part. One is left with considerable doubts. Before we leave the subject, it is worth noting that the *Kipling Journal* for September 1983 published Roger Lancelyn Green's ingenious dead-pan chronological and topographical investigation of "Mowgli's Jungle," hitherto only available in a privately published volume.[16]

Kipling was born in 1865, the year in which Dr. James Barry died. Barry, a small, peppery army doctor with a curious voice, fought a duel in South Africa, berated Florence Nightingale during the Crimean War, and in the course of forty years served also in Jamaica and other parts of the West Indies, St. Helena, Malta, and Canada (as inspector general of hospitals in the latter). Soon after Barry's death, it was rumoured that "he" was a woman, and many fantastic romances have been woven on this basis. It was not until 1958 that Isobel Rae, in *The Strange Story of Dr. James Barry*, produced a well-researched and balanced account, drawing on official records to confirm the truth of the rumours. June Rose's *The Perfect Gentleman* is a more recent account with a few additional facts. If Dr. Barry's sex was a deception, her medical ability and combative character were not, and her achievements were considerable for a man or a woman.[17]

If James Barry was a woman, what of John White, a Canadian member of Parliament who died in 1894? In the view of Don Akenson, White was a woman, also known as Eliza McCormack. The book that puts forward this theory, *At Face Value*, is written as a novel, and though it contains twenty-one pages of sources, these are sources for the social and political background in Ireland and Canada, not for the theory. "The known facts of White's life fit the hypothesis," asserts the author, "but the reality can never be known and that is just the point; in a culture where most historical records have been made and preserved by males it is very difficult to get at the true stories about women's lives." This appears to be a recipe for making lack of evidence a form of proof. It is left for the reader to decide whether the bearded married man with eight children was really a woman. Incidentally, Dr. James Barry makes a brief appearance in the book.[18]

While Dr. Barry was in South Africa in 1837, she visited the town of Knysna and its patriarchal resident, George Rex. Rex made no claims on his own behalf, but his curious name, a certain reticence about his origins, and his alleged likeness to the Hanoverian monarchs gave rise to the theory that he was the son of King George III, who as Prince of Wales was alleged to have contracted a secret marriage with a Quakeress, Hannah Lightfoot. Many books and articles have been written on the subject, the most comprehensive being *George Rex of Knysna; the Authentic Story*, written by a descendant, Sanni Metelerkamp. However, a book published in 1939, *Princess or Pretender*, by M.L. Pendered and Justinian Mallet, included an appendix by the latter (who was actually Evans Lewin, the distinguished librarian of the Royal Empire Society) establishing that an English family named Rex might well be his genuine forebears. The matter was finally settled by Ian Christie's research on the Rex family in England, and that of Patricia Storrar on George Rex in South Africa. Her book, *George Rex, Death of a Legend*, embodies both Christie's discoveries and her own.[19]

Three other characters – a Caribbean plantation owner, an ex-slave, and a Scottish soldier – also fall, like George Rex, into the category of legends created by other people. "The White Witch of Rose Hall" is a famous figure of Jamaican history, and the original of the much-married, murderous, and lustful Mrs. Palmer has been sought in three different ladies of that name. Modern research, summed up in Glory Robertson's article "The Rose Hall Legend," has examined details of all their lives, and the colourful story, however useful to the tourist industry, is clearly fiction.[20]

F.W. Butt-Thompson's *King Peters of Sierra Leone*, though written as a novel, purports to tell the story of Thomas Peters, from his boyhood as a slave, through his work as spokesman for the Nova Scotian ex-slaves, his share in the settlement of Sierra Leone, and his later activities, including visits to England, to his appearance as a venerable old man at the jubilee of the Nova Scotians in 1837. All that is wrong with this story is that he died in 1792, within four months of landing in Sierra Leone.[21]

Other famous figures who met untimely ends have been credited in popular legend with survival in some other guise – Lawrence of Arabia is one example. One of the oddest of these yarns holds that General Hector MacDonald (Fighting Mac) did not commit suicide in 1903 but was smuggled into Germany and became Field Marshal Von Mackensen. This theory is rejected by Trevor Royle in his biography *Death before Dishonour*.[22] And Lennox Robinson, Irish director of the Abbey Theatre, wrote *The Lost Leader*, a play that blends fact and fiction, playing with the idea that Charles Stewart Parnell did not die in 1891 but survived to return to Irish political life at a crucial moment.

And then there is the famous Canadian who overcame the disadvantages of never having existed to the extent of being the subject of at least three statues and many "portraits." Evangeline is one of the two "uncanonized saints" of the Maritimes, the other being Anne of Green Gables. Longfellow's poem, first published in 1847, tells of an Acadian girl who, separated from her sweetheart Gabriel in the deportation of 1755, spends the rest of her life looking for him, succeeding only at his deathbed. Her statue stands in the evocative historical park at Grand Pré, the end of the tourist-oriented "Evangeline Trail." Longfellow drew the bones of his story from an episode told him by the Reverend H.L. Conolly, but the name of his heroine was his own invention, as were the details of her saga. Nonetheless, Acadians in Louisiana have their own claimant to the identity of Evangeline, and there is a Longfellow/Evangeline Memorial Park not far from her alleged burial place in St. Martinville and a statue given by the actress Dolores Del Rio, who played Evangeline in a silent film.[23]

There are other tales: the story of "Prince Makarooroo" and "Prince Shervington," who at different times posed as African princes but turned out to be Jamaicans; or the one about Robert Turk, whose "diary" of the Uganda Railway led the publishers and some reviewers to regard Ronald Hardy's *The Iron Snake* as fact rather than skilled fiction; or the diversity of revelations contained in *The Invention of Tradition*, edited by Eric Hobsbawm and Terence Ranger.[24]

It would be difficult and rather pointless to try to draw any ponderous conclusions from the varied stories touched on in this paper. Let Sir Walter Scott have the last word:

> *O what a tangled web we weave*
> *When first we practice to deceive.*

Donald Simpson, born in 1920, began library work in 1938, and after war service with the Royal Air Force, including at Malta, he joined the staff of the library at the Royal Empire Society (later the Royal Commonwealth Society) in 1945. He was appointed librarian in 1956, a post he held until retiring in 1987, when he was appointed honorary archivist. A fellow of the Library Association, 1946, he was awarded an honorary M.A. by the University of Edinburgh in 1975, and was appointed O.B.E. in 1983. He was chairman of the Standing Conference on Library Materials on Africa 1964–68 and 1973–77, and the first editor of its newsletter; chairman of the working party on library holdings of Commonwealth literature 1970–84; and president of the African Studies Association of the U.K. 1976–77 and of the British Association for Canadian Studies 1984–86. He was the first chairman of the committee for awarding the Northern Telecom medals for services to Canadian studies. Joint editor of "Drawings by William Westall" (1962), he wrote "Dark Companions: The African Contribution to the European Exploration of East Africa," published in 1975; founded and edited the Royal Commonwealth Society "Library Notes," 1957–87; and edited several volumes of the library's printed catalogue. He has written many articles, reviews, and pamphlets, among them several published by the Twickenham Local History Society, of which he is vice-president. His British Association for Canadian Studies (BACS) presidential address in 1986 was "Ivy-Mantled Tower and Settler's Cabin: Some Thoughts on Local History in Britain and Canada" (*British Journal of Canadian Studies* 1, no. 1 [June 1986]: 1–14). He is particularly interested in biography, and his work in building up this aspect of the Royal Commonwealth Society Library is one of the sources for this paper.

Notes

1 Richard Hall, *Stanley, an Adventurer Explored* (Boston: Houghton Mifflin, 1974); Frank McLynn, *Stanley, the Making of an African Explorer* (London: Constable, 1989); and Frank McLynn, *Stanley, Sorcerer's Apprentice* (London: Constable, 1991).

2 Richard Aldington, *Lawrence of Arabia: A Biographical Enquiry* (London: Collins, 1955).

3 *Dictionary of Canadian Biography (DCB)*, vol. 1, *1000–1700*, edited by George W. Brown (Toronto: University of Toronto, 1979), 266–75; and *DCB*, vol. 3, *1741–1770*, edited by Francess G. Halpenny, 308–13.

4 A.H.C. Gardner, *Soldier and Traveller* (Edinburgh: Blackwood, 1898); and Charles Grey, *European Adventurers of Northern India, 1785 to 1849*, edited by H.L.O. Garrett (Lahore: Government Printer, Punjab, 1929), 265–91.

5 Margaret Carnegie and Frank Shields, *In Search of Breaker Morant* (Armadale: Graphic Books, 1979).

6 A.L. Moffat, *Mongkut, the King of Siam* (Ithaca: Cornell University Press, 1961), 220–25; and W.S. Bristowe, *Louis and the King of Siam* (London: Chatto & Windus, 1976), 23–31.

7 Douglas Woodruff, *The Tichborne Claimant, a Victorian Mystery* (London: Hollis & Carter, 1957); and Michael Roe, *Kenealy and the Tichborne Cause* (Melbourne: Melbourne University Press, 1974).

8 Hugh Trevor-Roper, *Hermit of Peking* (New York: Knopf, 1977); and Hope Danby, *The Dictionary of National Biography 1941–1950*, edited by L.G. Wickham Legg and E.T. Williams (London: Oxford University Press, 1937), 31–32.

9 Frederick Philip Grove, *In Search of Myself* (Toronto: McClelland and Stewart, 1946); Douglas Spettigue, *Frederick Philip Grove* (Toronto: Copp Clark, 1969), 1–33; Douglas Spettigue, *Frederick Philip Grove: The European Years* (Ottawa: Oberon Press, 1973); Desmond Pacey, ed., *The Letters of Frederick Philip Grove* (Toronto and Buffalo: University of Toronto Press, 1976), which includes some by Greve; and Douglas Spettigue, "The Grove Enigma," *Queen's Quarterly* 79, no. 1 (Spring 1972): 1–2.

10 Will Wyatt, *The Man Who Was B. Traven* (London: Cape, 1980).

11 Lovat Dickson, *Half-breed* (London: P. Davies, 1939); Lovat Dickson, *Wilderness Man* (Toronto: Macmillan, 1973); and Donald B. Smith, *From the Land of Shadows* (Saskatoon: Western Producer Prairie Books, 1990).

12 Grey Owl, *Men of the Last Frontier* (London: Country Life, 1931); Buffalo Child Long Lance, *Long Lance* (New York: Cosmopolitan Book Corporation, 1928); and Donald B. Smith, *Long Lance, the True Story of an Imposter* (Toronto: Macmillan, 1982).

13 Leslie Monkman, *A Native Heritage: Images of the Indian in English-Canadian Literature* (Toronto: University of Toronto Press, 1981); Annie H. Foster, *The Mohawk Princess, being some Account of the Life of Teka-Hion-Wake (E. Pauline Johnson)* (Vancouver: Lion's Gate Publishing Co., 1931); and Betty Keller, *Pauline* (Vancouver: Douglas & McIntyre, 1981).

14 Charles Barrett, *White Blackfellows* (Melbourne: Hallcraft Publishing Co., 1948); Michael Alexander, *Mrs. Fraser on the Fatal Shore* (New York: Simon & Schuster, 1971); Patrick White, *A Fringe of Leaves* (London: Cape, 1976); and J. Drummond, *John Rutherford, the White Chief* (Christchurch: Whitcombe and Tombs, 1908).

15 William Jackman, *The Australian Captive*, edited by Rev. I. Chamberlayne (Auburn: Derby & Miller, 1853); and Geoffrey Maslen, *The Most Amazing Story a Man Ever Lived to Tell* (Sydney: Angus & Robertson, 1977).

16 R. Harbord, ed., *Reader's Guide to Rudyard Kipling's Works*, vol. 7 (privately published), 3026; Charles Maclean, *The Wolf Children* (London: Allen Lane, 1977); and Roger Lancelyn Green, "Mowgli's Jungle," *Kipling Journal*, no. 227 (September 1983): 29–35.

17 Isobel Rae, *The Strange Story of Dr. James Barry* (London: Longmans, Green & Company, 1958); and June Rose, *The Perfect Gentleman* (London: Hutchison, 1977).

18 Don Akenson, *At Face Value: The Life and Times of Eliza McCormack/John White*

(Montreal: McGill-Queen's University Press, 1990). For an analysis of the book, see Ann Barry and Ged Martin, "Stanger than Fiction?" *BACS History Group Newsletter*, no. 1 (October 1991): 5–7.

19 Sanni Metelerkamp, *George Rex of Knysna; the Authentic Story* (Cape Town: H. Timmins, 1955); Mary L. Pendered and Justinian Mallet, *Princess or Pretender?* (London: Hurst & Blackett, 1939); Patricia Storrar, *George Rex, Death of a Legend* (Johannesburg: Macmillan, 1974); and *Notes and Queries*, January 1975, 18–23. (Judging by the number of copies stolen from the Royal Commonwealth Library in London, the Metelerkamp book is the most popular.)

20 See *The Legend of Rose Hall Estate* (Falmouth, Jamaica: Falmouth *Post*, 1868); J. Shore, *In Old St. James* (Kingston, Jamaica: Sangster's Book Stores, 1911); H.G. de Lisser, *The White Witch of Rosehall* (London: Macmillan Caribbean, 1982); and Glory Robertson, "The Rose Hall Legend," *Jamaica Journal* 2, no. 4 (1968): 6–12.

21 F.W. Butt-Thompson, *King Peters of Sierra Leone* (Manchester: Religious Tract Society, 1927); Christopher Fyfe, "Thomas Peters: History and Legend," in Arthur T. Porter, ed., *Eminent Sierra Leoneans* (Freetown: Government Printer, Sierra Leone, 1961), 9–14.

22 Trevor Royle, *Death before Dishonour* (New York: St. Martin's Press, 1982).

23 The story is more complex, and the author has a substantial file of published and unpublished material on the topic.

24 W.F. Elkins, "The Black Princes of Jamaica," *Caribbean Studies* 15, no. 1 (1975): 117–22; Ronald Hardy, *The Iron Snake* (New York: Putnam, 1965); and Eric Hobsbawm and Terence Ranger, eds., *The Invention of Tradition* (Cambridge: Cambridge University Press, 1983).

Chapter 13

Canadians in
The Dictionary of National Biography

Claire England

Dictionaries of national biography recall, posthumously, the lives of people who contributed to a nation. These dictionaries are a monument to a nation and, as such, are venerated as major reference works of scholarship and considerable prestige. To be recorded therein with a biographical essay is to be given a distinction, although any close consideration of national biographies often raises questions of definition and inclusion. The great progenitor of national, monumental biography for English-speaking peoples is the century-old and still-published *Dictionary of National Biography (DNB)*. It is possible to find Canadians in this pre-eminent British national biography, and their presence lends some insight into nineteenth-century collective biography in the days of empire.

The *DNB* discussed here is the main set and its supplement documenting lives from the earliest times to January 1900 (exclusive of twentieth-century continuation).[1] The set was initiated and financed by London publisher George Smith, who decided upon a major biographical work as a public contribution and fitting culmination to his career. In 1882 Leslie Stephen began as the editor; he was shortly joined by Sidney Lee, who saw the main set to its completion. The first of the sixty-three original *DNB* volumes was published in 1885; the last volume of the main set came from the press in 1901, with a corrigendum and supplement in 1903. Its volumes were produced with regularity and at an extraordinary pace that would not be matched nowadays.

The dictionary was to supply "full, accurate and concise biographies of all noteworthy inhabitants of the British Islands and the Colonies (exclusive of living persons) from the earliest historical period to the present time" (that is, 1900). It claims to record 29,120 persons, and "it is believed that the names include all men and women of British or Irish race who have achieved any reasonable distinction in any walk of life ... whose career presents any feature which justifies its preservation from oblivion."

George Smith and his editors wanted the dictionary to commemorate nationals. By commemoration, Leslie Stephen meant an enumeration of lives. He thought that the value of a national dictionary lay not in simply retelling the lives of great men and women for whom "there are fuller and better notices in any library," but in recording second-ranked or minor persons whose lives are pieced from research in obscure and ephemeral sources.

Any biographical compilation is only as good as the several factors that bear upon its creation, and compilations like the *DNB* reflect the biographical fashion, knowledge, and publishing standards of their time. A century later, the *DNB* retains its solid reputation and glorious adequacies.

The principles upon which British North Americans were admitted to the *DNB* are largely stated in the prefatory remarks. The entry of persons "has been generously interpreted," and the editors included, as nationals, "the early settlers in America, or natives of these islands [Great Britain] who have gained distinction in foreign countries, or persons of foreign birth who have achieved eminence in this country." Some 830 names (less than 3 percent of the total number of *DNB* entries) contain a North American reference: Britons with some North American connection, Americans, and Canadians. Most of the North American references are British or American.

Noteworthy Britons are the *raison d'être* for the *DNB*, and many had a North American connection. American references begin with the first colonists and come well into the nineteenth century, even though there is little apparent connection with, let alone contribution to, the British nation to qualify citizens of the United States for inclusion in the *DNB*. This record of names seems to reflect Leslie Stephen's personal admiration for America. Both Stephen and Lee visited the United States and were familiar with its history and people. Neither man, however, left any documented evidence of similar knowledge or interest in Canada, but the country could hardly be neglected by the *DNB* editors. Within the set of British North American names, a definition of "birth" or "residency" plus "noteworthiness in a Canadian context" provides a guideline for counting Canadians. While many references are to people who were of consequence to Canada, many more with some Canadian mention are of little consequence to the country. These passing references range from early mariners to later travellers, and from colonizers, absentee landlords, uninterested officials, and military personnel to the entrepreneurs and casual callers who stopped in Canada.

The early references to Canada are related to discovery, colonization, exploration, or exploitation. John Cabot does not have his own entry but is mentioned in the biography of his son, Sebastian. John is recorded as a Venetian who settled in England, and a dispute about son Sebastian's birthplace is noted, the *DNB* biographer decreeing Bristol the place. Readers comparing entries in other biographical dictionaries find Venice given as Sebastian's birthplace, and they can choose between the various claims and speculative proofs of the biographers. Modern national biographies would give John Cabot the separate entry he deserves, since he was the first recorded fifteenth-century mariner actually to set foot on mainland North America, at Cape Breton in 1497. The *DNB* records that Sebastian Cabot sailed, on that voyage, with his father and brothers, under licence of Henry VII, to "discover Nova Scotia."

With a seeming randomness, *DNB* compilers record some mariners and overlook others who sailed around Canada's coasts. Richard Hore, who is not recorded, brought a group of English gentlemen-tourists to Cape Breton and Newfoundland in 1536, and among them was Armagil Waad, who is recorded. Waad's son described his father as the "first English explorer of America" and had his tombstone enscribed "the English Columbus." "Waad has no more title to the name than his companions," claims Waad's biographer, "and infinitely less than the sixteen Englishmen who accompanied Sebastian Cabot, not to mention the possibility that there were English sailors among Columbus's crews."

A decade or so earlier, in 1527, John Rut, who is not in the *DNB*, had commanded the first English ship to sail from Newfoundland to Florida for Henry VIII. A member of this expedition sent the first-recorded letter from the New World describing Newfoundland and Labrador. Not surprising, however, is the substantial entry for Sir Walter Ralegh (or more commonly Raleigh), who sailed the same Atlantic seaboard in the 1580s. Arguably, Ralegh's voyages were of more consequence, and his sovereign, Elizabeth I, was more interested in the New World than her father had been.

In 1606 John Knight searched for the Northwest Passage, but his ship was crippled in a Labrador gale. Going ashore, he and three companions "went inland over a hill, and were never seen again. It was concluded that they were killed by the natives – little people, tawny-coloured, flat-nosed with thin or no beards."

The mariners who brought the colonists, and the colonists themselves, are not as often recorded in the *DNB* as are the entrepreneurial and more influential instigators of colonization. European monarchs gave and sold poorly defined and conflicting land grants and trade charters in the New World. In 1578 Elizabeth I gave Sir Humphrey Gilbert a large portion of the northeast. He began colonization in Newfoundland, and he served there as governor for five years. Having sold baronetcies in Northern Ireland to advance plantation, King James extended the idea to America. Sir Robert Gordon became the first Baronet of Nova Scotia in 1625, and he supported a colonization scheme. Sir Thomas Temple, also Baronet of Nova Scotia and governor of Acadia, organized colonies and resisted French claims in Acadia in the 1660s. Perhaps the most enthusiastic early organizer of colonies was the energetic Scotsman Sir William Alexander. He had promoted American baronetcies to King James, and he later became Earl of Stirling and Viscount Canada. Like Gilbert before him, Alexander received a prodigious grant in 1621 to land in the northeast, and he had "jurisdiction over Nova Scotia and Canada." Although Alexander never travelled to Canada, he published a "weighty and vigorous and statesmanlike *Encouragement to Colonies*," in which he applauded royal support for colonization. He also outlined world colonization, praised the British people as colonizers, and gave a history and description of the American colonies.

Other people came to exploit Canada's resources and to visit its landscape. Thomas Tryon, manufacturer of beaver hats, did not actually visit Canada, except perhaps in his imagination. According to the *DNB*, he attempted to extend "his trade in 'beavers'" by visiting the Barbados in the 1660s. John Lambert came to Canada in the early 1800s to cultivate hemp, with the aim of making Great Britain independent of a European supply endangered by Napoleon. Failing in this objective, he "determined to remain in America and explore those parts rendered interesting by the stories of a Wolfe and a Washington." His *Travels through Lower Canada & the U.S.* focused primarily on the United States and was well received as a description of the "different impressions produced upon Englishmen by Americans of the second and third generation after the revolution." Edward Trelawney, author and adventurer, was a nineteenth-century tourist whom the *DNB* biographer credits with two "Canadian" achievements. He held actress Fanny Kemble in his arms to give her a view of Niagara, and he swam across the river between the rapids and the falls. While accepting the adventures as factual, the biographer does record that Trelawney was known as a "brilliant but inaccurate conversationalist."

Like other hierarchical institutions of Church and State, the military keeps good records. Military service is normally noted in a biographical dictionary, and during the Seven Years' War there was a large British military commitment in North America. At one point, there were at least twenty-nine British infantry battalions. A battalion had ten companies, and each company, in theory, had a hundred men. Major figures, such as Amherst, Arnold, Burgoyne, Shirley, and Wolfe, receive attention in the *DNB*, as do some minor figures. Eighty entries show military service in a Canadian area, while nearly another eighty show service in the American War of Independence or on a "North American station." Attempts at tracing specifics of service in Canada would rarely repay the effort. Rank and file military service is noted, usually without details, in national biographies.

More celebrated is the activity of the explorers and traders who discovered the country. There are about forty names in this category, including almost all of the English names that spring to mind as the foremost explorers of Canada (Baffin, Cook, James, Vancouver, Hearne, Mackenzie, Fraser, Frobisher, Franklin and some of his searchers). Even though some names are overlooked (Thompson, Pond, Kelsey, Henry), the list of familiar British explorers and navigators in the *DNB* is substantial.

Henry Hudson's biographer notes that Hudson wanted to cross the North Pole to the "islands of spicery," but "though he explored further than his predecessors [he] discovered neither the bay, nor straits, nor river called after him." Hudson found neither passage nor happy fate in Canada's inland waters, but the company named after the Bay and Hudson did find fortune and did contribute significantly to the country. Many people associated with the Hudson's Bay Company (HBC) are in the *DNB*. Brief mention of the misnamed "Hudson Bay Company" is in a paragraph in Prince Rupert's long entry, and the mention, although technically correct in phrasing, leaves a false impression about the charter voyage. There is mention of two ships despatched to Hudson's Bay [sic]. It is implied that both ships made the voyage, and one ship is identified as the *Eaglet*. In fact, the *Eaglet* turned back near Ireland, and only one ship, the *Nonsuch*, made the trip that resulted in the HBC charter. Two Frenchmen, Radisson and Groseilliers (Radishes and Gooseberries to generations of Canadian schoolchildren), were associated with this initial voyage and with the HBC, but they are not in the *DNB*, although Groseilliers and Zachariah Guilliam (or Gillam), a Bostonian, are named in the reference to the company, under Prince Rupert.

Neither here nor in a separate entry is there any mention of Charles Bayly (or Bayley), the first governor of the Hudson's Bay Company's territory in North America. Other sources must supply the details on Bayly, a Quaker, who was promoted from imprisonment for treason in the Tower of London to governorship of a colony. By all accounts a good governor, Bayly formalized treaties between the HBC and the native peoples. He reinforced English claims to territory with exploration and construction of forts, and he worked for the consolidation of British interest in the face of French rivalry for the same empire.

North American aboriginal peoples are unrepresented, perhaps because of limited documentation, but even the well-known names of Tecumseh and Joseph Brant are missing from the *DNB*. Further, the extensive and fundamental French contribution in Canada is also largely unrecorded, except for a few political appointees. Not surprisingly, a *DNB* policy of inclusiveness extending to "foreign noteworthy inhabitants" breaks down in the case of North America. The difficulties of knowing, and the sheer bulk of recording, all colonial worthies in the vast British Empire work against accomplishment of the task.

Political figures are often assured mention in a national biography. In all, the *DNB* has eighty-five political Canadian entries plus ten or so that are Britons with titles or other references pertaining to Canada. However, for some of these British entries, a specific contribution or even a presence in Canada is difficult to determine. Office holders like those early baronets of Nova Scotia, various other British appointments, and governors of Canada are noted. Four prime ministers (called premiers) of Canada departed life before 1900, and all four (Macdonald, Alexander, Abbott, and Thompson) are in the *DNB*.

A fair "Fathers of Confederation" test for the *DNB* would require agreement on who, among the thirty-six delegates at the Confederation conferences, was noteworthy. Of eleven delegates who attended all three conferences (Charlottetown, Quebec, London), five are in the *DNB*. In all, ten persons linked with Confederation are recorded. They are Archibald, Brown, Campbell, Cartier, Galt, Macdonald, McGee, Mitchell, Taché, Tilley. Among the few missing possible noteworthies is William Henry of Nova Scotia, who was reputed to have helped draft the British North America Act in London. The Glasgow-born Sir John A. Macdonald has the longest

Canadian entry, a eulogy in which the main "Father" of Confederation is called "the foremost statesman in the American continent" and the organizer of "civilisation throughout Canada."

In addition to figures noteworthy in the categories of exploration, politics, and economics, a national biographical dictionary has also to reflect people in a wide range of professions, from science to letters. In this Victorian biography, the sciences are largely applied, and the few Canadians named were surveyors, geographers, engineers, and builders of towns, roads, and canals. The fine arts are poorly represented. Paul Peel is the only truly Canadian artist mentioned. His Canadian-ness is an accident of birthplace; he trained in the United States and studied and lived in Paris. Readers of his biography are left to draw their own inference from the statement that Peel painted "subjects entirely French in character."

Religion is better represented. Two nineteenth-century Canadian clerics in the *DNB* are James Gillis and John Strachan. Gillis, Montreal-born son of Scots parentage, returned to Scotland to become a Catholic bishop. The *DNB* lists three items about him: he founded a convent for Ursuline nuns, the first religious house in Scotland since the Reformation; he delivered a paper on Robert Burns's pistols to the Society of Antequaries of Scotland and gave the pistols to the society; and most unusual of all, he praised Joan of Arc in the Cathedral of Orleans in France and, "as a tribute of thanks for the eloquent panegryic," was given "the heart of Henry II, King of England, who died at the Castle of Chinon on the Loire in 1189." Gillis went from Canada to Scotland to achieve distinction, while John Strachan came the other direction to become the influential first Anglican bishop of Toronto and a founder of universities.

Canadian letters has the widest *DNB* representation. There are a few archivists and historians. William Kingsford, a soldier, engineer, and historian of Canada is noted, and so is another historian, Francis [sic] Garneau. Their histories of Canada, are occasionally cited as sources by *DNB* biographers. Several authors are travellers writing of their journeys; some are diarists; some are journalists whose main discourse is politics; and a few write in a more creative vein.

Poetry is represented by Joanna Picken and Peter Allan. Of Picken, there is little to say; she wrote verses for the *Glasgow Courier* and the *Literary Garland*. Of Allan, there should be less or nothing said. A Halifax lawyer, Allan had some poetry published in a local Canadian journal and decided to pursue a career in literature. Unfortunately, he died before he was twenty-three and before his single small book of verse appeared. His biography records "an absence of any striking originality," and the years since have produced no challenge to that judgment. Other Canadian entries are Gustave Strauss, Anna Jameson, Susannah Moodie, Sam Strickland, and Thomas Chandler Haliburton. Strauss, who appears to have had little talent, was an early expatriate. Anna Jameson, though with a Canadian literary reputation, was also a passerby in Canada. She came to "New England" and Canada in 1836–38 to visit her husband. The *Edinburgh Review,* as quoted in the *DNB,* called her "a rudely neglected wife, who as an authoress, made capital of her talent." The remark seems to describe precisely her Canadian-ness, since her visit produced *Winter Studies and Summer Rambles.* Catharine Parr Traill, Susannah Moodie, and Sam Strickland are in the *DNB* under the entry for their sister, Agnes Strickland, who was a better-known author at the time. Most of the information on Susannah is found in an entry inserted after the entry for her husband, John, who himself is an entry inserted under his brother, Douglas Moodie. Thus Susannah is in her brother-in-law's entry, and her first and last books are mentioned. Of the last, *The World Before Them,* the biographer quotes critical opinion on Mrs. Moodie's writing as the "handiwork of a sensible, amiable, refined and very religious lady ... innocent and negative." Thomas Chandler Haliburton, who qualifies for political as well as a literary noteworthiness, is the Canadian literary giant in the *DNB.* His biographer credits him with starting a peculiarly American sense of humorous writing with his character Sam Slick.

Several literary figures are missing from the *DNB,* such as Goldsmith, Richardson, Sangster, Lampman, Carmen, Roberts, Scott, and Dunlop. Some of them are post-Confederation and unlikely perhaps to come to the attention of an insular and contemporary Victorian literary establishment. It seems clear that, for Canadian arts and letters, the *DNB* compilers relied on older works that recorded primarily the early or pre-Confederation writers and journalists.

What editorial decisions exclude some names while including others? In any national and collective biography, certain categories of people are likely to be recorded, including those of noble birth or of high rank, those who hold an official post, and those who receive the pay and notice of monarchs and governments. Once noted, archival tradition ensures that such record continues. Leslie Stephen argued that "an ideal dictionary would be a complete codification or summary of all previously existing collections" and would include "all names which have appeared in any respectable collection of lives [and] a great many names which for one reason or another have dropped out, but which appear to be approximately of the same rank." Creators of biographical lists tend to look backward from the era in which they live and see a crowd of people from earlier times.

The compilers of Canadian names likely used some of the same sources for deciding on entrants that contributors subsequently used to write the biographies. Biographers consulted two or three Canadian collective biographies, although the citation of the titles is sometimes too brief to be clear. *Morgan's* and *Rose's* are mentioned. George Rose edited and published *A Cyclopedia of Canadian Biography* (Toronto, 1886–88), covering some 2,000 persons – "chiefly men of the time" – in commercial, professional, and political life. *Morgan's* probably refers to one of two titles by Henry James Morgan, whose *Bibliotheca Canadensis* (Ottawa, 1867) surveyed pre-Confederation Canadian literature with biographical sketches of the writers. Finding few people of letters to record, he wrote that newspaper writers and journalists "in our young country [held] no unimportant position in literature." He also compiled some 460 biographies of pre-Confederation notables of Upper and Lower Canada in his *Sketches of Celebrated Canadians* (Quebec, 1862). *Appletons' Cyclopedia of American Biography* (6 vols., New York, 1887–89) is also cited for Canadian names. Aside from these collective biographies, the roster of Canadian sources is a very few miscellaneous or primary documents, the newspapers, a few individual biographies, and a handful of Canadian general histories.

The choice of Canadian entries is a variable strength. From early times, the Puritans and colonial Americans, the explorers, the landholders, and the British contributors to Canada are represented. In later times, politicians come to the fore, with letters represented modestly well in number and only modestly in quality. As the centuries progressed and development westward occurred, the gaps increased. Nevertheless, British North America seems as well or better represented than the other parts of the British Colonial Empire, and the entries, whether of indigenous or colonial personality, are written in similar manner.

Editors Stephen and Lee exhorted *DNB* contributors to write a factual account, without extraneous detail, opinion, or interpretation. Stephen, in particular, wanted "unembroidered fact and unromantic accuracy," not "vague conjecture and sentimental reflection." In spite of Stephen's impatience with other people's prose, "antequarian research," and "archaeological details," he tolerated anecdote and occasional embroidery.

Of Sir William Logan, the distinguished Canadian geologist who was educated in Edinburgh and called "the father of Canadian science," the *DNB* records that his writings "although accurate and precise are deficient in power of expression and hardly convey an adequate impression of the vast store of [his] original information ... [and his] keen and systematic observation." That may also be a comment on the *DNB* itself, where the important contribution is not style, organization, analysis, and absolute accuracy but creation of a record. The *DNB*'s strength is in its publisher's and editors' vision of commemorating an imperial nation's people, a vision that comprehended those persons who contributed to the exploration, development, politics, and culture of Canada.

Claire England is a reference librarian and professor of library science. She has taught at the College Librarianship Wales and now teaches reference resources and collections at the Faculty of Library and Information Science, University of Toronto. She is the consulting editor of the *Guide to Reference Materials for Canadian Libraries* (8th ed., University of Toronto Press, 1992). The evaluation of major reference sets, particularly in biographical writing, is an expression of her interest in biography as reading material and as a genre for study.

Note

1 The collective biography discussed here is *The Dictionary of National Biography from Earliest Times to 1900*, edited by Leslie Stephen and Sidney Lee, 63 vols. (London: Smith, Elder & co., 1895–1901); with *Supplement*, 3 vols. (1903); and *Errata* (1904). The sixty-six–volume set was compressed into twenty-two volumes (1908–1909), and reissued in this familiar form many times over. *An Index and Epitome to the Main Work* (1903) is a key to entries and is better known under a later title, *Concise Dictionary of National Biography, I: To 1900*. Oxford University Press has owned and issued the *DNB* since 1917. (The twentieth-century supplements, not considered here, contain biographies of people who died in the years 1901–85.) Quotations in this essay are taken from the *DNB*'s biographies; preface and statistical accounts (vol. 1, 22-vol. reissue); entries for Leslie Stephen (1901–11 vol.), and Sydney Lee (1912–21, 1922–30 vols.).

Part 5

Cultural Migration

Chapter 14

Scottish Emigration and Political Attitudes: Old Wine in New Bottles

Barbara Murison

Touring the Western Isles in the late eighteenth century, Dr. Johnson noted that whole groups of Highlanders had departed for America[1] and commented that such emigrants "carry with them their language, their opinions, their popular songs, and hereditary merriment: they change nothing but the place of their abode." In his book *The Emigrant*, Sir Francis Bond Head, lieutenant-governor of Upper Canada during the 1837 Rebellion, made the identical point, in more flowery Horatian manner: "Coelum, non animum, mutant qui trans mare currunt."[2] Some of the recent literature on emigration has found this idea valuable: the notion that the impact of the emigrant's home background is a lasting one and that the "folkways" of the emigrant are vital to the development of the new society. The cultural baggage of the emigrant, in other words, is as crucial as the physical.[3]

Yet this point is often insufficiently stressed. As a recent review of a volume of the *Dictionary of Canadian Biography* pointed out,[4] most of the entries on immigrants to Canada tend to assume that careers began, essentially, at the moment that the migrant set foot in British North America. The point is confirmed if one glances at an assortment of biographies of one famous immigrant to British North America, William Lyon Mackenzie. Mackenzie's life in Scotland before emigration to Upper Canada receives twenty-two pages from Lindsey, eight pages from Kilbourn, and three pages from Flint.[5] To be sure, Mackenzie had hardly become a public figure before he emigrated at the age of twenty-five, and the impact of his Upper Canadian and American experiences would be profound; nonetheless, analysis of the political background from which he emerged is clearly helpful in understanding his actions on the other side of the Atlantic. Mackenzie was born just north of Dundee, went to school in the city, and at fifteen was the youngest member of the commercial news room of the local newspaper. The knowledge that Dundee was a centre of violent political protest in Scotland and that nearby Perth was an established stronghold of reform ideas is surely valuable information when one considers Mackenzie's later role in Upper Canadian politics.[6] Similarly, Robert Gourlay's actions in Upper Canada a few years earlier and the radical views he expressed there owe their origins to his experiences as a Fife laird and his notions about land reform in Scotland.

Work of a wider scope than the biographies of individuals also frequently neglects crucial formative influences on immigrants. A survey of Scots as politicians in Canada suggests that once the immigrants had acquired a home and means of livelihood, "many of them, accustomed to years of struggle for economic and political freedom in their own land, began to turn their attention to public affairs."[7] But the writer is silent on what that struggle had implied and what effects it might have had on these Scottish politicians.[8]

Furthermore, recent assessments by historians of eighteenth- and nineteenth-century Scotland have provided new insight into the pace, and the distinctive nature, of political, economic, and religious change in Scotland.[9] As a result, we need to reconsider our ideas about the nature of the Scottish background and its influences on the immigrant's behaviour. The 1820s and 1830s were years of increasing emigration to Upper Canada, particularly by Scots, for whom it was the favoured destination in British North America;[10] they were also years of political disturbance on both sides of the Atlantic. Thus, they provide a useful period within which to consider the question of the transfer of ideas.

The political experiences of the Scottish immigrant were not those of the English or the Irish.[11] Before the Reform Bill of 1832, Scotland had the narrowest, most oligarchical franchise in Britain; perhaps 4,000 out of a population of 1.5 million had the vote, and the electoral system fostered corruption. County voters did not have to be resident, so that the wealthy outside a constituency could buy properties within it, qualifying them for the franchise. Fictitious freeholds were systematically created, and the system became patronage ridden. As for the burghs, here the MPs were chosen by the corporations, most of which elected their own successors. "Omnipotent, corrupt, impenetrable" was Cockburn's description of the town council of Edinburgh.[12] No wonder that burgh reform became the dominant political issue of the 1820s and that political unions, descendants of the local radical societies of the 1790s and the post-Napoleonic War period, were set up to organize agitation for a reform bill.

Pressure for reform mounted, encouraged by the growth of an opposition press such as Edinburgh's *Scotsman*, the country's first liberal newspaper, founded in 1817. The middle classes soon became accustomed to attacks upon authority, and a coherent opposition was forming. Among the advocates of reform were the Hope family, tenant farmers in East Lothian. George Hope attended various meetings in 1831 and 1832 in Edinburgh and Haddington. "Had the Tories not yielded," Hope recalled, "our freedom would have been achieved with blood."[13] Adam Hope, George's brother, emigrated from East Lothian to Upper Canada in 1834, and another brother followed; it was with this kind of reform background that they observed the growth of the reform movement in Upper Canada. They had been active and informed citizens in Scotland; would they not be the same in British North America?

Even after the Scottish Reform Act of 1832 and the Municipal Corporations Act the following year, there was still a great deal of corruption in the Scottish political system and a marked difference between it and the English one. Whereas in England, post-1832, one adult male in five had the franchise, in Scotland it was one in eight. Nonetheless, that represented a sixteenfold increase in the electorate and the Whigs reaped the benefit of the measures they had introduced; the Tories had, in the main, to accept the fact that the Scottish burghs were a lost cause for them after 1832 and that in the counties there were many more contested elections. Though the Scottish Reform Act of 1832 was flawed and poorly drafted, it did provide a framework within which greater political pressure could be exerted.[14]

This, then, was the political background that shaped many Scottish emigrants of the 1820s and 1830s, one of a growing political consciousness, of reform agitation, and of some achievement. Like other British emigrants, these Scots were not a homogeneous group. They included unemployed handloom weavers from the west of Scotland, some of whom had left Scotland for Lanark, Upper Canada, in the early 1820s with a certain amount of government assistance. Radical unrest was a staple of life in the west (witness the troubles of 1820 and the 1837 textile workers' strike), and leaving the country was in some cases an alternative to continuing the fight for reform at home.[15] There were poor Highland crofters and fisherfolk, victims of agricultural dislocation and the collapse of the kelp industry after the Napoleonic Wars. Reliance on landlord paternalism died hard in the Highlands, but by the 1820s and 1830s it must have been clear to many inhabitants that the modernizing objectives of landowners, some of them newcomers to the area, were inconsistent with the struggle for subsistence of an ever-increasing Highland population. There were also middle-class emigrants seeking expanded business or farming opportunities, such as Adam Hope of East Lothian or Edward Collins of Glasgow.[16]

The timing of emigration had a crucial effect on behaviour in the New World. Many earlier Scots emigrants, such as William Dickson or James Crooks, had been drawn into the orbit of the controlling oligarchy of Upper Canada, the Family Compact, and early in the century the government was often referred to as "the Scotch faction," "the clan," or, more hostilely, as a "Shopkeeper Aristocracy" of "scotch Pedlars."[17] Naturally those who had shared "the pickings of Tory governments" might, as Patrick Shirreff suggested after his tour of North America, desert their Whiggism.[18] The solicitor general of Upper Canada pointed out to Adam Fergusson, another visiting Scot (and soon to settle in the province), that "however turbulent or discontented individuals may have been prior to their arrival in the province, comfort and plenty soon work wonders."[19] But this was a Tory pleading a case to a visitor who might well be influential in drumming up suitable (from a Family Compact point of view) conservative Scots settlers.

In some cases emigration makes conservatives of radicals, but that oversimplifies the matter. It is important to compare the political background in Scotland of two groups, those who migrated before 1815 and those who did so after that year. After the end of the Napoleonic Wars, turbulence and discontent were much more a fact of Scottish life than before. Scottish emigrants of the 1820s and 1830s, particularly those who came from the urban centres, were likely to have experienced political and economic protest, either as participants or spectators. Devine's work on internal migration in Scotland suggests that many Highlanders, too, must have had some experience of Lowland protest.[20] Such emigrants, much more numerous than in the previous period,[21] were likely to find the political system of Upper Canada oppressive. To be sure, they no longer laboured under the same franchise restrictions in Upper Canada as they had at home, since the possession of a freehold worth 40 shillings per acre was not difficult to achieve and the urban voting qualification was similarly modest. However, from 1814 there was a property qualification for members of the assembly, and after 1821 the vote was denied to holders of location tickets who had not yet received their freehold patents,[22] a regulation that irritated recent immigrants. There were other irritants, from land regulations to the clergy reserves, to annoy the independent-minded Scot who was accustomed to the tactics of protest.

The Upper Canadian authorities considered Scots settlers partial to reform, which, given their numbers, was a worrying thought for the government. They were, for example, the second-largest group in the western part of the province.[23] The government anxiously awaited the Scots reaction to the disturbances of 1837 and 1838, and fears were expressed even about the long-established Scots settlement in Glengarry, famously loyal in the War of 1812.[24]

Yet the Scots settlers of Upper Canada did not rise en masse to support their fellow Scot, William Lyon Mackenzie; the term "Scotch Rebellion," applied by some contemporaries to the disturbances, was in many ways inappropriate. Research into the origins of over 200 rebels and their accomplices involved in the rising in the western part of the province shows no Scots. Similarly, detailed study of the Yonge Street rebellion reveals only limited rebel activity by Scots of the Home District and only a few signs of a favourable response to Mackenzie's actions by the Gaelic speakers of Nassagaweya Township in Gore.[25] The frontier raids from the United States in 1838 served only to strengthen the loyalty of the majority of Scots settlers. As Lieutenant-Governor Sir George Arthur observed to Sir John Colborne in December, "The Scotch part of the Community have come round very much lately – so that I have less apprehension than I had of our own people, & consequently care less for the movements of the Brigands."[26]

However, aversion to rebellion was one thing; aversion to reform was another. It was the "Yankee" features of Mackenzie's program that alienated some Scots, not his basic reforming stance. As government officials soon learned, the very name of Tory was anathema to most Scots, for it meant to them a party which for fifty years and more had ruthlessly manipulated Scottish politics in its own interests.

This partiality to reform was strongly affected by religious factors, and no proper understanding of the political attitudes of emigrant Scots is possible without reference to their religious background.[27] This too was varied. There were Scots Catholics, Presbyterians of various stripes, and Dissenters. Every effort was made by the Catholic Church and by the Kirk to translate traditional Scottish social control mechanisms to the Upper Canadian environment. Shortage of priests and ministers was a problem, but perhaps not more so than in Scotland, where there was also a rapidly growing population and where urbanization was proceeding at a faster pace than anywhere else in Europe.[28] In the 1820s and 1830s, the colonial Catholic establishment played an important role in directing the political attachments of its flock in a Tory direction. A confidential report on the political state of the inhabitants of Upper Canada in 1839 expressed confidence in the loyalty of the Scots settlers of the Bathurst District, of the Perth military settlement, and of the Lanark area. The Roman Catholic priest John Macdonald was instrumental in drafting a Catholic declaration of loyalty in these areas.[29] Bishop Macdonnell of Kingston similarly did his best for the Tory cause. The Kirk did likewise; the Church of Scotland had already received financial recognition in its campaign for a share of the clergy reserves and thus had practical as well as philosophic reasons for supporting the government. The Reverend Alexander Ross of Aldborough in Middlesex County and the Reverend Donald McKenzie of the Highland settlement of Zorra in Oxford County preached the doctrines of Toryism, as well as those of the Kirk. It was well known in Zorra that the Scottish settlers "hold their attachment to the kirk of Scotland" and that they did not back the reform cause.[30] The Church of Scotland had traditionally exercised a more independent and important position in Scotland than the Anglican Church did south of the border, with a consequent contrast in the degree of influence exercised over congregations. In this, as in so many other areas, the experiences of the Scots emigrants were different from those of the English.

Religious developments in Scotland also shaped the emigrants of the years after the Napoleonic Wars. Because of population growth and redistribution associated with industrialization, traditional churches had difficulty satisfying the spiritual needs of the Scots. A growing religious radicalism arose to parallel the political radicalism discussed earlier. Urban radicals were often religious dissenters, the two main groups of Presbyterian dissent being the Original Secession and the Relief. Together with more minor groups, these Presbyterian dissenters accounted for approximately one-fifth of the population by the time of the 1851 census. Secession churches were thriving in the 1820s and 1830s, and independent or Voluntary churches became very common in the expanding urban centres.[31] In Edinburgh and Glasgow, the Church of Scotland attracted less than 45 percent of churchgoers in the 1830s, and by 1851, following the Disruption of 1843, only 32 percent.

Typical of those who found the orthodox churches unsatisfactory was the reformer George Hope of East Lothian. Unitarian ideas seemed to suit him best, and the two Hope brothers who emigrated to Upper Canada were of the same persuasion. Unitarian support of political reform, in this instance the Reform Bill, is demonstrated in the prayer for the king and the royal family by a Unitarian minister in Edinburgh in 1832, as reported by one of George's brothers: "We pray for our Sovereign the King; O impart unto him that firmness and decision of mind which he seems to stand so much in want of. We pray especially for the members of his illustrious family, who are standing in opposition to the declared wishes of a whole empire. O show them the folly of their way."[32]

Scots emigrants carried their religious as well as their political prejudices with them across the Atlantic. As it had been in Scotland, so must it be in Upper Canada, and they were anxious to acquire ministers of their own religious denomination as quickly as possible. Again, the political potential of religious dissent was recognized by the Upper Canadian authorities, who suspected that it implied disloyalty or worse.

The general themes discussed above can be illustrated by an examination of the careers of certain Scottish emigrants of the 1820s and 1830s. The case of the Reverend William Proudfoot is well documented. Proudfoot had supported the cause of reform in Scotland, and he followed its fortunes from across the Atlantic; soon after his arrival he arranged with a friend a joint subscription to the *Edinburgh Review* and the *Quarterly Review*.[33] As a member of the Presbyterian United Secession Church, he favoured complete separation of church and state; he was delighted when he heard that hundreds of Scots petitions were being presented to the Reformed Parliament asking for the abolition of the Church of Scotland, seeing this development as "the wholesome workings" of a new spirit in Scotland.[34]

It was inevitable that Proudfoot's liberal principles should find expression in a colonial context. Although he confided to his diary that his business was not with the politics of this world, disassociation was impossible.[35] He was soon subscribing to the St. Thomas *Liberal*, whose editor, John Talbot, was a leader of reform in the London District; soon he was contributing articles to it on the church question. Talbot urged him to use his influence in the reform cause in the 1836 Upper Canadian elections; as Proudfoot well knew, the Anglican minister Cronyn was "all over the township – electioneering – bah!"[36]

The events of 1837 and 1838 had Scottish parallels. Mackenzie's political unions were reminiscent of similar organizations formed in the post-Napoleonic period and in the early 1830s in Scotland, particularly in hotbeds of unrest such as Dundee. The Upper Canadian government's reaction to Mackenzie's uprising, with every reformer suspect and "any meeting to get up petitions" regarded "as a disturbing of the public peace,"[37] was all too familiar to Scots who had witnessed the savage Tory repression of such disturbances as the Glasgow strikes of 1820. In the late 1830s, it was the industrial unrest of the west of Scotland and the harsh government actions in response to it that banished the Canadian rebellions from editorials of the Scottish newspapers.

Proudfoot soon had proof of how the government viewed his reform sympathies. Although he was no backer of rebellion and was mortified when his spendthrift nephew from Edinburgh, James Aitchison, got himself involved in the Patriot raid on Windsor, Upper Canada, in late 1838, his appeals to Lieutenant-Governor Arthur for clemency in his nephew's case brought only vice-regal accusations of Proudfoot's disloyalty and the unwelcome news that accusations had been lodged against him in the government office. As Proudfoot bitterly reflected in a letter to Thomas Parke, a Reform member of the assembly, the members of his congregation had been made to feel they were part of a den of thieves.[38]

Making sense of Proudfoot's attitudes in the 1830s is possible only within the framework of his Scottish experiences. The same is true of Adam Hope and his brother, emigrants to Upper Canada in the early 1830s. Like Proudfoot, they retained a keen interest in politics at home, worrying in a letter on the eve of the British general election of 1841 that the county of East Lothian was "doomed to be Tory-ridden." And like Proudfoot, they brought their anti-Tory bias to Upper Canadian politics. The same letter that discussed the British election also described every detail of the 1841 Upper Canadian one; the Hope brothers were strong supporters of the moderate reformer, Parke, and were pleased that, in the St. Thomas area where they lived, there was no chance of returning a Tory if the Liberals were united behind a single candidate.[39] Adam, the older brother, was appointed to the Commission of the Peace and soon became an important figure in the growing Reform Party of the western area of Upper Canada. He was ultimately appointed to the Senate (1877), where he virulently denounced the protectionist National Policy; he was a life-long freetrader.[40] What should be pointed out here is that such ideas owed their origins to his youth in East Lothian, where the Hopes stood strong in the Anti-Corn Law agitation – for the prosperous tenant farmers of southeast Scotland, where Scottish agriculture was as efficient as ever it got, stood in no need of the protection of the Corn Laws.[41]

The cases of Proudfoot and the Hopes are particularly well documented. They were members of the middle class – well-educated, possessed of a certain leisure, able to afford the postage and to keep in touch with home through correspondence and visits. Other Scots emigrants are less easy to document, but the evidence at least allows for some suggestions to be made about their behaviour. Consider the case of David Gibson, participant in the 1837 Rebellion. After Gibson had fled to the United States, a friend wrote to him in Syracuse expressing surprise that "men of good sense like you and others could be involved in so absurd and hopeless a project." And indeed it is a puzzle that this "man of integrity, good sense, and amicable character," as a testimonial put it, got himself dragged into the affair,[42] especially since this moderate and sensible reformer apparently knew nothing of the rebellion until two days before it started.[43]

Perhaps a little geographical backtracking can be of assistance. Gibson, a surveyor who came out from Scotland in 1825 and settled in York Township in 1829, was originally from Glamis, a few miles up the road from Dundee, where William Lyon Mackenzie lived for some years. What could be more likely than that these two men had acquaintances in common and that this common background helped to bring them together politically in the 1830s in Upper Canada?[44] Mackenzie had connections in Glamis, and his illegitimate son was born in that parish. Gibson had relatives in Dundee, and his apprenticeship to a surveyor in Forfar took him all over that area. Gibson's Dundee cousin wrote to him in 1834 that he sometimes saw in Dundee a copy of the paper edited by William Lyon Mackenzie, and he presumed that Gibson saw the British papers regularly in Upper Canada.[45] In other words, here too the transatlantic connection was carefully preserved. There was a continuous two-way flow of information and ideas, facilitated in the late 1830s by the introduction of the transatlantic steamship, which made communications easier, quicker, and cheaper.

The evidence presented does not, to be sure, lend itself to categorical conclusions. Nonetheless, it simply is not possible to understand how Scots emigrants functioned in their new society without an adequate understanding of the Scots society from which they sprang.[46] The increasing radicalism of Scottish politics and religion in the years after 1815 could not fail to affect the emigrants of the period, emigrants who in numbers, we should remember, far overwhelmed the earlier Scottish settlers. For some years, the impact of their Scottish experiences, less diluted than it might have been in other periods by the influence of well-established settlers, was bound to be particularly strong. Of course there were some who wished, like one of the Reverend William Proudfoot's acquaintances, to bury all distinctions that had prevailed in Scotland and to go forward on a new, harmonious basis. But Proudfoot himself knew that this pleasing idea was impractical, for religious pluralism was a fact of life. "Other churches keep up their peculiar distinctions," he explained, "and so must we [the United Secession Church], as a reason why we do not belong to them."[47] And just as the peculiar religious distinctions had crossed the Atlantic with the settlers, so too had the political distinctions. Collectively, the Scots had been formed by a background different from that of the English and the Irish. As our knowledge of nineteenth-century Scottish history advances, our assessment of emigrant behaviour must similarly become more sophisticated. Individually, of course, these emigrants differed. But no one could doubt that, as the Reverend William Fraser observed in 1835 of the Scottish settlement in the township of West Gwillimbury, Upper Canada, "all their attachments and prejudices have been imported along with them."[48] It was very much a case of old wine in new bottles.

Dr. Barbara Murison is assistant professor of history at the University of Western Ontario, London, Canada. Her Ph.D. was in imperial history and she has published a number of articles in this field, including papers in the *Journal of Imperial and Commonwealth History* and the *British Journal of Canadian Studies*. She spent a post-doctoral year at the Centre of Canadian Studies at the University of Edinburgh, pursuing research on Scottish emigration to Upper Canada; the present paper is a result of that work. She has recently completed an essay on the colonial impact of the Disruption of the Church of Scotland for a book to be published by Edinburgh University Press in 1993. Dr. Murison is particularly interested in the problems posed by writing biography. Her most recent publication was a piece on the seventeenth-century imperial administrator William Blathwayt for *History Today*, and she is at present working on a full-scale biography of Blathwayt.

Notes

1 The term was often used indiscriminately in the eighteenth and nineteenth centuries to refer both to British North America and to the United States.

2 Samuel Johnson, *A Journey to the Western Islands of Scotland* (Oxford: Oxford University Press, 1924), 87; and Sir Francis Bond Head, *The Emigrant* (London: John Murray, 1846), 116.

3 See, in particular, B. Bailyn, *The Peopling of British North America, an Introduction* (New York: Alfred A. Knopf, 1986); and D. Hackett Fischer, *Albion's Seed: Four British Folkways in America* (New York: Oxford University Press, 1989); together with the discussion and response by Fischer in *William and Mary Quarterly*, 3rd series, 48, no. 2 (April 1991): 223–308.

4 Ged Martin, review of *Dictionary of Canadian Biography (DCB)*, vol. 7, *1836–1850*, edited by Francess G. Halpenny (Toronto: University of Toronto Press, 1988), *Journal of Imperial and Commonwealth History* 18, no. 2 (May 1990): 238–39.

5 Charles Lindsey, *The Life and Times of William Lyon Mackenzie*, 2 vols. (Toronto: P.R. Randall, 1862); William Kilbourn, *The Firebrand* (Toronto: Clarke, Irwin, 1956); and David Flint, *William Lyon Mackenzie, Rebel against Authority* (Toronto: Oxford University Press, 1971). In each case, the Scottish background is dealt with briefly at the beginning of the work.

6 For example, Dundee was the scene of the most serious Scottish riots in the radical disturbances of 1792; it took two troops of dragoons to restore peace after a week of disturbances (J. Binns, "Scotland and the French Revolution," *Scottish Records Association Report*, no. 12 [September 1989]: 19). The city remained a centre of radical protest in the early nineteenth century.

7 A.M.M. Evans, "The Scot as Politician," in W. Stanford Reid, ed., *The Scottish Tradition in Canada* (Toronto: McClelland and Stewart, 1976), 273.

8 There are exceptions: J.M.S. Careless, *Brown of the Globe* (Toronto: Macmillan, 1959 and 1963), is sensitive to the Scottish background, and a recent study of a group of migrants describes their background in depth: Marianne McLean, *The People of Glengarry: Highlanders in Transition, 1745–1820* (Kingston and Montreal: McGill-Queen's University Press, 1991). But the general argument holds.

9 For a discussion of this point and an introduction to some of the literature, see T.M. Devine and Rosalind Mitchison, eds., *People and Society in Scotland*, vol. 2, *1760–1830* (Edinburgh: John Donald Publishers in Association with the Economic and Social History Society of Scotland, 1988).

10 The Upper Canadian population increased by nearly 50 percent between 1830 and 1833, mainly through immigration, and tenfold between 1815 and 1850. See G.M. Craig, *Upper Canada, the Formative years, 1784-1851* (Toronto: McClelland and Stewart, 1972), 228; and K.D. McRae, "The Structure of Canadian History," in Louis Hartz, *The Founding of New Societies* (New York: Harcourt, Brace & World, 1964), 245; see also emigration statistics in H. Cowan, *British Emigration to British North America: The First Hundred Years* (Toronto: University of Toronto Press, 1961), appendixes.

11 The following discussion is based on M. Fry, *Patronage and Principle:. A Political History of Modern Scotland* (Aberdeen: Aberdeen University Press, 1987), esp.

chap. 1; and I.G.C. Hutchison, *A Political History of Scotland, 1823–1924* (Edinburgh: John Donald, 1986), chap. 1.

12 R.M. Mitchison, *A History of Scotland* (London: Methuen, 1982), 370.

13 *A Sketch of the Life of George Hope, Compliled by His Daughter*, private publication (Edinburgh, 1879), 15.

14 For the general quickening of public interest in politics, see, for example, *A Sketch of the Life of George Hope*, 15.

15 In the unrest of 1820, twenty-seven Glasgow men were arrested and accused of planning an uprising; in 1837 a cotton spinners' strike soon spread to all the skilled trades and was only broken up by savage repression and resultant trials and transportation of the prime movers. Cowan, *British Emigration*, 60, suggests a division among weavers beginning with Peterloo (1819), one group seeking salvation through reform and the other asking for emigration assistance or a minimum wage. Individual weavers moved back and forth between these objectives.

16 For the Collins correspondence, see Scottish Record Office, GD177/Box 3/File 4.

17 This last observation, that of Judge Thorpe in 1806, is cited in A.R.M. Lower, *Canadians in the Making* (Toronto: Longmans, Green, 1958), 159; see also biographical information in A. Ewart and J. Jarvis, "The Personnel of the Family Compact," *Canadian Historical Review*, 7, no. 3 (September 1926): 209–21.

18 P. Shirreff, *A Tour Through North America; Together with a Comprehensive View of the Canadas and the United States As Adapted For Agricultural Emigration* (Edinburgh: Oliver and Boyd, 1835), 104.

19 A. Fergusson, *Practical Notes Made during a Tour in Canada*, 2nd ed. (Edinburgh: W. Blackwood, 1834), 115. Fergusson settled in Upper Canada in 1833 and soon acquired considerable political influence.

20 T.M. Devine, "Temporary Migration and the Scottish Highlands in the Nineteenth Century," *Economic History Review*, 2nd series, 32 (1979).

21 See note 10.

22 For the details see John Garner, *The Franchise and Politics in British North America* (Toronto: University of Toronto Press, 1969), 82–91.

23 Colin Read, *The Rising in Western Upper Canada 1837–8: The Duncombe Report and After* (Toronto: University of Toronto Press, 1982), 23, 50.

24 The Glengarry fears proved groundless. See Elinor Senior, "The Glengarry Highlanders and the Suppression of the Rebellions in Lower Canada, 1837-8," *Journal of the Society of Army Historical Research* 56 (1978): 143–59.

25 See Read, *The Rising in Western Upper Canada*; and R.J. Stagg, "The Yonge Street Rebellion of 1837: An Examination of the Social Background and a Re-assessment of Events" (Ph.D. diss., University of Toronto, 1976).

26 Arthur to Colborne, 7 December 1838, in C. R. Sanderson, ed., *The Arthur Papers* (Toronto: Toronto Public Libraries and University of Toronto Press, 1957), vol. 1, 424.

27 The discussion of the relationship between Scottish religion and political radicalism in S.D. Clark, *Movements of Political Protest in Canada* (Toronto: University of Toronto Press, 1959), is marred by inadequate knowledge of the Scottish

religious groups; the same criticism applies to Clark's *Church and Sect in Canada* (Toronto: University of Toronto Press, 1948).

28 A further indication that the Scottish experience must be differentiated from the English or the Irish.

29 Memorandum, May (?) 1839, in Sanderson, *Arthur Papers*, vol. 2, 137; and Colin Read and R.J. Stagg, eds., *The Rebellion of 1837 in Upper Canada* (Toronto: Champlain Society in co-operation with the Ontario Heritage Society, 1985), 263–65.

30 J. Carruthers, *Retrospect of Thirty Six Years Residence in Canada West* (Hamilton: Printed for the author by T.L. McIntosh, 1861), 119.

31 Fry, *Patronage and Principle*, 38; and Hutchison, *A Political History of Scotland*, 16.

32 *A Sketch of the Life of George Hope*, 15, 18.

33 University of Western Ontario library, Regional Room (UWOLRR) Proudfoot Diary, B 4273, 13 May 1833.

34 Ibid., Proudfoot Diary, 15 December 1832.

35 Ibid., 7 July 1834.

36 Talbot to Proudfoot, 15 June 1836 in L.R. Gray, ed., *Ontario History* 44, no. 4 (October 1952): 140; and UWOLRR, Proudfoot Diary, 23 June 1836.

37 UWOLRR, Proudfoot Diary, 1 November 1838.

38 UWOLRR, Proudfoot Papers, Proudfoot to Parke, [?] December 1841.

39 Charles Hope to his father, 14 June 1841; and SRO, RH1/2/612/5.

40 Douglas McCalla in *DCB*, vol. 11, *1881–1890*, edited by Francess G. Halpenny (Toronto: University of Toronto Press, 1982), 422–24.

41 In 1842 George Hope won an Anti-Corn Law League prize for an essay on the repeal of the Corn Laws; it was circulated in Upper Canada, partly through his brothers' efforts. (See *A Sketch of the Life of George Hope*, 93, 97.)

42 Archives of Ontario (AO), Gibson Papers, MS 95, item 123, Marshall S. Bidwell [?] to Gibson, 6 March 1838; and testimonial in the same hand.

43 R.J. Stagg, *DCB*, vol. 9, *1861–1870*, edited by Francess G. Halpenny (Toronto: University of Toronto Press, 1976), 313.

44 That was the case with the Lesslie family, who had known Mackenzie in Dundee. One Lesslie brother went out on the same emigrant ship as Mackenzie; two others were active in the radical wing of the reformers and, though not actually participants in the rebellion, were arrested afterwards because of their known sympathies. (See J.M.S. Careless, *DCB*, vol. 11, *1881–1890*, edited by Halpenny, 516–19.)

45 AO, Gibson Papers, MS 95, item 97, John Manson to David Gibson, 17 July 1834.

46 Moreover, it is possible to fall into a whole variety of traps without a proper knowledge of the background; the word "Presbyterian" is a landmine in itself.

47 UWOLRR, Proudfoot Diary, 9 September 1833.

48 *Transactions of the London and Middlesex Historical Society*, part 4 (1930), 141, Rev. William Fraser to Rev. William Peddie in Edinburgh, 10 May 1835.

Chapter 15

Timothy Eaton:
Canadian Capitalist, Irish Saint

Leon B. Litvack

Timothy Eaton was born at Clogher, County Antrim, two miles from Ballymena, in 1834. He was the youngest of nine children, his father dying two months before he was born. At the age of thirteen he was apprenticed to the draper and retailer William Smith of Portglenone. In 1853, following a well-trodden path, he packed his bags and set sail for Canada, the land to which two of his brothers had emigrated several years earlier. He first settled in Georgetown, where his brother Robert had a farm. He went into business with his brother James in 1856, trading as "J. & T. Eaton" in Kirkton, ten miles northwest of St. Marys. Timothy was the more active partner, and in 1860 he moved to St. Marys. He was now on his own, and his business began to flourish. In St. Marys he abandoned the credit system once and for all, in favour of cash and one fixed price; for the remainder of his career, he staked his reputation on the slogans "The greatest good to the greatest number" and "Money refunded if goods are not satisfactory." It was his belief that an honest storekeeper should promise his customers "not only bargains, but that every article will be found just what it is guaranteed to be ... use no deception in the smallest degree ... nothing you cannot defend before God and man."[1]

In 1869 Eaton moved to Toronto and proceeded to trade in groceries and dry goods on Front Street. Realizing that this was not a prime location, in 1870 he moved to 178 Yonge Street. To bypass the Canadian wholesalers, he began to order goods directly from Britain and elsewhere. Such innovations, combined with Eaton's own business acumen, resulted in increased profits and the need to expand. Annual sales went from $24,000 in 1870 to over $200,000 in 1882. In 1883 he moved to 190 Yonge Street, north of Queen, which many still remember as "Eaton's Queen Street." He constantly introduced innovations, such as hydraulic elevators, a massive boiler that provided heat for the entire store, and electric lighting throughout the store, a novelty in Toronto in the early 1880s. By 1885 sales had reached almost $335,000 and staff totalled 250.

By 1890 Eaton operated a mammoth emporium fronting on three main downtown streets. As the store grew, so too did the services offered to the customer. It was possible by 1895 for the Eaton shopper to browse through the largest selection of merchandise in the city, enjoy cool drinks and ice cream in the summer and hot meals all year round, have shoes repaired, obtain magazine subscriptions, and take advantage of the free bus service linking the store to certain boats and trains, which ensured that customers would not be tempted to enter competing establishments. It was also possible to purchase goods from the Eaton's catalogue, which accounted for a significant percentage of the company's sales. At the end of the century, the Eaton store had become a national retailing institution, with sales of some $5 million a year. It still lagged behind such retail giants as Macy's, but compared favourably with Harrod's and Bloomingdale's. By the time of Timothy Eaton's death in January 1907, the company employed over 6,000 people, and had annual sales of $22.5 million. Eaton left two thriving stores (Winnipeg Eaton's had been opened in 1905), numerous manufacturing establishments, and a firm foundation on which the enormous Canada-wide chain would be built.

It is sometimes asked whether entrepreneurs are passive or creative forces in the historical process. Are they self-determining entities and thereby engines of change? Or are they variables themselves to be explained by other independent historical factors?[2] Considering only the Irish part of Timothy Eaton's background, the answer seems to be that this portion of his history had little effect on subsequent events. Growing up on a farm in mid-nineteenth-century Ulster, Eaton was exposed to the seasonal aspects of rural life. Regular visits to the market in Ballymena, by then the country's largest linen market, made him aware of the urban commercial world, albeit on a small scale. Little documentation exists on his early years in Ireland, but it is believed that he attended the local national school for several years. Following this he was sent for a short period to an academy in Ballymena, an experience he later pronounced to be somewhat unproductive. On the advice of the master, his mother removed him from this establishment in 1847. It is unclear whether his departure was primarily due to lack of interest in academic subjects or to financial problems arising from the potato famine that had devastated vast areas of Ireland in 1846.

The store in Portglenone at which Eaton served his apprenticeship was a thriving business; the owner, William Smith, operated twelve transport wagons and three river freighters. His involvement with both produce and a wide variety of merchandise provided the young Timothy with a diversified background. As he became familiar with the many different aspects of a large general store, he learned to assess the quality of grain and linen, deal with agricultural produce and groceries in large and small quantities, and serve drams of liquor to farmers on their way to the market.

While no documentation exists for the years of Eaton's training and apprenticeship, one can gain some insight into such a period of service, albeit a generation later, from the notebook of another young Irish apprentice. Harry McGee, who became Eaton's right-hand man in 1883 and a company director in 1893, began his business career as an apprentice at a general store in County Wicklow. It was 1878, and McGee was seventeen. Working without wages for four years, McGee kept a daily record of his expenditures, accounting for every single expenditure, however small. Personal appearance for an apprentice was obviously very important, and clothing in the form of suits and shirts necessitated a regular semi-annual disbursement. Food and board were provided, but arrangements had to be made for personal laundry. Large regular payments to cover this service were made to the local washerwoman. Lead pencils, costing a penny, postage for letters home, church collections, and notebooks were all dutifully recorded and monthly totals noted. In four years Harry McGee spent £31.6.4. (about $155) on personal items. The bulk of this expenditure was directed towards keeping himself respectably clothed, with only token amounts spent on luxuries such as fruit.[3] These years of apprenticeship were but an extension of one's education for the real world, a time in which frivolity had little place.

Although related to Eaton,[4] Smith maintained a strict master-employee relationship. Timothy long remembered the unfairness of being obliged to walk nine miles home to Clogher each Sunday to visit his family, while Smith drove by in his carriage on his way to church in Ballymena. Eaton also disliked the task of sorting the rags collected by Smith and at one point appealed to his mother to terminate the apprenticeship. Rather than forfeit the £100 bond posted for him, Margaret Craig Eaton persuaded him to continue.

Tradition insists that at the end of his apprenticeship Eaton received a silver watch along with repayment of the £100 bond. This he probably returned to his family to offset personal expenses, similar to those listed by McGee, incurred during the preceding five years. He subsequently worked for a short period for a man named Lyttle in Portglenone, presumably to acquire funds for his move to the New World.

Emigration received encouragement and added impetus from press reports and advertisements as well as from activities undertaken by shipping companies. In the first decades of the nineteenth century, Irish newspapers throughout the country not only publicized the offers of land and aid made to settlers in Canada, but contained regular advertisements urging passengers to take advantage of the free crossing to Liverpool. Each spring, shipping agents visited principal towns on market days to make the necessary arrangements for prospective emigrants. The westward migration continued steadily through the 1830s and into the 1840s. In 1846 it became a flood that lasted until 1854, when more than 150,000 people left Ireland to seek a new life elsewhere. Among them was Timothy Eaton.

This is all that can be said with certainty concerning the Irish element in Timothy Eaton's existence, a frustrating problem for the modern biographer who wants to trace patterns from childhood through the adult life and career.

The list of major Eaton biographies runs as follows: in 1919 a golden jubilee volume was anonymously compiled by Edith MacDonald and published by the company; in 1923 G.G. Nasmith was paid by Eaton's to write *Timothy Eaton*; in 1963 Mary Etta Macpherson was paid by the company to compile *Shopkeepers to a Nation: The Eatons*; and in 1969, William Stephenson was commissioned to write a centenary tribute to the Eaton Company, entitled *The Store That Timothy Built*. In 1990 Joy Santink issued *Timothy Eaton and the Rise of His Department Store*, a fine academic study developed from a Ph.D. thesis whose primary intention is the history of a business in relation to other businesses of the time. It only mentions in passing Eaton's Irish roots.[5] All but the last perpetuate myths about Eaton's life in Ireland, such as the fact that he slept under the counter in Smith's shop, identified in the jubilee volume as "a college of hard work."[6] There was also a good deal of meddling on the part of the family in order to uphold the Eaton name. For instance, Robert Young Eaton, Timothy's nephew, born in Northern Ireland and eventually company president, on reviewing Edith MacDonald's manuscript before publication, wrote her a memo pointing out that William Smith's wife was a relative of Timothy Eaton's mother. "Dont rub [it] in about the merchant's harshness," he advised MacDonald.

"He was no worse than other merchants of his day. And his second wife lives in Toronto. Also his daughter."[7] By the time Mary Etta Macpherson came to write her book, R.Y. Eaton had died, and so, with the relatives born in Northern Ireland out of the way, Macpherson was able to milk additional sympathy for poor Timothy from fabricated hard times during his apprenticeship:

> Through these years he was to learn many things about merchandise and qualities and customers' ways, but, more significantly, he learned about the type of employer he would never wish to be. The image of Smith and his inhumanity to the workers who did his bidding was burned into Tim's mind for ever. He might have accepted the sixteen-hour day, the rushed meals over the shop, if such conditions had been accompanied by ordinary Christian kindness. But Smith never relaxed the master-slave relationship. Often on a Sunday, the boy, walking the nine miles to Clogher, would be caught up by the Smith carriage driving to church. Inevitably it whirled by without pause for greeting or the suggestion of a lift. In the lad, standing there brushing the dust from his one good suit, was born an implacable hatred of class distinctions, based on the power of wealth.[8]

The company's Irish connections seem to have been a great source of pride for employees, and the archives, once established, was encouraged to work on confirming and building the list of Irish connections. For example, in 1963 Kitty McPhedran, then Eaton's archivist, noted that "there have been many through the years from Ulster employed by Eaton's." Not long before, she had overheard an Irishman remonstrating "when a fellow employee showed ignorance about the whereabouts of Ballymena."[9] There were indeed many emigrants from Northern Ireland employed by Eaton's, but this does not reflect a pervasive favouritism on the part of the founder or his descendants, but only the settlement patterns of the times: many Ulster men and women gravitated to Toronto and its environs. It appears that there is only one recorded instance of Eaton's displaying any loyalty to his Irish brethren, and it comes from the Eaton staff magazine, *Flash*, in 1943: a retired employee, William Elder, recalled that he had been hired because his mother had known Timothy at Portglenone. He began work in 1875 at the age of fourteen, driving the first delivery wagon.[10] More than this cannot, however, be substantiated: there is no record of Elder's application for employment.

Yet the myth of employee favouritism persisted. In the *Winnipeg Free Press* of 18 September 1958, which covered the visit of the Lord Mayor McKee of Belfast to Canada, Mckee is reported as saying that Ulstermen regarded Toronto as a second Belfast. The writer of the article then speculates that "this had probably been started by Ballymena-born Timothy Eaton, founder of the T. Eaton stores, who had given a 'gentleman's promise' that every Ulster immigrant would be given employment."[11]

A more striking article appeared the following year in the *Drayton (Ontario) Advocate*:

> Of the many who came to the Maritimes and to Central Canada the name of Timothy Eaton from County Antrim stands out. The founder of Canada's greatest retailing enterprise always found a place in his organization for a fellow expatriate from N. Ireland. The story is told that an Asiatic landed in Toronto seeking employment armed with three powerful words, "Me Ballymena Man." We have no doubt Mr. Eaton took him on.

The article closes with this generalisation: "As Hugh Shearman, in his book *Northern Ireland* says, 'an Ulster origin, an Ulster ancestry or an Ulster family tradition is a very precious gift, both to the individual who possesses it and to any other community outside Ulster to whose life and activity he or she may contribute.' "[12]

Timothy Eaton's descendants did not forget their origins. In 1909, for example, Sir John Craig Eaton, the founder's son, made a pilgrimage to the old burying-ground at Kirkinriola. There the company president arranged for the refurbishment of the graves of his grandparents and unveiled a plaque at the site of William Smith's store, recording the fact that the founder of the T. Eaton Co. had spent his apprenticeship there. But these token remembrances are dwarfed by the actions and expressed sentiments of R.Y. Eaton, who first worked in the company's European offices from 1897 to 1902, when he was appointed secretary of the company by his uncle Timothy. When Sir John Craig, R.Y.'s cousin, died in 1922, the latter took over the presidency of the company, retaining this position for twenty years, until the youngest of Sir John's sons reached the age of twenty-seven, at which time the company directors would choose one son to succeed him.

Born in Northern Ireland, and the only member of the family for whom an Ulster origin was precious, R.Y. named his Toronto house

"Killyree" and always maintained a keen interest in events in Northern Ireland. In 1949, he donated £1,000 to the Mid-Antrim Sports Association for the development of the Eaton Park playing fields in Ballymena. For this and other acts of generosity, he was honoured in 1954 as a Freeman of the Borough of Ballymena, the second time that this rare honour was bestowed. Only too often, Mayor Thomas Wilson remarked, those who had risen from comparative obscurity had found it convenient to forget the old homestead in the luxury of their new surroundings. "But not so with the Eatons," he added. "The family homestead was remembered and visited. Many of the old relations, neighbours and acquaintances were given a helping hand in the new world at a time in their lives when help was most needed." The mayor pointed out that the Eatons had put Ballymena on the map and had set "a new standard of values as between man and man; a standard of values which will never be beaten and is unlikely to be equalled."[13]

Such laudatory remarks gave R.Y. cause to rejoice about his family. The *Belfast News-Letter* records R.Y. Eaton saying that the late Timothy Eaton had an abiding affection for the land of his birth and that it was natural for him and his successors to give practical effect to that sentiment by extending a welcome to the immigrants from the "old sod." He pointed out that because the Eaton name was so widely and favourably known by residents of Ballymena and district, it was only natural that they should choose Eaton's Co. Ltd. when seeking employment in Canada. "Quite a number remained with us 20, 30 or 40 years," he added, "many having risen to positions of high responsibility in the company, as also have many of their sons and daughters." The newspaper reported that both Sir John Eaton and his son, John David, who had succeeded R.Y. Eaton as president in 1942, "manifested similar leanings towards Ulster." It was only natural, R.Y. said, that he, the founder's nephew and, for twenty years after his death, president of the firm, should desire to welcome newcomers from Northern Ireland and from time to time renew memories of the land of his birth.[14] It should be noted that when R.Y. undertook the Northern Irish tour, he had not been president, or even associated with the company, for many years. Frederik Eaton, current chairman, notes that R.Y.'s visit "was in the nature of a swan song," of the sort that elicits such speeches. In contrast, when Frederik visited Northern Ireland with his father and brother the year before (1953), they were not met with any form of public display.[15] Thus, R.Y., the last living link with the old country, took advantage of a golden opportunity to perpetuate Eaton myths, one of them being employee favouritism.

From the time R.Y. Eaton took the helm of the company in 1922, the Northern Irish connections mushroomed. In 1938 the Ulster Tourist Development Association, urged on by R.Y., made enquiries concerning the exact location of the farm where Timothy Eaton was born, so that a plaque could be affixed to it. The association wrote back to Eaton to say that the occupant of the farm was reluctant to carry out such a plan, for fear of

Timothy Eaton (1834–1907), whose fondness for the "auld sod" was more invention than actuality. (Courtesy P.J. Wilson, Manager, Company Community Relations, Eaton's, Toronto.)

intruding visitors.[16] On 3 July 1944 the Museum and Art Gallery at Stranmillis, Belfast, wrote to R.Y. to request a portrait of Timothy Eaton for a collection of "portraits of Ulstermen who became eminent outside their own country, in administration, business or other capacity."[17] The Eaton myth was growing.

Newspapers and magazines played their part in keeping "St. Timothy" alive. From the time of R.Y.'s recognition by Ballymena in 1954 until at least 1985, articles have appeared in the *Ballymena Guardian*, the *Ballymena Observer*, the *Ulster Commentary*, the *Belfast News-Letter*, and the *Belfast Telegraph*, with such titles as "Portrait from the Past," "Ulsterman with the Midas Touch Founded Canada's Biggest Store," and "County Antrim's 'Canadian Explorer' Born 150 Years Ago." Some Canadian papers followed suit. When Terrence O'Neill, Northern Ireland's minister of finance, visited Toronto in 1959, he presented Mayor Phillips with a letter from Alderman Wilson of Ballymena, O'Neill's home town. In an article entitled "Auld Sod Thanks Eatons," the Toronto *Telegram* reprinted the letter: "'The name of Eaton (The T. Eaton Co. Ltd.) is a household word in Ballymena and District,' wrote Ald[erman] Wilson. 'The founder of these famous stores – the late Mr. Timothy Eaton, as you probably are aware, was born in the Ballymena area, and his lifelong interest in this district has been fully maintained by succeeding family members of the Eaton family to the gratification of our citizens.'"[18]

Eaton's connections with Ulster are impossible to substantiate. In many cases, they were fabricated or distorted by his descendants, admirers, and employees in order to build up a saintly picture of this man and his department store. His religious character, another asset of supposed Irish foundation, is worthy of emulation, his venerators imply: "Remember that he was born and bred a kirkman. Clogher developed in him a profound veneration for the Sabbath"; or, "On Sunday behold the sturdy, blue-eyed youth trudging through mud or snow ten miles to Clogher to change his clothes and go to the kirk for a dour, Calvinistic sermon"; or, "On the Calvinistic stock he grafted Methodist growth. He joined the Methodist Church, of which until the day of his death he remained a pillar."[19]

Without doubt the Eatonian claim to Irishness resulted in posthumous gestures of goodwill on both sides of the Atlantic. However, heartfelt sentiments for the "auld sod" were absent from Timothy Eaton's character. His only reason for keeping in touch with Ireland was his brother John's residence there until his death in 1895. Even references to this branch of his family are few and perfunctory. In 1870 he wrote to his brother James, who was living in St. Marys, Ontario, telling him about a letter from John: "They are all well. He has got the flax mill in operation. Flax this year is a good crop."[20] Again in 1875 he wrote to James, advising him to return home to Ireland, for "it will do you good all over to see old Ireland & John."[21] Timothy never returned to Ireland (although he did take his wife on a cross-country motor trip in England), and never mentioned the place of his birth in his correspondence after the death of John. The only lasting visible acknowledgment of an Irish descent was his sporting a sprig of shamrock in his buttonhole on St. Patrick's Day.

A tough, single-minded business genius, Timothy Eaton took it upon himself to change the whole concept of retail trade in Canada. He was a self-determining entity, a maker of history, who developed a commercial system far more efficient, expansive, and competitive than anything then in existence. In all that he did, he saw himself as a Canadian first and foremost. In 1893 he wrote to an associate in South Dakota: "We Toronto people think there is no such place under the sun as our own City and Country."[22] He was clearly proud of what he had achieved, not as an Irishman, but as a Canadian.

Dr. Leon Litvack is a lecturer in the School of English at the Queen's University of Belfast, Northern Ireland. Born and raised in Toronto, he is a graduate of the University of Edinburgh (Ph.D., 1989). He has worked extensively on ethnicity and multiculturalism in Canada, in both literary and sociological contexts, and has lectured and taught about these subjects in Europe and in the Far East. From 1987 to 1990 he served as the visiting professor of Canadian studies at Kwansei Gakuin University in Nishinomiya, Japan, and as the coordinator of Canadian studies for Western Japan. In 1991, while on a sessional lectureship in Scotland, Dr. Litvack lectured on the Jews of Canada in a multicultural setting, at the Centre of Canadian Studies, University of Edinburgh. Currently he is a member of the British Association of Canadian Studies Council and is vice-director of the Centre of Canadian Studies at the Queen's University. He is teaching a course on "Multiculturalism in Canadian Literature" in the School of English, as well as courses in Romantic and Victorian literature, his other areas of expertise. Having settled in the United Kingdom, he hopes to continue to lecture on the Canadian multicultural model, with lessons for Europe. Timothy Eaton is of special interest to Dr. Litvack, not only because of his proximity to Eaton's birthplace, but also because members of his family have worked for the T. Eaton Co. In the near future he will begin work on a book on multiculturalism in Canadian literature. Leon Litvack is the author of *John Mason Neale and the Quest for Sobornost* (Oxford: Oxford University Press [pending]).

Notes

1 Archives of Ontario (AO), Eaton Archives, F 229, Memorandum in Timothy Eaton's handwriting, series 221, box 5. I would like to thank P.J. Wilson, Eaton's Community Relations Department, for his kindness and for granting me access to restricted archival materials, and Frederik S. Eaton, high commissioner for Canada to the United Kingdom, for sharing with me his personal insight into the Eaton family.

2 John H. Dales, "Approaches to Entrepreneurial History," *Explorations in Entrepreneurial History* 1, no. 1 (1963): 10.

3 AO, F 229, series 221, box 1, Harry McGee, notebook.

4 By marriage to the Craig side of the family.

5 Mary Etta Macpherson, *Shopkeepers to a Nation: The Eatons* (Toronto: McClelland and Stewart, 1963); G.G. Nasmith, *Timothy Eaton* (Toronto: McClelland and Stewart, 1923); Joy Santink, *Timothy Eaton and the Rise of His Department Store* (Toronto: University of Toronto Press, 1990); and William Stephenson, *The Store That Timothy Built 1869–1919* (Toronto: McClelland and Stewart, 1969).

6 Edith MacDonald, *Golden Jubilee* (Toronto: privately printed, 1919), 71.

7 AO, 229, series 221, box 5, R.Y. Eaton's notes to Edith MacDonald re. jubilee book.

8 Macpherson, *Shopkeepers to a Nation*, 7.

9 AO, F 229, series 221, box 5, letter from Kitty (McPhedran) Fells to N.C. Mitchel, lecturer in geography, the Queen's University of Belfast, 27 June 1963.

10 Santick, *Timothy Eaton*, 85.

11 "Lord Mayor of Belfast Likes Canada's Colleens,"*Winnipeg Free Press*, 18 September 1958, 6.

12 Brock B. Davis, "Me Ballymena Man," *Drayton Advocate*, 16 April 1959, 4.

13 "Freedom of Borough conferred on Mr. Robert Young Eaton," *Ballymena Weekly Telegraph*, 17 September 1954, 8.

14 "Mr. Eaton made freeman of Ballymena," *Belfast News-Letter*, 16 September 1954, 8.

15 Personal letter, Frederik Eaton, Canadian High Commission, London, England, to author, 19 December 1991.

16 AO, F 229, series 221, box 6, UTDA to R.Y. Eaton, 12 April 1938.

17 Ibid., Gallery to R.Y. Eaton, 3 July 1944.

18 *Telegram* (Toronto), 5 October 1959, 7.

19 MacDonald, *Golden Jubilee*, 72, 73.

20 AO, F 229, series 6, box 1, T. Eaton to J. Eaton, 9 Oct 1870.

21 Ibid., T. Eaton to J. Eaton, 8 June 1875.

22 Ibid., T. Eaton to W.G. Scougal.

Part 6

Laurier and McCarthy: Two Solitudes

Chapter 16

Écrire sur la carrière politique de Wilfrid Laurier: Quelques réflexions et hypothèses sur la biographie de personnages politiques au Québec

Réal Bélanger

Professor Bélanger's *Wilfrid Laurier: Quand la politique devient passion* (Presses de l'Université Laval, 1986) was the first biography of Laurier written by a French Canadian historian. As well as examining Laurier through the eyes of French Canada, Réal Bélanger attempts to explain in this paper why fellow historians in French Canada have ignored the Liberal leader (1887–1919) and prime minister of Canada (1896–1911). The strong nationalism of French Canadian intellectuals in this century may be one explanation. Beyond that, however, lies an aversion to political history, including political biography, on the part of Francophone historians since 1960, in spite of efforts to enlarge the horizons of traditional biography in Quebec and elsewhere. Bélanger concludes with a definition of modern biography, its strengths and limitations, and its contribution to our understanding of the past.

Centré sur la biographie de Wilfrid Laurier, ce texte présente aussi quelques réflexions et hypothèses sur la biographie de personnages politiques telle que perçue par la communauté historienne canadienne-française. Il se partage en deux parties. La première est consacrée à une brève vue d'ensemble de la carrière politique de Wilfrid Laurier tandis que la deuxième tente d'expliquer le peu d'engouement des historiens canadiens-français pour cet illustre homme politique et aborde la place de la biographie dans les études historiques au Québec. La conclusion montre comment la biographie que j'ai écrite sur Wilfrid Laurier[1] s'inscrit en partie dans le courant dit de la "nouvelle histoire" et participe pleinement de l'histoire qu'elle contribue à faire avancer.

Je commence avec la carrière politique de Wilfrid Laurier – ou, du moins, les grandes lignes de sa carrière telles que perçues par un historien canadien-français du Québec. Je me concentrerai d'abord sur les principaux moments de la vie de Laurier, premier Canadien français à devenir premier ministre du Canada, puis je dégagerai sa place dans l'histoire canadienne et québécoise.

L'homme naît en 1841 dans une famille très modeste de Saint-Lin, paroisse agricole, en très grande majorité canadienne-française et catholique du Québec, que son père, un arpenteur et cultivateur passionné de politique, et sa mère sont venus habiter en 1834. Wilfrid Laurier fait des études de droit à McGill, l'université anglaise de Montréal; il devient avocat en 1864 et pratique aussitôt le droit à Montréal. Comme plusieurs des avocats du Canada-Est de l'époque, il se transforme aussi alors en journaliste. Dès 1866, sa santé chancelante – elle le sera toute sa vie – l'oblige à quitter le grand centre qu'est Montréal pour vivre dans l'air pur de la campagne: il choisit la région des Bois-Francs, Québec, où il s'installe définitivement en janvier 1867.

C'est là, à Victoriaville puis à Arthabaskaville, où il gardera une résidence jusqu'à la fin de ses jours, qu'il commence vraiment sa vie d'adulte. C'est là, véritablement, qu'il fera ses premiers pas en journalisme et en politique et qu'il épousera la cause du parti Rouge du Québec, un parti considéré comme radical à l'époque, vigoureusement opposé au projet de Confédération que propose alors le parti Conservateur dirigé par John A. Macdonald. Ce projet prévoit la réunion de quatre colonies britanniques de l'Amérique du Nord pour former une fédération, le Canada, et une nation nouvelle, la nation canadienne, bilingue et biculturelle, dans laquelle deux peuples fondateurs acceptent de cohabiter sans se fusionner. Or Laurier s'y objecte avec force car, croit-il, la Confédération deviendra le tombeau de la race canadienne-française. Pour lui, l'avenir du Canada-Est passe par l'obtention d'un gouvernement libre et séparé.

Laurier et les Rouges, on le sait, n'obtiendront pas gain de cause. En homme pragmatique – il dira toujours qu'il faut prendre les choses comme elles sont – Laurier, comme d'ailleurs la plupart des membres de son parti, se ralliera progressivement à la Confédération. Et, fait capital, il décide dès lors, à titre de Libéral, d'en défendre l'existence à l'Assemblée législative de la province de Québec, de 1871 à 1874, puis à la Chambre des communes du Canada, où il arrive inconnu le 26 mars 1874.

Commence alors une carrière politique qui marquera l'histoire canadienne – une carrière dont l'ampleur se mesure d'abord par l'importance des fonctions détenues ainsi que par la durée de leurs mandats. Laurier sera député fédéral de 1874 à 1919, année de sa mort, soit pendant 45 ans; il deviendra chef du parti libéral du Canada en 1887 et le restera jusqu'à sa mort, soit pendant 32 ans; et il occupera le poste de premier ministre du Canada de 1896 à 1911, soit pendant 15 ans.

Mais il y a plus. Même si certaines de ses actions servent mal la cause qu'il prétend défendre, on doit admettre que son oeuvre transforme le Canada, le Québec et le parti Libéral du Canada. Souvent présenté comme le digne successeur de John A. Macdonald, il est, de fait, l'architecte du Canada moderne. Certes l'homme ne travaille pas en vase clos: il n'est pas responsable de tout et il est secondé par une équipe de Libéraux capables et ce, à un moment où la société canadienne attend impatiemment qu'un tel leader se pointe. Mais il figure au centre de l'action à un moment clé de l'histoire; il lui dicte très souvent la seule voie à suivre; il l'imprègne d'un sens politique aiguisé, surtout d'un sens du compromis indispensable, selon lui, à une société comme la nôtre; il la guide de son autorité qu'il a toujours exercée franchement aux dires mêmes de ses plus influents ministres; il l'enveloppe en tous temps de son charisme exceptionnel et de sa personnalité attachante pour mieux la faire accepter de la majorité des Canadiens.

Indéniablement, la connaissance de l'histoire canadienne de la fin du XIXe siècle et du début du XXe siècle passe par une meilleure connaissance de Wilfrid Laurier, grand seigneur de la politique pour les uns, le pire Machiavel pour les autres, mais un homme qui s'est toujours perçu lui-même tel un infatigable indolent, amoureux des charmes romantiques de la campagne, ardent passionné de lecture.

Que réalise donc cet homme politique au cours de sa si longue carrière? On peut, grossomodo, partager ses réalisations en deux grandes parties. D'abord celles effectuées à la tête de son parti, puis celles accomplies à la tête du gouvernement canadien.

À la tête de son parti, Laurier réussit deux exploits qui marqueront la société canadienne de l'époque et les structures politiques du pays. Sous sa direction amorcée en 1887, le parti Libéral sort d'abord des terres froides de l'Opposition et se déleste de son esprit plutôt régionaliste et de son purisme peu rentable électoralement pour devenir un parti vraiment national, pragmatique et bi-racial dans lequel, pendant près de trois décennies, soit précisément jusqu'en 1917, les Canadiens français et les Canadiens anglais coopèrent de manière généralement satisfaisante.

Le plus beau fleuron toutefois de la couronne de Laurier reste d'avoir amené le Québec dans le giron de son parti. Il s'agit d'une véritable révolution politique pour l'époque. Pour la comprendre, il faut savoir que le Québec de la deuxième moitié du XIXe siècle est imprégné d'un courant idéologique très conservateur que domine un clergé catholique très opposé à tout ce qui concerne le libéralisme. Pour ce clergé, être libéral, donc être Libéral en politique, signifie être anti-clérical, vouloir la séparation de l'Église et de l'État, être révolutionnaire et briseur de l'ordre social. Pour ce clergé très écouté de la population, un seul parti politique doit être encouragé: le parti Conservateur de John A. Macdonald.

Or Laurier arrive, met l'accent sur la modération, la tolérance, propage l'idée que les Libéraux du Québec souscrivent seulement au libéralisme de type britannique fondé sur l'ordre, la liberté individuelle, le progrès et le développement économique. Les Canadiens français l'entendent, puis l'appuient: le parti Libéral devient dès lors crédible au Québec et plus, le Québec devient même la base de ses nombreuses victoires électorales dans le cours du XXe siècle. Laurier, sans conteste, demeure l'âme de ce revirement, le centre de ce mouvement d'opinion qui a participé à renverser les mentalités au Québec, l'initiateur d'une transformation du système de parti canadien. Il s'agit d'un rôle capital dans l'histoire canadienne.

À la tête du pays, Laurier pose des gestes d'envergure multiples, guidé par son ambition de réaliser le plan canadien de John A. Macdonald, de développer territorialement et économiquement le Canada, de réaliser l'unité canadienne. Le XXe siècle, dira-t-il, sera le siècle du Canada. Dans ma biographie, je montre ces exploits remarquables mais je développe aussi la thèse que les stratégies de compromis de Laurier sur l'unité nationale conduisent à deux conséquences: le commencement de la fin d'un Canada bi-culturel et le confinement territorial obligé des Canadiens français au Québec.

Cette oeuvre de Laurier et de son équipe ne peut être comprise qu'en la situant dans le contexte qui la fait éclore. Lorsque Laurier devient officiellement premier ministre, le 11 juillet 1896, le Canada, nation projetée plutôt que nation formée, se débat dans une situation précaire: la dépression économique sévit tandis qu'éclatent les particularismes régionaux, que s'intensifiient les querelles ethniques entre Canadiens français et Canadiens anglais, que menace l'agressivité du puissant voisin américain et que s'ébauchent les divergences face à l'impérialisme britannique.

Or, Laurier paraît et, se fondant sur les principes et ambitions mentionnés précédemment, exploitant une conjoncture internationale profitable, coordonnant une brillante équipe qui l'inspire et le fouette à l'occasion, il assume le plan de la Confédération et contribue à faire du Canada une nation. Les réalisations du gouvernement qu'il dirige vont du développement de l'Ouest canadien par une vigoureuse politique d'immigration jusqu'à la création d'un chemin de fer transcontinental en passant par la formation de deux nouvelles provinces, l'Alberta et la Saskatchewan, l'expansion industrielle de l'Est et la résistance tenace et fructueuse aux assauts de centralisation impériale qui taille une place au Canada dans l'Empire et prépare la voie au Commonwealth britannique. Petit à petit, entre 1896 et 1911, un esprit de plus en plus canadien surgit au pays. Plus, Laurier sait répondre à plusieurs des besoins de la société canadienne: on peut même affirmer que pendant une bonne partie de cette époque une quasi-symbiose se vit entre le premier ministre et un grand nombre de Canadiens. C'est un autre fait capital de l'histoire canadienne.

Bien que cette carrière politique soit éclatante, elle subit néanmoins des ratés et connaît des échecs retentissants. Passons outre aux défaites électorales de 1911 sur la réciprocité commerciale avec les États-Unis et de 1917 sur la conscription; passons outre aussi au fait que Laurier n'adapte pas, à la longue, son libéralisme aux aspirations de la nouvelle société industrialisée et urbaine qui s'était progressivement formée; passons outre enfin au fait que le transcontinental ne s'avérera pas rentable à moyen et à long termes. Passons outre à tout ceci pour nous arrêter à l'aspect que je considère le plus décevant de cette carrière, soit les compromis consentis pour régler le sort des minorités catholiques canadiennes-françaises hors Québec, en particulier lorsqu'il s'agit des écoles séparées.

Ici, l'illustre chef perd une partie de sa gloire. Retenons deux cas, celui du règlement Laurier-Greenway en 1896 sur les écoles du Manitoba et cet autre, le fameux deuxième article 16 lors de la création de l'Alberta et de la Saskatchewan en 1905. Dans ces deux exemples, les compromis de Laurier conduisent à faire accepter une vision tronquée de la nation canadienne, ce qui menace au plus haut point le caractère bi-culturel du pays. Certes, il lui faut alors composer avec une situation très tendue. Certes le compromis est nécessaire dans un pays comme le Canada. Mais quand le compromis s'accompagne de trop d'ambiguïtés, d'équivoques, d'opportunisme et qu'il s'aligne régulièrement sur les seules vues de la majorité, ce compromis ne joue plus son rôle et provoque frustrations et désenchantements chez la minorité. Or Laurier est tombé dans tous ces travers, espérant qu'aux moments décisifs la majorité canadienne-anglaise saurait à son tour faire les concessions qu'il fallait pour servir la cause suprême. Laurier a mal calculé car la majorité canadienne-anglaise, sincère pourtant elle-même dans ses convictions, ne le suivra jamais jusque-là. Par son attitude faite de reculs sur reculs, Laurier met alors en péril la survie même du dualisme inscrit dans la lettre et dans l'esprit de la Constitution de 1867.

À la fin de sa vie, Laurier a toutes les raisons du monde d'être amer et désabusé. La crise de la conscription de 1917–18 ruine d'abord l'unité du parti Libéral qu'il avait mis tant d'années à construire (des Libéraux canadiens-anglais favorables à la conscription rompent alors avec lui pour se joindre au Gouvernement d'Union de Robert Laird Borden formé pour imposer la conscription), puis elle fracasse l'unité nationale au nom de laquelle, a-t-il si souvent répété, il avait oeuvré depuis ses débuts en politique fédérale (les Canadiens français combattent vigoureusement la conscription alors que les Canadiens anglais l'approuvent majoritairement). En somme, deux des clés majeures de son système s'écroulent en même temps. Et l'homme en est profondément touché. Mais il reste les autres acquis, et ils sont nombreux. Laurier en est bien conscient et, à la veille de sa mort, le 17 février 1919, il garde, malgré tout, l'espoir que le travail accompli depuis le début des années 1870 n'aura pas été effectué en vain.

Convenons qu'à ce jour l'Histoire a rendu justice à Wilfrid Laurier et lui a assuré une place d'honneur dans ses plus belles pages. Ma biographie s'inscrit dans ce courant bien qu'elle n'écarte aucune des réserves sérieuses mentionnées précédemment. Sans indulgence mais avec une constante et lucide volonté de compréhension, elle laisse à ce personnage immense assez d'éclat pour lui permettre de vivre dans la mémoire des Canadiens.

Personnage immense! Mais comment expliquer que ce Canadien si important dans l'histoire canadienne ait fait l'objet d'attentions particulières de la part de Canadiens anglais (pensons aux travaux de O.D. Skelton, de John W. Dafoe, de Joseph Schull, de H. Blair Neatby, de Richard Clippingdale)[2] mais qu'il ait été tant négligé par les historiens canadiens-français? En effet, je fus le premier historien canadien-français à m'intéresser sérieusement à ce personnage et à sa place dans l'histoire canadienne.[3] Les historiens canadiens-français, les biographes canadiens-français, ont boudé Sir Wilfrid Laurier. Pourquoi?

Trois raisons principales expliquent, selon moi, cette situation. La première est liée à l'influence sur les intellectuels du courant nationaliste dominant au Canada français depuis la mort de Laurier, ou du moins de celui qui apparaît le plus véhiculé ouvertement et de manière la mieux articulée qu'il soit. Plus centré sur la défense, la protection et le développement du Québec et des Canadiens français, et plus récemment sur la séparation même du Québec du Canada, ce nationalisme a conquis la majorité des historiens canadiens-français qui ont consacré leurs recherches au Québec. Il restait alors bien peu de place dans leurs préoccupations pour le Canada en général et pour ceux qui l'avaient défendu, qu'ils soient canadiens-anglais ou canadiens-français, qu'ils aient été importants ou pas. Certes, quelques hommes politiques canadiens-français ayant oeuvré à Ottawa ont trouvé grâce aux yeux de certains historiens, mais ils sont l'exception[4] et, surtout, ils ont moins marqué leur époque qu'un Laurier, grand défenseur du nationalisme pan-canadien.

La deuxième raison de l'absence de Laurier dans l'historiographie canadienne-française relève du type d'histoire fabriqué au Québec depuis bon nombre d'années mais surtout depuis les années 1960. Et ici, il faut le dire, les historiens francophones du Québec ne font pas bande à part, s'inscrivant plutôt dans un courant quasi occidental. L'historien Fernand Ouellet a très bien résumé la situation québécoise francophone dans un article paru en 1985.[5] "Jusqu'en 1963," écrit-il, "l'historiographie était ... restée, dans l'ensemble, politique et cléricale, non seulement dans son contenu mais, tout autant, dans son personnel." Or, vinrent le développement des universités québécoises et le mouvement de professionnalisation des historiens qui firent éclore un nouveau type d'historien et un nouveau type d'historiographie qu'inspirera considérablement (il faut dire que le marxisme apportera aussi sa contribution) l'École française des *Annales* qui défendait "l'image d'une histoire sociale axée sur l'idée de totalité et appuyée principalement sur l'économique," une histoire qui valorisait aussi la démographie, les perspectives théoriques, l'utilisation de modèles et le recours aux méthodes quantitatives, qui débouchait sur "les interactions entre les diverses composantes de la vie en société," sur "l'étude des structures et des mouvements sociaux," sur "une plus grande sensibilité aux ferments communautaires et à leur signification au plan culturel."

Cette historiographie nouvelle, conclura Ouellet,

> assumée par un personnel renouvelé, sans doute préoccupé avant tout par la question nationale mais quand même ouvert à des options idéologiques variées quant au social, multipli [a] ses intérêts et ses domaines de recherche en fonction des besoins de la société contemporaine.[6]

L'histoire économique, l'histoire sociale et l'histoire socio-culturelle étaient devenues la mode au Québec. Haro donc sur l'histoire dite traditionnelle au centre de laquelle se trouvent l'histoire politique et l'histoire cléricale. Haro, en conséquence, sur la biographie qui a tant servi, au Québec, ce genre d'histoire.[7] Si bien que, depuis 1965, la biographie touchant à des personnages politiques et produite par des historiens professionnels canadiens-français[8] est en nette régression au Québec comme l'est, d'ailleurs, l'histoire politique, laquelle n'est presque plus pratiquée, à part chez nous à l'université Laval et quelque peu à l'université du Québec à Montréal et au collège universitaire de Saint-Jean, et ne fait plus l'objet d'ateliers lors des congrès de l'Institut d'Histoire de l'Amérique française (IHAF), le rassemblement le plus important d'historiens québécois.[9]

Vous comprenez mieux pourquoi Laurier n'a pas suscité l'intérêt d'historiens-biographes canadiens-français. Le contexte historiographique ne s'y prêtait pas et la biographie de personnages politiques était de moins en moins prisée par la communauté historienne. Dans des discussions privées aujourd'hui, des historiens peuvent prétexter le manque de ressources du milieu, de taille si réduite, et aligner les quelques biographies récentes produites le plus souvent par des politicologues et des journalistes pour tenter d'enrayer cette interprétation. Ils ne réussissent toutefois pas à convaincre.

La troisième raison du peu d'engouement qu'a soulevé Laurier est liée à la deuxième. Elle tient compte de la perception erronée que plusieurs historiens francophones du Québec ont encore de la biographie. En fait, comme un certain nombre d'autres historiens à travers le monde, bien qu'en France, aux États-Unis et en Grande-Bretagne le retour à la biographie soit très évident,[10] ils se méprennent sur le sens réel de la biographie. Je dois avouer, ici, toutefois, que j'extrapole car peu d'historiens francophones ont osé écrire sur le sujet. Mais leur comportement et leurs propos tenus lors de congrès me font dire que je suis assez près de la réalité en soulevant cette hypothèse et que ces historiens épousent encore trop aujourd'hui ce qu'on a véhiculé et publié ailleurs dans les années passées.

Qu'a-t-on véhiculé ailleurs? Que la biographie, réduite au terme peu flatteur de "genre historique", reste une façon de faire de l'histoire dépassée, peu utile, partielle, au corpus documentaire rudimentaire, peu critique et peu scientifique, simplement descriptive, trop souvent hagiographique plutôt qu'explicative, élitiste, qui ne provient pas et ne répond pas ni aux nouvelles méthodologies ni aux questions fondamentales posées par la nouvelle histoire, qui simplifie au maximum la complexité de l'histoire et, pire, qui déforme la réalité en la présentant sous l'oeil réducteur de l'individu, un individu, au surplus, identifié à une sorte de héros porteur d'une mission spéciale. La biographie est, en somme, une oeuvre d'édification qui propose un modèle de comportement. Il s'agit d'une manière de faire de l'histoire qui empêche de parvenir à l'histoire totale tant recherchée, qui néglige "les forces profondes," qui se désintéresse trop de l'étude de la société sous toutes ses formes et groupes et celle des changements dans le temps et qui, pour produire un effet littéraire, modifiera la vérité, cultivera l'imaginaire, organisera même la vie du héros selon une chronologie artificielle. On n'hésite donc pas à parler de "l'illusion biographique," du peu de possibilités du discours biographique qui rétrécit ainsi l'histoire à l'élaboration d'une accumulation de vies les unes toutes aussi incertaines et difficiles à cerner que les autres.[11]

Dans ce contexte, on comprend encore mieux pourquoi Laurier n'a bénéficié que tardivement d'une biographie établie par un historien canadien-français. Au Québec, il faut presque encore se défendre de faire de la biographie alors que, je le répète, une tendance autre prévaut dans certains pays où, comme en France, un Pierre Goubert n'a pas craint d'écrire récemment sur *Mazarin*.[12]

Certains, toutefois, pourraient nuancer cette constatation en s'appuyant sur le fait que plusieurs membres de la communauté historienne ont quand même participé avec enthousiasme à l'élaboration du prestigieux *Dictionnaire biographique du Canada*, que l'IHAF a institué en 1985 le prix Maxime-Raymond, qui couronne la meilleure biographie scientifique portant sur un individu de l'Amérique française, enfin que des biographies touchant à des personnages de divers horizons, mais de haute qualité, ont été reconnues par le milieu universitaire.[13] À cet égard, des historiens signalent même, aujourd'hui, une "reprise d'intérêt" pour la biographie au Québec.[14]

Mais ne nous méprenons pas. Au-delà de ces réalisations, l'esprit décrit plus haut domine, selon moi. En fait, il me semble que plusieurs historiens ont encore trop en tête l'image de la biographie telle qu'élaborée dans le Québec francophone du XIXᵉ siècle et de la première moitié du XXᵉ siècle laquelle, il faut l'admettre, était tombée dans plusieurs des travers mentionnés précédemment comme l'a bien démontré l'historien Serge Gagnon dans son excellent livre *Le Québec et ses historiens de 1840 à 1920*, paru en 1978.[15]

Pourtant ces historiens, qui regardent de haut la biographie en ces heures de crise des paradigmes, de critiques sévères des modèles interprétatifs et du retour à l'individu, devraient se rendre compte que cette façon de faire de l'histoire a évolué au Québec comme ailleurs et que les historiens canadiens-français qui écrivent des biographies ont modifié la manière de les construire, sans en contrecarrer toutes les limites, d'une façon qui permet d'en exploiter plusieurs des possibilités et, ce faisant, contribue davantage à l'explication historique et à l'histoire en général.

Des quatre principales approches à la base de la confection des biographies et qui les définissent aux dires de Giovanni Levi, soit celles de la "prosopographie et de la biographie modale", de la "biographie et contexte", de la "biographie et les cas limites" et de la "biographie et herméneutique,"[16] les biographes du Québec se sont davantage adonnés à la deuxième, celle qui insère la singularité individuelle dans une époque, dans un milieu et dans un environnement qui participent à l'explication historique. Or ils l'ont fait, plus souvent que certains ne le croient, selon une méthodologie renouvelée qui a élargi les horizons de la biographie et l'a conduite en partie dans le courant de l'histoire dite nouvelle.

En effet, de plus en plus, la biographie québécoise – ce qui comprend évidemment celle centrée sur les personnages politiques – confectionnée par des historiens canadiens-français de métier étudie l'individu mais elle le confronte à l'épreuve de l'histoire politique et sociale, plus larges dans leurs perspectives et dans leurs problématiques. L'étude biographique, ignorant la fiction, est devenue aussi plus critique, plus analytique, ce qui amène le biographe à mieux choisir, à mieux déterminer, à mieux construire un personnage en un acte authentique de création qui écarte le piège des textes où le spectaculaire commande la construction du sens. Cette biographie fait en outre appel à des sources nouvelles et diversifiées et aux sciences connexes que sont la science politique, la sociologie, l'anthropologie, la démographie, l'économique, la psychologie, la graphologie. Plus, elle lie désormais vie privée et vie publique dans une dynamique évolutive, elle situe l'homme dans les mouvements sociaux de l'époque examinée; elle place l'individu dans son cadre, ce qui entraîne entre autres l'étude du mode de vie et des habitudes sociales, des relations et des solidarités, des attitudes, des fortunes même.

Ainsi, la biographie exerce dans le Québec francophone, comme l'a démontré pour la France Philippe Levillain, "une fonction à mi-chemin entre le collectif et le particulier", elle identifie une "figure dans un milieu"; elle examine "le sens pris par une éducation distribuée selon les mêmes modèles à d'autres"; elle analyse "les relations entre dessein personnel et forces concourantes ou concurrentes"; elle fait "le bilan entre héritage et acquis dans tous les domaines." L'individu devient alors le miroir d'une société à un moment précis de son destin. La biographie représente, pour reprendre les beaux mots du même Levillain, "le lieu par excellence de la peinture de la condition humaine dans sa diversité si elle n'isole pas l'homme de ses dissemblables ou ne l'exalte pas à leurs dépens."[17]

Certes, il faut être réaliste au Québec: tout n'est pas parfait et définitif. L'exigence de correctifs à apporter à la confection des biographies demeure. Il faut aussi admettre que toutes les biographies n'ont pas pris la tangente mentionnée plus haut. Des limites perdurent; des craintes apparaissent dont celle de produire des biographies hybrides qui ne seraient, au fond, qu'une moitié de biographie et qu'une moitié de monographie d'histoire sociale et culturelle; des difficultés inhérentes à cette façon de faire de l'histoire restent.[18] En somme, s'agitent ici – comme ailleurs – encore aujourd'hui les relations avec les sciences sociales, les questions liées aux échelles d'analyse, aux rapports entre règles et pratiques, aux restrictions à la liberté et à la rationalité humaines.[19] Mais, de fait, ne sont-ce pas là les interrogations méthodologiques les plus courantes de l'historiographie contemporaine? Il faut donc demeurer vigilant comme biographe et attentif à toute critique, à toute nouveauté méthodologique. Mais, disons-le franchement aussi, il faut être fier des modifications apportées ces dernières années au Québec à la manière de produire des biographies, manière qui s'inscrit dans le courant du renouveau de la biographie.[20]

La biographie que j'ai écrite sur Laurier s'intègre en bonne partie à ce courant, et la critique l'a bien perçue ainsi.[21] Il me semble qu'une biographie ainsi construite peut appuyer l'explication historique. Mieux, elle peut devenir une contribution irremplaçable à l'histoire totale tant recherchée et si difficilement accessible. Car la reconstitution d'une vie n'est-elle pas l'unique manière de comprendre vraiment l'ensemble d'une époque sur le mode du vécu? Et l'étape ultime de la vérification théorique ne se retrouve-t-elle pas réellement dans la confrontation avec des individus d'une société donnée? Décidément, il m'apparaît juste d'affirmer que la biographie telle que proposée est beaucoup plus qu'un simple "genre" dont l'histoire pourrait se passer: elle participe pleinement de l'histoire par le récit qu'elle offre et "qui rythme, selon les mots de Daniel Madelénat, les invariances et les circonstances de ce module existentiel fondamental, le cours d'une vie humaine."[22]

Né le 30 septembre 1943, à L'Islet, province de Québec, le professeur **Réal Bélanger** a obtenu son Ph.D. en histoire en 1979 de l'Université Laval, où il enseigne depuis ce temps. Son enseignement et ses recherches portent sur l'histoire politique du Canada et du Québec contemporains, en particulier sur l'histoire des partis et du personnel politiques ainsi que sur l'histoire des nationalismes canadiens et québécois. Il a publié plusieurs articles et quatre livres dont trois biographies d'hommes politiques: *Albert Sévigny et les Conservateurs fédéraux, 1902–1918* (Les Presses de l'Université Laval, 1983), *Paul-Émile Lamarche, Le pays avant le parti, 1904–1918* (Les Presses de l'Université Laval, 1984) et *Wilfrid Laurier, Quand la politique devient passion* (Les Presses de l'Université Laval, 1986), qui lui a mérité le prix Maxime-Raymond offert par la Fondation Lionel-Groulx à la meilleure biographie sur un personnage de l'Amérique française publiée entre les années 1986 et 1990.

Il prépare actuellement deux livres: la biographie d'Armand Lavergne (1880–1935), un autre personnage politique ayant oeuvré sur les scènes canadienne et québécoise, et, en collaboration, une histoire des grands débats parlementaires à l'Assemblée nationale du Québec de 1792 à 1992. Il va sans dire que c'est son expérience à titre de biographe d'hommes politiques qui l'a conduit à réfléchir sur la biographie telle que pratiquée chez les historiens canadiens-français, l'objet de son article dans ce volume. Il a contribué, par ailleurs, à plusieurs organismes et à plusieurs associations d'historiens dont l'Institut d'histoire de l'Amérique française dont il fut secrétaire et vice-président. Il est actuellement membre du comité de rédaction de la *Revue d'histoire de l'Amérique française*. En 1989, il fut le président du Comité organisateur du Congrès de la Société historique du Canada tenu à l'Universié Laval de Québec.

Notes

1 Réal Bélanger, *Wilfrid Laurier: Quand la politique devient passion* (Québec et Montréal: Les Presses de l'Université Laval et Les Entreprises Radio-Canada, 1986). Les informations qui suivent sur la carrière politique de Laurier proviennent de cette biographie.

2 Oscar Douglas Skelton, *Life and Letters of Sir Wilfrid Laurier* (Toronto: Oxford University Press, 1921); John W. Dafoe, *Laurier* (Toronto: Allen, 1922); Joseph Schull, *Laurier* (Montréal: HMH, 1968); H. Blair Neatby, *Laurier and a Liberal Quebec* (Toronto: McClelland and Stewart, 1973); Richard Clippingdale, *Laurier: His Life and World* (Toronto: McGraw-Hill Ryerson, 1979).

3 Robert Rumilly, dans *Sir Wilfrid Laurier, Canadien* (s.l.: Ernest Flammarion, 1931), et Raymond Tanghe, dans *Laurier Artisan de l'unité canadienne, 1841–1919* (Tours:

Mame, 1960) ont été les seuls, pratiquement, à écrire sur Laurier. Mais leur travail n'est vraiment pas très étoffé et solide.

4 Pensons à Andrée Désilets, qui a écrit la biographie définitive d'Hector-Louis Langevin: *Hector-Louis Langevin (1826–1906)* (Québec: Les Presses de l'Université Laval, 1969).

5 Fernand Ouellet, "La modernisation de l'historiographie et l'émergence de l'histoire sociale," *Recherches Sociographiques* 26, nos 1-2 (1985): 11–83.

6 Ibid., 13, 47 et 16.

7 Voir à ce sujet Michael D. Behiels, "Recent Quebec Historiography: Reinterpreting French Canada's Past," *American Review of Canadian Studies* 13, no 2 (1983): 95–6; et Paul-André Linteau, "La nouvelle histoire du Québec vue de l'intérieur," *Liberté 147* 25, no 3 (juin 1983): 34–47.

8 Des journalistes et des politicologues ont comblé en partie le vide créé par les historiens de l'histoire politique. Pensons, entre autres, aux travaux de Dale C. Thomson, de Denis Monière, de Pierre Godin, de Michel Vastel, de Bernard Saint-Aubin. On peut enfin ajouter des publications d'autobiographies et de mémoires qui ont aussi, à leur façon, pris la relève.

9 La seule exception véritable fut le congrès de l'IHAF tenu à Saint-Jean, Québec, en octobre 1990, dont le thème fut "Pouvoirs et politique en Amérique française." Mais ce n'est vraiment pas suffisant pour parler d'une popularité nouvelle pour l'histoire politique. Comme ne sont pas suffisants non plus, à cet égard, les colloques sur les leaders politiques organisés à l'université du Québec à Montréal.

10 En ce qui concerne la France, il faut lire le trop bref article de Jacques Le Goff, "Comment écrire une biographie historique aujourd'hui," *Le Débat*, no 54 (mars-avril 1989), pp. 48–53.

11 De bons résumés de ces arguments se retrouvent dans: Carl Berger, *The Writing of Canadian History* (Toronto: Oxford University Press, 1976), p. 222 ss; Philippe Levillain, "Les protagonistes: de la biographie," dans René Rémond, dir., *Pour une histoire politique* (Paris: Seuil, 1988), pp. 121–59; Giovanni Levi, "Les usages de la biographie," *Annales ESC*, no 6 (novembre-décembre 1989), pp. 1325–36; Pierre Bourdieu, "L'illusion biographique," *Acte de la recherche en sciences sociales*, no 62-3 (juin 1986), 69-72.

12 Pierre Goubert, *Mazarin* (Paris: Fayard, 1990).

13 Outre celle de Réal Bélanger sur *Laurier* déjà citée en note l, nous pouvons mentionner celles de Nive Voisine, *Louis-François Laflèche* (Saint-Hyacinthe: Edisem, 1980); de Brian Young, *George-Etienne Cartier: Bourgeois montréalais* (Montréal: Boréal, 1982); et de Hélène Pelletier-Baillargeon, *Marie Gérin-Lajoie* (Montréal: Boréal, 1985).

14 Voir à ce sujet deux excellents articles de Guy Laperrière, "Biographies et mémoires: le Québec du XXe siècle," *Revue d'histoire ecclésiastique* 86, no 1 (janvier-mars 1990): 41–77 et no 2 (avril-juin 1990), 343-58; voir aussi Jean-Claude Robert, "La recherche en histoire du Canada," *Revue internationale d'études canadiennes* 1-2 (printemps-automne 1990): 24.

15 Serge Gagnon, *Le Québec et ses historiens de 1840 à 1920* (Québec: Les Presses de l'Université Laval, 1978).

16 Levi, "Les usages de la biographie," 1329–32.

17 Levillain, "Les protagonistes: de la biographie," 146 et 159.

18 Sur ces difficultés que rencontre l'historien-biographe, voir P.B. Waite, *Reefs Unsuspected: Historians and Biography in Canada, Australia and Elsewhere* (Sydney: Macquarie University, 1983); et Daniel Madelénat, *La biographie* (Paris: Presses universitaires de France, 1984).

19 Levi, "Les usages de la biographie," 1326.

20 Comme il faut apprécier aussi, à cet égard, l'effort fait au Canada anglais. Voir Reg Whitaker, "Writing about Politics," dans John Schultz, ed., *Writing about Canada: A Handbook for Modern Canadian History* (Scarborough: Prentice-Hall Canada Inc., 1990), pp. 6–8. Il faut regretter toutefois que le professeur Whitaker, à l'instar de plusieurs de ses collègues canadiens-anglais, ignore presque complètement la production des historiens canadiens-français.

21 Voir, à ce sujet, le compte rendu de Carman Miller, "La couronne de Laurier," *Recherches sociographiques* 30, no 1 (janvier–avril 1989): 91-100.

22 Madelénat, *La biographie*, 9.

Chapter 17

D'Alton McCarthy, Jr.: A Protestant Irishman Abroad

J.R. Miller

"There is properly no history; only biography,"[1] Ralph Waldo Emerson (1803–82) once claimed. His contemporary, Thomas Carlyle (1795–1881), contended that "history is the essence of innumerable Biographies."[2] Today such views of the collective past are as unfashionable as Carlyle's even more famous aphorism, "No great man lives in vain. The History of the world is but the Biography of great men."[3] Nevertheless, Carlyle's and Emerson's biographical orientation remains an acceptable approach to history.

Biography has at least three points in its favour. First, along with the narrative, it remains the most accessible path into the study of the past. Mercifully free of graphs and tables, often dispensing with maps that too often are indecipherable, biography focuses on a large and disorienting panorama. Its chronological narrative line makes it simpler to follow than statistically burdened analyses that purport to sketch an age. To appreciate biography's accessibility to historical understanding, consider J.M.S. Careless's two-volume life of George Brown, *Brown of the Globe*, still the most easily understood and comprehensive introduction to such subjects as the evolution of Canadian Presbyterianism, the development of Canadian liberalism, the emergence of Toronto's urban ambitions, and Ontario's role in the creation of Confederation.[4] More readable than works belonging to other historical genres, biographies continue to attract readers, especially among the "educated general public."

Second, biographies sometimes serve as the building blocks of a more general history. For a long time what little we knew of organized labour and working-class movements in Canadian history came in the form of institutional studies of labour bodies or biographical sketches of labour notables. Prior to the advent of methodologies that claimed to give voice to those who were historically inarticulate, biographies of leaders of minority causes served as mouthpieces for the vast silent numbers who supported them. Taken to its logical conclusion, this biography-as-building-block method of doing history results in prosopography, or collective biography. And few would argue that Sir Lewis Namier and his followers have not greatly enriched our understanding of both politics and respectable society in eighteenth-century Britain by their prosopographical examination of Parliament. Conversely, a critical mass of individual biographies could, at least in theory, permit a student to draw general analytical conclusions about mass movements, particular epochs, or historical phenomena. In this sense, at least, Carlyle was right in contending that "history is the essence of innumerable Biographies."

Third, and finally, biography is invaluable to historians because studies of lives and careers permit researchers to test the validity of generalizations arrived at by other forms of investigation. So, for example, consideration of the lives of Gabriel Dumont or Pierre Vallières might enable a student of anarchism to test general theories of that ideology's development, its influence upon historical actors, and its historical significance, the specific, as it were, testing the general. For example, when Sarah Carter examined agriculture on some Prairie reserves in the 1880s and 1890s, she discovered that George Stanley's claim that Canadian agricultural policy for Indians failed because Plains Indian culture was inimical to horticulture was without foundation – at least on the basis of the parts of Treaty 4 that she examined so carefully.[5] Likewise, an examination of the life and career of D'Alton McCarthy might also lead to qualifications or revisions of established interpretations of some events in Canada's post-Confederation political life.

D'Alton McCarthy, Jr., was born in Ireland in 1836, the son of a successful lawyer who eleven years later emigrated to North America.[6] The family settled near Barrie, Canada West, where the younger D'Alton completed his schooling and the senior McCarthy attempted to establish himself as a gentleman farmer before continuing his legal career. The older McCarthy quickly fell into a pattern of Toryism, practising law with D'Arcy Boulton of the family of Compact fame and emerging as a major figure in the Loyal Orange Association of the western part of the province in 1867.

D'Alton, Jr., emulated his father's penchant for law and his pretensions to gentry status, but he substituted something else for the elder McCarthy's Orangeism. The younger McCarthy became a practising lawyer late in the

1850s, was elected a bencher of the Law Society of Upper Canada in 1871, and was named Queen's Counsel in the following year. He soon emerged as a prominent urban lawyer, and in 1877 he established a Toronto firm, McCarthy, Hoskin, and Creelman, which was expanded in 1882 when McCarthy joined with the Liberal B.B. Osler to form the legal powerhouse of McCarthy, Osler, Hoskin, and Creelman. In 1879 he bought a house on Toronto's Beverley Street. At the same time, he retained his post as solicitor for Simcoe County, and he never relinquished his ties to the squirearchical life in the Lake Simcoe region, where he rode to hounds on a country estate, "the ideal residence of a county magnate of the old school."[7]

After unsuccessful attempts to gain Simcoe North's Commons seat in two general elections and a by-election between 1872 and 1874, McCarthy finally succeeded in joining Macdonald's Conservatives with a by-election victory in a safe seat, Cardwell, in 1876. The Conservative prime minister saw fit to encourage and facilitate McCarthy's entry into politics for two reasons: the two men were connected by marriage – McCarthy's second wife was the widow of the Old Chieftain's brother-in-law; and, more important, by the early 1870s Macdonald judged McCarthy to be a promising politician. For at least the first decade of his Commons career, McCarthy repaid Macdonald's support, almost without question.

Too little appreciated is the degree to which McCarthy, down to the early 1890s, was an intensely partisan and energetic Conservative. In 1873, following his first unsuccessful by-election attempt, he assumed the presidency of the Simcoe Conservative riding association, and he led the local branch of his party in the provincial general election of 1875. After his entry into the Commons in 1876, he became one of the most ferocious Conservative critics of the Mackenzie government. Outside Parliament, as the Old Chieftain began to warm up for the coming general election battle, McCarthy was Macdonald's principal legal agent for fighting the Grits in controverted election cases. McCarthy's career reached a new plateau in 1878, when he was finally returned for his home constituency, Simcoe North, in the Conservative sweep of that year.

Throughout most of the 1880s, McCarthy continued to be a partisan and loyal Conservative flag-bearer. In the courts he was Macdonald's choice to represent the federal government's argument in a trio of constitutional cases that unsuccessfully tested the swelling pretensions of Ontario and its premier, Oliver Mowat. On a more practical level McCarthy made himself useful to Macdonald as one of the leaders in the movement to prop up weakening Conservative support in Ontario, where McCarthy helped to form the Liberal-Conservative Union of Ontario, one of the first post-Confederation political organizations. He also helped Macdonald find a new voice among Toronto's newspapers. As the time for calling an election in 1887 approached, Macdonald found it necessary to disown the *Toronto Daily Mail* for its intensely anti-Quebec editorial line, formulated during the Northwest Rebellion of 1885. McCarthy was one of the loyal Conservatives who moved to fill the vacuum by founding the *Daily Standard*, a short-lived vehicle of Conservative propaganda, soon succeeded by the *Empire*, also founded with McCarthy's money and influence. Twice in 1884, in recognition of McCarthy's talents and partisan labours, Macdonald offered McCarthy the justice portfolio. However, McCarthy declined, arguing that substantial debts – maintaining his country estate and the lifestyle of a gentleman proved costly – made it necessary for him to maintain his large and prestigious legal practice.

As it turned out, had he accepted, McCarthy would have been an embarrassment to his leader. Between 1887 and 1892, McCarthy's disquiet about the political orientation of Quebec, articulated tentatively in the early 1880s and more vehemently after the Riel affair, deepened into alarm and alarmist proposals whose roots were both ideological and partisan. He recognized that Quebec's strong attachment to provincial rights was anathema to his own belief in a highly centralized federal structure. Also, Quebec's strong attachment to the Montreal-based Canadian Pacific Railway was both an obstacle to the railway schemes of Barrie and district and a source of Quebec Conservatives' opposition to federal government regulation of railways by means of a board of railway commissioners. To McCarthy, the thoughtful non-partisan, Quebec was a barrier to "progressive legislation," an enemy of Ontario's economic interests, and a foe of healthy federalism.[8]

There was also, however, a strongly partisan streak to McCarthy's growing disenchantment with Quebec after 1885. In forming the Liberal-Conservative Union and establishing the *Empire*, McCarthy was motivated largely by his recognition that Ontario support for the Conservatives was eroding at the same time that Quebec was steadily distancing itself from the party. After the emergence of Honoré Mercier in 1886–87 and Wilfrid Laurier's assumption of the federal Liberal leadership in 1887, McCarthy feared that Quebec's attachment to the Liberals would increase. At the same time, rural Ontario's growing unrest over financial strain in the farm sector was pushing Ontario yeomen towards the Liberals, who in 1888 adopted a policy of unrestricted reciprocity that was designed to capitalize on rural malaise. That, as McCarthy coldly explained to Macdonald early in 1889, was a major reason for his support of federal disallowance of Quebec's Jesuits' Estates Act. Vetoing the measure that was highly popular in Catholic Quebec and intensely disliked in Protestant Ontario would solidify Protestant support for Macdonald and the Conservatives in Ontario.[9] For neither the first nor last time, Macdonald rejected this divisive advice, and during his remaining two years of life he attempted in vain to knit the religious and language communities back together.

Equally troublesome, in view of the prime minister's desire to conciliate Quebec, was McCarthy's prominence in the imperialist movement that emerged in Canada in the latter half of the 1880s. Although he served as the first president of the Canadian branch of the Imperial Federation League from 1885 to 1891, McCarthy was not by any means a major thinker or advocate among Canadian imperialists. He frequently represented Canadian imperialists at meetings in London, often, one suspects, because business before the Judicial Committee was taking him there in any event. Nor did McCarthy make explicit a linkage between his imperialist views and his hostility to the French language outside Quebec. In fact, at the urging of Principal Grant of Queen's University, McCarthy resigned the presidency of the league in 1891 because imperialists feared that his prominence in the Equal Rights Association would make the league's relations with French Canada more difficult than they needed to be.[10] Still, McCarthy's prominence among Canadian imperialists, like Tupper's in Britain, was an occasion for criticism by French Canadian Conservatives. For his part, McCarthy's unhappiness with Quebec was increased by the animosity that French Canadian Conservative leaders showed towards the imperial cause.[11]

During the last decade of his career, McCarthy paid less attention to imperialism than to his anxiety over rural Ontario and his antipathy to the anti-national features of Quebec. Frightened by the narrowness of the Conservatives' victory in the general election of 1891, McCarthy worked energetically to convince the party to adopt tariff reform. His failure to persuade either Sir John Abbott or Sir John Thompson induced frustration in McCarthy and boldness in some of his enemies. When the editor of the *Empire* attacked him on tariff policy, he waited for Thompson to defend him. When the leader, with whom McCarthy had never been close, failed to do so, McCarthy declared his independence from the Conservative Party. His championing of tariff reform for the benefit of agriculture was the basis for cooperation between his new political movement, the Equal Rights (or McCarthyite) League, and the Patrons of Industry. It also provided a comfortable pretext for his growing sympathy and support for Laurier's government after 1896. The Fielding tariff of 1897, with its rate reductions and imperial preference, represented the sort of change McCarthy had been urging on his own party for years.

The other major preoccupation of D'Alton McCarthy's career in the 1890s was Quebec and French Canadian nationalism. Partly for reasons noted earlier and partly because McCarthy had been influenced by British and continental thinkers who linked uniformity of language and national unity, he had come to view cultural diversity and bilingualism outside Quebec as "the great danger to the confederacy."[12] In Max Muller and E.A. Freeman, McCarthy found analyses and arguments to answer his own questions about the sources and potential of growing disunity between French and English in Canada. The country could only be united and powerful if it were homogeneous, and to McCarthy that meant that outside Quebec there should not be any official recognition of the French language. That – not sectarian motives – was why he had played a prominent role in protecting the province of Manitoba's dismantling of official bilingualism and the Roman Catholic schools that were a bulwark of the Franco-Manitoban community in 1890 legislation. The issue was not creed; it was culture. And since the settlement of the question in 1897 protected a number of minority language groups without recognizing French particularly, McCarthy could, once again, lend at least grudging support to Laurier's young government.

McCarthy's career came to a swift and unforeseen end in the spring of 1898, on the eve of a significant event. Apparently he and Laurier had only recently agreed to terms by which McCarthy was to enter the Liberal cabinet as minister of justice. However, a carriage accident in Toronto led to his premature death and terminated one of the most curious and misunderstood political careers in post-Confederation Canadian political history.

How can the life of a single lawyer and politician serve the history of nineteenth-century Canada? What generalizations can it test? What are the results of such tests? McCarthy's career in fact throws light on a number of features of Canadian public life. His biography serves as a miniature case study of several issues: immigration and Orangeism; the character of Canadian imperialism; the reasons for the emergence of the Manitoba Schools Question; and the evolution of political liberalism in the hands of Laurier.

McCarthy does not fit the stereotype of the Irish immigrant who becomes a Tory in Canada. Although he came from impeccable Irish Protestant roots, and although his father was a prominent Orange leader in Ontario, D'Alton, Jr., showed little interest in the Loyal Orange Association and he never joined the order. In fact, his antipathy to what it stood for manifested itself in his refusal to allow the brethren into his house when they came in full regalia to mourn his deceased father.[13] Such behaviour, when coupled with his giving shelter and support to a Roman Catholic stepdaughter, was frequently thrown up to McCarthy in the latter years of his career, when his political independence and championing of the Manitoba government over the schools issue brought him into direct and bitter conflict with Orange politicians such as the Conservative minister Clarke Wallace.[14] Nor had McCarthy much sympathy for virulently anti-Catholic organizations such as the Protestant Protective Association, which he regularly deprecated in 1893 and 1894, even though he tried to exploit its membership politically at election time.[15] The reason for McCarthy's religious tolerance and for his refusal to associate himself with groups that emphasized their Protestantism along with their loyalty was his conviction that North America was no place for the sectarian quarrels of Ireland. It was, he told an Orange audience in 1889, a belief he had "formed early in life" that "in this new Canada of ours, it was unnecessary to import the feuds and strifes of the Old World."[16] A close examination of McCarthy's career and convictions casts doubt on the notion that Orangeism was easily transmitted to British North America along with Irish Protestant immigrants.

Scrutiny of McCarthy's religious views and actions also gives cause to modify the former conventional view of the origins of the Manitoba Schools Question. According to the likes of John W. Dafoe, O.D. Skelton, and Lovell Clark, it was the bigotry of D'Alton McCarthy, expressed most forcibly at Portage la Prairie in August 1889, that accounted for the outbreak of an assault on Catholic schools in a hitherto-peaceful Manitoba.[17] In fact, as already noted, McCarthy was no religious bigot, whatever he might have been on the language question. He rarely made allusion to Catholicism as a problem; instead, he concentrated upon what he described as "this demon of dualism," or bilingualism, outside Quebec.[18] His address to an Orange audience in 1889 at Stayner was in fact an attempt to direct the brethren's anger against the Liberal Party, and his speech at Portage the next month – the spark that supposedly set the plains afire – made almost no allusion to religion. And yet McCarthy and his so-called campaign are supposed to have initiated an assault on denominational education in Manitoba! The truth is that others, such as Joseph Martin, James Smart, and Thomas Greenway, had begun to push for abolition of

THE WOMEN FOLKS ALARMED!

THAT DREADFUL BOY McCARTHY HAS BROUGHT A LIVE ISSUE INTO THE HOUSE!!

"The Women Folks Alarmed" by J.W. Bengough in Grip, *1 February 1890, on the occasion of D'Alton McCarthy's motion in the House of Commons to abolish official French in the Northwest Territories. The frightened "women" in this sexist (1992) cartoon include Sir Hector Langevin,* derrière le rideau; *a slim Wilfrid Laurier, nearest snake; John Thompson, escaping through window; Sir John A. on chair; Sir Richard Cartwright, pigeon-toed, between Laurier and Macdonald; and Edward Blake, leaving on all fours. (Courtesy University of Saskatchewan Archives, Saskatoon, #869.)*

Catholic education in Manitoba long before McCarthy showed up.[19] Research during the last two decades has led to the conclusion that at the heart of the Manitoba educational dispute lay a desire to end linguistic dualism and discourage the development of cultural diversity. And this was to be accomplished through the establishment of a culturally uniform system of education. Had historians paid serious attention to McCarthy's career, they might have noted his expostulation on the Manitoba schools issue, which both encapsulated his views on religion and language and captured the essence of the Manitoba question: "Let them remain Catholic but not French. That is the object ... to make the people homogeneous."[20]

If McCarthy's biography can help to correct the conventional view of Manitoba schools, how can it enhance historians' understanding of the Canadian version of imperialism? Although he was a unilingualist, McCarthy did not use arguments based on notions of a supposedly superior "Anglo-Saxon race" to buttress his support for closer imperial cooperation. Rather, his case for imperialism was based on considerations of strategic advantage and commercial opportunity. Closer cooperation with the mother country was necessary in the 1880s because of the American menace. "Canadian independence ... could not last forty-eight hours with an aggressive neighbour to the south," he argued. Besides, there was such a community of interest between Britain and Canada that "in defending England Canadians would be defending themselves." Surely no Canadian would be "so mean-spirited" as to "ask England to spend money and shed blood and not be ready to make a return in kind."[21] Canada "was growing out of childhood and it was time it should share the burden of manhood."[22]

Closely allied to defence strategy was that of trade and commerce. The United States was Canada's commercial rival, whereas Britain was its potential partner. Since Canadian and American agricultural products were essentially similar in type, the U.S. and Canada could hardly be compatible trading partners. McCarthy recognized that the "great market for both countries, as for the whole of this continent, is the British market."[23] Besides, reducing duties on British products so as to create an imperial preference and stimulate trade with Britain would particularly help "our overburdened farmers"[24] and perhaps keep them from defecting to the Liberals and commercial continentalism. But certainly neither strategic advantage nor commercial opportunity was to be purchased at the cost of diminishing Canada's self-governing status. He and his imperialist colleagues had no intention of agreeing "to surrender one jot or tittle of the self-government entrusted to her by the mother country."[25] On the contrary, imperialism was "the best plan for attaining the complete national development of Canada."[26] McCarthy's imperialist career strongly supports Carl Berger's conclusion that Canadian "imperialism was one form of Canadian nationalism."[27]

Finally, McCarthy's life and career draw students of the Victorian transformation of Canadian liberalism to a fuller appreciation of Laurier's skill in fashioning an effective national party out of the elements that he inherited from Mackenzie and Blake. Thanks to Blair Neatby, Laurier's talent and patience in reworking the Parti Rouge fragments of the 1870s into the moderately Liberal Quebec phalanx of 1896 and beyond is now well understood. Less appreciated is the Liberal leader's triumph in establishing himself and his Quebec colleagues with Ontario voters in the 1890s. He did receive help from such Liberal worthies as Sir Oliver Mowat and John Charlton, two Presbyterian stalwarts whose support for Laurier and his policies convinced others that the Liberal Party under his leadership would not sell out Canada to the Pope. D'Alton McCarthy's move away from the party of Sir John and towards the party of Sir Wilfrid was a barometer of Laurier's increasing support in Protestant Ontario in the 1890s. McCarthy's strong advocacy of tariff reform to help the hard-pressed farmers, especially after the election of 1891 delivered such a fright, made it easy for the member for North Simcoe to applaud the Fielding tariff in 1897 and to agree to join the Liberal cabinet in 1898. Moreover, Laurier's cunning resolution of the Manitoba Schools Question – a denouement that gave the Manitoba minority far less than Tory coercion would have – made it possible for someone opposed to "this demon of dualism" to acquiesce. If Laurier by 1897 had become sound enough on issues such as imperialism, trade, and denominational education to satisfy D'Alton McCarthy, surely the Liberal Party under his direction was a safe vehicle for the ambitions and prejudices of Ontarians. And if that was so, had Laurier not worked a transformation in Ontario that was as astonishing as the metamorphosis he had brought about in Quebec?

"Read no history, nothing but biography, for that is life without theory,"[28] advised Benjamin Disraeli (1804–81), a contemporary of Emerson's and Carlyle's. Biography is, admittedly, only one of many historical forms, but it is a useful one. As argued here, it is a tool to modify or to corroborate the received wisdom arrived at by other historical methods. Perhaps what Disraeli should have said is that biography is history that goes beyond mere theory and *a priori* assumptions or conclusions. But, as Disraeli well knew, biography for many people is better than history because it is a more congenial means of access to the complexity of the past. Like the narrative, that other neglected and under-appreciated historical form, biography focuses the gaze and simplifies the observed. If it is not exactly "life without theory," then certainly it is history with the theory suppressed in the interests of intelligibility and comprehension. However precisely one phrases it, biography has been, and promises to remain, a useful and enjoyable form of history.

J.R. (Jim) Miller received his doctorate in history from the University of Toronto for a thesis on a controversy between French- and English-speaking Canadians in the nineteenth century. Part of the work for his dissertation involved the Ontario Conservative D'Alton McCarthy, Jr., whose short, but influential, career in Canadian politics (1876–98) had been misunderstood because historians' antipathy to his anti-French and pro-Empire views had clouded their view of him. An examination of D'Alton McCarthy was a prominent part of publications stemming from Miller's Ph.D. dissertation. These included *Equal Rights: The Jesuits' Estates Act Controversy* (McGill-Queen's University Press, 1979); "'As a politician he is a great enigma': The Social and Political Ideas of D'Alton McCarthy," *Canadian Historical Review* 58, no. 4 (December 1977); and "Anti-Catholic Thought in Victorian Canada," *Canadian Historical Review* 66, no. 4 (December 1985). Since 1970 Miller has been a member of the faculty of the University of Saskatchewan, where he holds the rank of professor of history. In recent years, his research has turned towards the history of native/non-native relations. He wrote *Skyscrapers Hide the Heavens: A History of Indian-White Relations in Canada* (University of Toronto Press, 1989; rev. ed. 1991) and edited *Sweet Promises: A Reader on Indian-White Relations in Canada* (University of Toronto Press, 1991). He is co-editor of the *Canadian Historical Review*. His current projects are a comprehensive history of residential schools for Indian and Inuit children in Canada and a biography of Big Bear for ECW Press.

Notes

1 Ralph Waldo Emerson, *Essays and Lectures* (New York: Library of America, 1983), Essays, 1st Series, Essay 1, "History," 240.

2 Thomas Carlyle, *Critical and Miscellaneous Essays*, Centenary Edition of the Works of Thomas Carlyle, 30 vols. (London: Chapman and Hall, 1905), vol. 27, *On History* (1830), 86.

3 Thomas Carlyle, *On Heroes, Hero-Worship, And the Heroic in History*, Atheneum Press Series, edited by Archibald MacMechan (1841; Boston: Ginn & Company 1901), "Lecture I: The Hero as Divinity," 33.

4 J.M.S. Careless, *Brown of the Globe*, vol. 1, *The Voice of Upper Canada*, and vol. 2, *Statesman of Confederation* (Toronto: Macmillan, 1959, 1963).

5 Sarah Carter, *Lost Harvests: Prairie Indian Reserve Farmers and Government Policy* (Kingston and Montreal: McGill-Queen's University Press, 1990); G.F.G. Stanley, *The Birth of Western Canada: A History of the Riel Rebellions*, 2nd ed. (1936; Toronto: University of Toronto Press, 1960), 218, 238–39.

6 Unless otherwise noted, information on McCarthy's life, ideas, and political career is derived from the following: L.L. Kulisek, "D'Alton McCarthy," *Dictionary of Canadian Biography*, vol. 12, *1891–1900*, edited by Francess G. Halpenny (Toronto: University of Toronto Press, 1990), 578–88; J.R. Miller, "'As a politician he is a great enigma': The Social and Political Ideas of D'Alton McCarthy," *Canadian Historical Review* (CHR) 58, no. 4 (December 1977): 399–422; J.R. Miller, "D'Alton McCarthy, Equal Rights, and the Origins of the Manitoba School Question," *CHR*, 54, no. 4 (December 1973): 369–92; and Curtis Cole, "McCarthy, Osler, Hoskin, and Creelman, 1882–1902: Establishing a Reputation, Building a Practice," in Carol Wilton, ed., *Beyond the Law: Lawyers and Business in Canada, 1830 to 1930* (Toronto: Osgoode Society, 1990), 149–66. I am indebted to Ted Regehr for bringing the Cole article to my attention.

7 'Amicus,' "The Late D'Alton McCarthy, Q.C., M.P., An Appreciation," *Canadian Magazine* 21 (1903): 31.

8 *Toronto Daily Mail*, 30 August 1886. See also Miller, "'Great Enigma,'" 407–10.

9 National Archives of Canada (NA), MG 26 A, Sir John Macdonald Papers, 228, 98613-19, McCarthy to Macdonald, 17 April 1889. These partisan calculations had been at the heart of McCarthy's attitude towards Quebec for some time. See also Macdonald Papers, 228, 98329-63, McCarthy to Macdonald, 16 October 1886.

10 On McCarthy's equivocal imperialism, see Miller, "'Great Enigma,'" 416–18.

11 NA, Macdonald Papers, 228, 98542-6, McCarthy to Macdonald, 20 August 1888.

12 Quoted in F. Landon, "D'Alton McCarthy and the Politics of the Later 'Eighties,'" Canadian Historical Association, Annual Report 1932, 46.

13 *Globe* (Toronto), 7 May 1896.

14 Canada, House of Commons, *Debates*, 1896, 4365-66; *Montreal Daily Witness*, 19 May 1896.

15 Kulisek, "McCarthy," 584; and E.J. Noble, "D'Alton McCarthy and the Election of 1896" (M.A. diss., University of Guelph, 1969), 52.

16 *Toronto Daily Mail*, 13 July 1889.

17 See the historiographical review of the question in Miller, "Origins," 369–73.

18 Canada, House of Commons, *Debates*, 1896, 3755.

19 T.S. Mitchell, "Forging a New Protestant Ontario on the Agricultural Frontier: Public Schools in Brandon and the Origins of the Manitoba School Question 1881–1890," *Prairie Forum* 11, no. 1 (Spring 1986): 33–49, esp. 46; and Joseph A. Hilts, "The Political Career of Thomas Greenway" (Ph.D. diss., University of Manitoba, 1974), chap. 4, esp. 176, 209, 216–21.

20 Canada, *Sessional Papers*, no. 20, 1895, 74.

21 *Toronto Daily Mail*, 21 December 1888.

22 *Globe* (Toronto), 12 January 1889.

23 Canada, House of Commons, *Debates*, 1888, 1070.

24 Ibid., 1887, 96.

25 *Toronto Daily Mail*, 26 March 1888.

26 Imperial Federation League in Canada, *Report of the First Meetings of the League in Canada held in Montreal*, 9 May 1885 (Montreal: Wm. Drysdale [1885]), 23.

27 Carl Berger, *The Sense of Power: Studies in the Ideas of Canadian Imperialism 1867-1914* (Toronto: University of Toronto Press, 1970), 259.

28 Benjamin Disraeli, *Contarini Fleming: A Psychological Romance*, new ed. (London: Longmans, Green, 1945; orig. pub. 1832), 133.

Part 7

History Enriched by Biography

Chapter 18

Lord Lansdowne in Canada, 1883-1888

John L. Gordon, Jr.

The Fifth Marquess of Lansdowne was governor general of Canada from October 1883 to May 1888, when he was in his late thirties and early forties. This was the first of several major administrative positions Lansdowne was to hold in the Empire and at home before his retirement from public life in 1917. This paper, a synthesis of a much larger work, reveals something of the nature of the office of Canadian governor general in the late Victorian period and assesses Lansdowne's tenure in that office.

Lansdowne was born Henry Charles Keith Petty-Fitzmaurice on 14 January 1845.[1] He had an impressive lineage that included Anglo-Irish, Scottish, and French ancestors, including Lord Shelburne, who was politically, socially, and culturally prominent during the reign of George III. As a leading Whig, he held various of the great offices of state during the 1760s and 1780s and was created First Marquess of Lansdowne.

The Fifth Marquess of Lansdowne owed much to his paternal Anglo-Irish heritage. It cast him as part of the aristocratic establishment that brought educational, social, economic, and political advantages. It bequeathed him a tradition of Whig political activity and statesmanship. It brought him important properties – Lansdowne House in London, Bowood in Wiltshire, and Irish lands in County Kerry and Queen's County. He was especially fond of Ireland, concerned with its problems, and dedicated in particular to the estate of Dereen in County Kerry, which was his favourite retreat. Ironically, Ireland was to be a source of great distress for Lansdowne. With estates totalling more than 121,000 acres, he was to be the target of verbal and press attacks by Irish nationalists and the victim of the Irish National Land League's withholding of rents. In 1886–87 his estates at

Luggacurran in Queen's (now Laois) County became the target of the league's new "Plan of Campaign." William O'Brien, one of the leaders of the campaign against Lansdowne's estates, brought the campaign to Canada in 1887 in hopes of discrediting Lansdowne as an oppressor of the Irish people. In time, under the 1888 and 1903 land purchase acts, the Lansdowne estates in Ireland were sold to tenants.

Lansdowne's mother, Emily, Fourth Marchioness of Lansdowne, was a Scottish heiress and the daughter of a Frenchman, Comte de Flahault, an aide-de-camp of Napoleon I and widely acknowledged to be the illegitimate son of Prince Talleyrand. This Franco-Scottish maternal background brought Lansdowne even more social eminence, close personal ties in France, and more properties.

Lansdowne's education was typical of that of young aristocrats in nineteenth-century Britain. His earliest formal education was at home, then at various boarding schools culminating in Eton, followed by Balliol College, Oxford, 1864–67, where his master was the noted Greek scholar Dr. Benjamin Jowett, who took a special interest in intelligent undergraduates with social position and a political future. He thought young Lansdowne had ability and promise, and invited him to spend the summers of 1865 and 1867 with him at his private retreat. During his Oxford years, Lansdowne devoted himself in part to his studies but did not neglect the revelry of an undergraduate's life. Disappointing both Jowett and himself, Lansdowne narrowly missed his First and had to be content with a Second. According to Jowett, the failure was due, not to a want of ability, but to a lack of scholarly dedication and the fact that his father died in 1866, thrusting upon him the family title and responsibilities.

Lansdowne began his public career in 1868 with a junior position in W.E. Gladstone's first Liberal government. He was a rising figure in Liberal circles until 1880, when he resigned because of the government's Irish policies generally and the bill to compensate evicted tenants specifically. For several years Lansdowne was politically more or less independent. By ancestry and temperament he was a Whig; he was still on closest terms with the Liberal lords Granville and Hartington; and he continued to support the general policies of the Liberal governments of the 1880s. However, he and Gladstone were not congenial, and he openly criticized Gladstone's Irish policy. After Gladstone's adoption of Home Rule in 1886, Lansdowne was among those who left the Liberal Party permanently, and subsequently as a Liberal Unionist he gravitated towards the Conservative Party. He was later to serve the Conservatives as viceroy of India (1888–

94), secretary for war (1895–1900), foreign secretary (1900–1905), and party leader in the House of Lords (1903–16).

Lansdowne was a small, trim, spare man, with classic features and a dark complexion. He presented a reserved image to casual acquaintances and the public in general. He was quiet and dignified, never assertive or demonstrative. He was the epitome of moderation when it came to eating, drinking, and other personal habits. He shunned notoriety. Although he held a series of high government offices, he was little known to the public in Britain; this was due in part to a lack of charisma and in part to an avoidance of the popular press. He was sometimes criticized for his aloofness and lack of appreciation for the common man. It was fortunate for Lansdowne that he held a seat in the House of Lords, for his temperament was hardly suited to the tumult of election campaigning. Lansdowne's reserve was not a significant liability in Canada, despite the egalitarian tendencies of British North American society. The governor general, as representative of the sovereign, was expected to act with dignity and propriety, and not to make himself too accessible or familiar to the public.

Lansdowne's immediate predecessor as governor general of Canada was the Marquess of Lorne, a Scottish Campbell, heir to the dukedom of Argyll and husband of Princess Louise, fourth daughter of Queen Victoria.[2] As Lorne's term drew to a close in 1883, the Gladstone government began the search for a successor. At that time, the imperial government was not obliged to consult dominion officials in choosing a new governor, and there is no evidence that the wishes of the Canadian government were sought during the crucial phases of decision making in 1883. The selection of Lord Lansdowne was apparently made quietly by Lord Derby, the secretary of state for the colonies, in consultation with Gladstone. The decision to appoint Lansdowne was reached in early May. On 8 May, Derby wrote Queen Victoria that "no one can be found fitter for the post than Lord Lansdowne. He has much judgment and ability; is an excellent public speaker; respected by all parties in England, moderate in his opinion; his manners are unusually prepossessing; his high rank is an additional recommendation."[3] Perhaps Gladstone was being magnanimous in appointing Lansdowne, who only three years previously had resigned from his government. Or perhaps he hoped the appointment would help in plastering over and checking the growing unrest within his party over Ireland. More probably, the appointment was a form of political exile – some contemporaries viewed it as such, including the editors of *Punch*.[4] In any case, the ministry had apparently settled on Lansdowne quickly, unani-

LORD LANSDOWNE

In his new Canadian costume, specially adapted to remaining for some time
out in the cold

(Reproduced by special permission of the Proprietors of "Punch")

Lord Lansdowne, on being appointed governor general, dresses for Canadian winters, from Punch, *May 1883. (Courtesy the Bodleian Library, Oxford.)*

mously, and without giving serious consideration to any other candidate.

Historians of post-Confederation Canada have not given the governors general a great deal of attention.[5] The tendency has been to view them, throughout the period, as formal constitutional heads of state with a position largely analogous to that of the sovereign of Great Britain. This is understandable, since the governors relinquished control of governmental policy to their ministers with the coming of responsible government in the mid-nineteenth century. However, a careful examination of the office of governor general under Lansdowne reveals not an impotent, purely titular figure, but an official with many functions, considerable influence, and some real power. His many responsibilities generally fell into three categories: he performed a host of ceremonial and social functions; he acted as an adviser and consultant to his ministers; and he served as the primary channel of communication between the Canadian and imperial governments.

The governor general's ceremonial and social obligations were numerous and diverse.[6] He was Canada's chief of state and its cultural and social leader. Arising from his position of titular head of state were certain official ceremonial tasks relating to the operation of the government generally and Parliament specifically. He served as commander-in-chief of the Canadian armed forces; he appointed various public officials; he delivered the speech from the throne at the opening of each parliamentary session; he summoned, prorogued, adjourned, and dissolved Parliament; and he gave the royal assent to bills passed by the legislature. A host of travel duties and nonofficial ceremonial obligations arose from the governor's position of cultural and social leadership. He was expected to visit cities and regions of the dominion; give attention to various ethnic, religious, cultural, economic, political, and other groups and their interests; lay cornerstones; receive addresses from municipal authorities and respond appropriately; open or at least attend exhibitions, museums, and other festive or cultural events; promote various fields of worthy endeavour such as education, music, art, literature, the theatre, and charities; entertain members of Parliament, judges, provincial and local officials, eminent Canadians, and foreign visitors of distinction; and, in general, perform the tasks expected of a monarch and, thereby, relieve the prime minister from such social and ceremonial activities in order that the latter might concentrate upon the task of governing the dominion. Lansdowne discovered that these activities occupied a large portion of his time and energy, probably as much as did his duties as adviser and correspondent combined. He conducted these routine official governmental functions without the slightest controversy, demonstrating a genuine interest in Canadian institutions and people. He identified himself with the life of the country and became generally respected and popular, except perhaps among Catholic Irish-Canadians.

In his capacity as an adviser, Lansdowne's real influence is difficult to determine. By the 1880s the governor general was required in nearly all cases to accept the decisions of his ministers on issues of policy. But he did not have to be a completely silent figure. He could offer his own opinions, criticize, suggest, and work for alterations in policies relating to both domestic and imperial matters, especially the latter. In his day, Prime Minister Laurier noted that although the position no longer allowed the governor general to determine policy, he was by no means a mere figurehead. "He has the privilege of advising his advisors," Laurier added, "and, if he is a man of sense and experience, his advice is often taken."[7] In the exercise of his advisory powers, Lansdowne faced a severe handicap, one common to most governors. On arrival, he knew little about Canada, apart from what he gleaned from some light reading in preparation for the job and the few letters Lorne had written apprising him of the Canadian situation – and Lorne had not stayed long enough to become an expert. On the other hand, fifteen years' experience in politics and government had taught Lansdowne ability, reserve, and tact; he brought with him the broader imperial view; and he had a budding interest in Canada that was to grow as his years in Ottawa passed.

Since Lansdowne, like Lorne, did not attend meetings of the Privy Council, his role as adviser to the cabinet was exercised mainly through his relationship with Sir John A. Macdonald, prime minister during Lansdowne's tenure. This was normal and understandable, especially in view of Macdonald's strong personality and pre-eminent position. However, the Lansdowne Papers reveal that there were occasional exchanges of correspondence between the governor and other cabinet ministers, some dealing with trivialities, others with matters of importance.[8] His most frequent correspondents, other than the prime minister, were two ministers of justice, Sir Alexander Campbell and Sir John Thompson;[9] the minister of marine and fisheries, Sir George Foster; and the minister of militia and defence, Sir Adolphe Caron. Private conferences between Lansdowne and individual members of the Macdonald cabinet seem to have been fairly infrequent, thus ruling out much oral advice from the governor on individual departmental matters.

Without question, Macdonald was the key figure in the connection between Lansdowne and the ministry. A close relationship between the governor and prime minister began to develop soon after Lansdowne's arrival. On the day following Lansdowne's inauguration, they exchanged their first letters.[10] Both the Lansdowne and the Macdonald papers reveal a steady correspondence between the two men throughout the governor general's stay in Canada. Lansdowne's letterbooks record more than 320 private letters to the prime minister,[11] and the Macdonald Papers contain a number of communications from the governor general that were not recorded in the letterbooks.[12] The Lansdowne Papers also reveal more than 300 letters received from Macdonald.[13] Some of these letters are brief and deal with trivial matters or do nothing more than arrange a meeting, but many others involve substantive issues. This correspondence is solid evidence of the confidence and good faith that existed between the two men, the extent to which the governor general was kept informed and involved in the affairs of state, and the frequency with which Lansdowne's advice was solicited.

This correspondence was supplemented by frequent conversations. The first exchange of letters on the day following the inauguration made arrangements for a private meeting.[14] Within a matter of weeks, Lansdowne extended Macdonald a standing invitation to visit Government House any time during the morning hours or for a 2:00 p.m. luncheon, whichever was more convenient for the prime minister.[15] When the two men were both in Ottawa, they saw each other almost every day and often more than once a day. What transpired in these conversations is lost to the historian, except for what can be surmised from references in letters and from actions taken. However, it is safe to assume that if they wrote letters about important matters, they also talked about them.

Since Canada enjoyed responsible government, the governor general did not make policy. But Lansdowne became much more than nominally involved. The eighties were critical years for Canada – issues arose with ominous consequences for the dominion for both the long and short range. Among the challenges faced by Ottawa in the Lansdowne era were the completion of the Canadian Pacific Railway, economic difficulties, farmers' unrest, rebellion in the Northwest Territories, conflicts with provincial governments, and fisheries disputes with the United States. To resolve these questions, Lansdowne worked side by side with Macdonald, gathering information, making suggestions, and supplying reports to the imperial government.[16] Even so, Lansdowne managed to keep his activities within the allowable limitation of a constitutional governor. This was not always easy, for at times he did not agree with Macdonald, and on occasion he became exasperated with the prime minister's habitual dilatoriness in dealing with seemingly critical matters. No doubt there were times when Lansdowne would have been pleased to shove Macdonald aside and implement the actions he deemed appropriate, but he never forgot that in the final analysis it was Macdonald who made and was responsible for Canadian domestic policy.

The governor general's most important role was as an instrument of communication between the Canadian cabinet and the Colonial Office. Until well into the twentieth century the governor was, in one sense, an imperial officer subordinate and responsible to the colonial secretary in London. He was the agent-in-chief of the Colonial Office in Canada. As Sir John Buchan has observed, the governor had the task of interpreting to Britain the ideals and aims of the dominion and at the same time expounding to the dominion the problems and interests of the mother country.[17] This involved an extensive communication,[18] nearly all of it in the form of dispatches, letters, and telegrams, since the governor in Ottawa was rarely able to converse with Colonial Office authorities. Lansdowne visited England only once during his appointment, in the fall of 1886.

The Colonial Office no longer exercised control over Canadian domestic matters, but for various reasons it wanted and needed to know what was transpiring on the British North American scene. The Queen, in whose behalf the Colonial Office functioned, was the sovereign of Canada, its government being conducted in her name. And the dividing line between purely domestic matters and imperial interests was indistinct, which underscored the limitations on Canada's sovereignty even in affairs that were essentially domestic in character. An issue apparently purely Canadian could have imperial ramifications. London's involvement might arise from constitutional right, from tradition, from perceived infringement on imperial interests, or from Canadian initiative. If the Canadians wanted economic assistance or needed support for a controversial stand, they actively solicited British participation. On other occasions, the Canadians resented the fact of British involvement. The British, for their part, did not evidence great eagerness to embroil themselves in Canadian problems. Colonial Office personnel, more often than not, sympathized with the Canadian point of view, while other departments of the Her Majesty's Government were more likely to see things from either the English or imperial perspective. Sometimes the different viewpoints produced internal conflicts in London that delayed decisions. Whatever the stance or issues, however, the imperial government rarely if ever moved to restrict further or interpret narrowly Canada's sovereignty. Generally speaking, it evidenced a desire to nourish Canada's sense of responsibility for its own affairs. The governor general, functioning as the imperial government's only representative in Canada, was inevitably in the middle of these dominion-imperial questions. He not only passed information back and forth between Ottawa and London, but also frequently offered his own opinions and advice in both directions. On most occasions, Lansdowne identified with the position of his Canadian ministers and no doubt helped contribute to the habitual pro-Canadian stance of the Colonial Office.[19] An examination of Canada's relations with the other parts of the British Empire and the United States during the 1880s reveals the governor general to be a more active figure than is often supposed. He served as the main medium for exchange of views and information between Canada and other imperial units. The bulk of his imperial correspondence was with the Colonial Office in London. By means of such correspondence, combined with work in Ottawa, he was able to carry out imperial projects that involved the dominion, such as organizing the Nile voyageur expedition of 1884 and arranging for Canadian participation in the first Colonial Conference in 1887. He was able to make the British aware of official and public opinion in Canada on questions that affected the Empire, such as the use of colonial troops in the Sudan, the improvement of Canadian and imperial defences, and the possibility of commercial union with the United States. On some issues whose direct effect upon the mother country was less than stupendous, such as prospects of Canadian union with Newfoundland or the British West Indies, the governor was able to communicate directly with these colonial governments. However, in such cases, Lansdowne was careful to keep London authorities informed about what was taking place.

Although many questions were viewed somewhat differently in London than in Ottawa, Anglo-Canadian relations were generally cordial in the Lansdowne era. The imperial government was careful to respect Canada's autonomy and sensitivities, even when it could have meant injury to British interests, as in the case of commercial union with the United States. The dominion under the guidance of Macdonald, an Anglophile who saw much advantage in the imperial tie, did not demand greater autonomy. The major point of discord revolved around issues of defence. Facing the reality of a changing world, the British sought greater Canadian effort, while Macdonald, viewing things from a relatively secure Canada and being cognizant of Canadian public opinion, was not inclined to undertake the cost involved in a greater effort. The result was procrastination and inaction.[20]

Lansdowne also played an important role in Canadian external relations. The British Foreign Office, in attempting to conduct Canadian external relations in accord with Canadian wishes, encountered the problem of maintaining satisfactory channels of communication with responsible authorities in Ottawa. London diplomats needed not only to comprehend Canadian interests and opinions, but also to acquaint Canadians with the broader imperial perspective. The division of labour in the British ministry required that the Foreign Office, which had the primary function of maintaining communications with foreign governments, depend upon the Colonial Office, which maintained communications with the colonial governments, for Canadian information and opinions. The Foreign Office never corresponded directly with Canada. The Colonial Office, in performing its intelligence-gathering function during the 1880s, was occasionally fortunate enough to have access to the fount of Canadian opinion, Sir John A. Macdonald, when he made periodic visits to London. Otherwise it had to rely on two sources – the governor general and the Canadian high commissioner.

The basic, long-standing, and most important medium for the exchange of information and opinions between London and Ottawa was the imperial representative in Canada, the governor general. The governor, British in background, with ready access to Macdonald and in almost constant communication with the Colonial Office, was in a good position to gather information and sense the official mood in Ottawa as well as transmit the imperial viewpoint to the Canadians. Nevertheless, the governor's effectiveness as an intermediary to the Colonial Office was lessened somewhat by the fact that he was not a Canadian, and thus not always capable of seeing and reporting the Canadian perspective, and by the inherent deficiencies of written correspondence.

By the 1880s the governor general was supplemented as an intermediary by the Canadian high commissioner. In the late 1870s the Macdonald government petitioned for permission to maintain an official resident minister in London. The British agreed to accept such a minister, who came to be known as the high commissioner, but refused to grant him full diplomatic status.[21] The high commissioner's activities were numerous and varied. He represented Canada in financial negotiations with the imperial government and British banking houses; he promoted immigration to

Canada; he worked to improve Canadian commercial relations with Europe; and he dealt with a host of lesser issues. In the 1880s he did not generally handle official communications with British authorities on major diplomatic questions, such as the North Atlantic Fisheries dispute with the United States. The high commissioner received instructions directly from Macdonald and other Canadian ministers. He seldom communicated with the governor general. His main interaction with the British government was through undersecretaries in the Colonial Office. Only rarely did he communicate directly with the secretary of state. He occasionally conferred with other departments of the imperial government, but only with permission of the Colonial Office.

The creation and development of the high commissioner's office were to have an important impact on the role of the governor general. Both Lansdowne and his predecessor, Lorne, approved of the new post, but both were concerned that it should complement the existing communication system and not reduce the importance of the governor's office. Lorne had requested and received permission to see all documents that were sent to the high commissioner from Ottawa. Lansdowne was accorded the same privilege, which served to reduce the high commissioner's potency, since the Colonial Office often knew in advance, via the governor general, what he was going to report or request. In the Lansdowne era the governor general remained important in external relations, both as an adviser to his ministers and as the primary link between Ottawa and the imperial government.[22]

Lansdowne's greatest influence was in the areas of dominion-imperial relations and external affairs. In both cases, Canada was subordinate to the imperial government, a circumstance that naturally permitted a greater role for the governor general, the only imperial representative in Ottawa. This, together with the respect Lansdowne commanded, allowed him to exercise influence in both capitals – to impress upon Macdonald the more cosmopolitan interests and concerns that shaped thinking in London and to interpret to the imperial government the interests and concerns of Canadians. Because Lansdowne usually tended to sympathize with the Canadian point of view, the Colonial Office, with which Lansdowne corresponded, was inclined to react positively to Canadian requests and positions. At least in this sense, Lansdowne made a positive contribution to the development of the concept and content of "responsible government" at a critical point in the development of Canada, and he emerges as one of the more constructive of the imperial proconsuls.

John L. Gordon, Jr., is professor of history and chair of the department at the University of Richmond. A native of Kentucky, he received his A.B. from Western Kentucky University and his M.A. and Ph.D. from Vanderbilt University. He was appointed to the faculty of the University of Richmond in 1967. He left the department in 1980 to serve the University of Richmond in several administrative roles, including dean of graduate studies and associate dean of the Faculty of Arts and Sciences, 1980–87; interim dean of the faculty, 1981–82; and interim vice president and provost, 1983. Professor Gordon returned to the Department of History in 1988 and became its chair in 1989. His teaching reponsibilies include both undergraduate and graduate courses in modern British, Irish, and Canadian history. He has presented and published papers in British, Irish, and Canadian history and is an officer in the Southern Conference of British Studies and the Southeast Council for Canadian Studies. He is currently working on a book-length study of the Fifth Marquess of Lansdowne.

Notes

1 Information on Lansdowne's life and career may be found in Lord Newton, *Lord Lansdowne: A Biography* (London: Macmillan, 1929); Dudley Barker, *Prominent Edwardians* (New York: Atheneum, 1969), 137–73; and *Dictionary of National Biography, 1922–1930*, edited by L.G. Wickham Legg and E.T. Williams (London: Oxford University Press, 1937), 667–75.

2 Lorne's tenure as governor general has been studied by William S. MacNutt, *Days of Lorne: Impressions of a Governor General* (Fredericton: Brunswick Press, 1955).

3 National Archives of Canada (NA), Fifteenth Earl of Derby Papers, reel A32, Derby to Queen Victoria, 8 May 1883.

4 A reproduction of a May 1883 *Punch* cartoon that projects this view appears in Newton, *Lord Lansdowne*, facing 24.

5 There is no comprehensive study of the governor general's office and functions. A helpful short account appears in Robert M. Dawson and Norman Ward, *The Government of Canada*, 4th ed. (Toronto: University of Toronto Press, 1963), 153–79.

6 For a discussion of this subject, see John L. Gordon, Jr., "Lord Lansdowne in Canada, 1883–1888: The Office of Governor General in a Self-Governing Dominion" (Ph.D. diss., Vanderbilt University, Ann Arbor, University Microfilms, 1972), 107–32.

7 Quoted in John Buchan, *Lord Minto: A Memoir* (London: Thomas Nelson and Sons, 1924), 122.

8 NA, Fifth Marquess of Lansdowne Papers, Canada, reels A623–A627.

9 Thompson succeeded Campbell as minister of justice in September 1885.

10 NA, Sir John A. Macdonald Papers, MG 26 A, Lansdowne to Sir John A. Macdonald, 24 October 1883, vol. 84.

11 NA, Lansdowne Papers, Letterbooks I–V, reels A623–A624.

12 NA, Macdonald Papers, vols. 84–88.

13 NA, Lansdowne Papers, reels A624–A625.

14 NA, Macdonald Papers, Lansdowne to Macdonald, 14 October 1883, vol. 84.

15 Ibid., 26 November 1883.

16 For a fuller account, see Gordon, "Lord Lansdowne in Canada," chap. 4.

17 Buchan, *Lord Minto*, 122. A noted author, Buchan was raised to the peerage as Lord Tweedsmuir and served as governor general of Canada, 1935–40.

18 Records of this communication for the Lansdowne period are contained in NA, Colonial Office Papers, CO 42 series, vols. 775–98, reels B610–631; and NA, Records of the Governor General's Office, series G 21. These papers are the major source of observations about the governor general–Colonial Office correspondence and relationship.

19 See Gordon, "Lord Lansdowne in Canada," chap. 5.

20 See ibid., chap. 6.

21 The establishment of the Canadian high commissionership is discussed in David M.L. Farr, *The Colonial Office and Canada, 1867–1887* (Toronto: University of Toronto Press, 1955), 253–70.

22 See Gordon, "Lord Lansdowne in Canada," chap. 7.

Chapter 19

The Challenge of Biography: The Case of Francis Hincks

G.A. Davison

Biography has been guilty of creating certain misconceptions about the period leading up to Confederation. Paradoxically, biography can also help to rectify and revise some of those misconceptions. There has been a natural focus on the career of John A. Macdonald, whose star began to rise after 1854; in the previous four years, from 1848 to 1854, he served as a member of the opposition. These four years, while not figuring prominently in a biography of Macdonald, were critical nonetheless. From the sidelines, Macdonald observed the French-English Reform alliance, the Francis Hincks–George Brown battles, the co-opting of the Clear Grits, and the links forged between business and politics. Thus did Macdonald learn how a "responsible government" could work. Hincks was actually the more important figure during the first half of the Union period, from 1841 to 1854. By focusing on Hincks, biography can lead to a new way of looking at the period before Confederation.

Of Anglo-Irish extraction, Hincks came to Canada in 1831 and had a varied business and editorial career before becoming a member of Parliament in 1841, inspector-general in 1842 and 1848, and premier in 1851. The political and economic history of mid-nineteenth-century British North America can hardly be discussed without taking into account Hincks's role in laying the groundwork for the English-French compact that lies at the heart of the Canadian system, in setting Canadian finances on a sound footing after the introduction of free trade, in encouraging the building of railways, and in attracting moderate businessmen into a coalition to promote the development of the province.

Historians who focus on political-constitutional developments, French-English relations, or economic history often ignore both the role of individuals and the wider context. More than a generation ago, Donald Creighton observed that Canadian politicians had too often been presented as "Robert Responsible-Government, Francis Responsible-Government and Wilfrid Responsible Government."[1] On the other hand, the biographical approach alone can also be limiting, leaving "little room to speculate about groups or parties, the links between business and politics, or the importance of class and ethnicity, beyond the particular character being studied."[2] And while Donald Creighton, Maurice Careless, and William Ormsby have provided written scholarly biographies of mid-nineteenth-century politicians, Hincks has been ill-served by historians.

Several recent biographies have influenced my work on Hincks's early career, including Keith Johnson's study of Sir John A. Macdonald and Brian Young's life of Sir George-Étienne Cartier, businessmen-politicians who were contemporaries of Hincks. Johnson's work on "the young non-politician" and the Kingston business community shows the close relationship between business and politicians, postulating "that Macdonald as Party Leader, as Prime Minister, as policy maker, as nation builder, was influenced in significant ways by the habits, the experience, the mentality of Macdonald the businessman." Johnson noted that such a connection needs "more extensive research than has so far been undertaken," as well as "a careful comparison in depth of the habits of mind, the code of beliefs, the rules of the game under which Macdonald operated in both his private and public capacities."[3] Recent biographical and historical trends and interpretations open up a series of questions about Hincks's role in the politics of the union, including his role in the development of the Reform Party's economic policy and in the political transformation that created the coalition of 1854.

Hincks had a crucial role in the formation of the united Reform Party. Between 1839 and 1841, he worked to convince Reform leader Louis LaFontaine that in order to preserve French cultural interests the best course was to join with Upper Canadian Reformers to win responsible government. Hincks also advocated "liberal institutions and economical government"[4] and the use of patronage to build up the party. He told Baldwin in 1843 that Reformers were fighting "the battle of the middle classes against the aristocracy" and that to keep on good terms with Governor General Lord Metcalfe, Reformers should persuade middle-class, business-oriented Tories "of good character," as well as "respectable farm-ers" with Conservative connections, to join with the Reformers so that when the Tories complained about Reform appointments, "they will hit their own friends & unite them on that point with us."[5] The Reform move-ment would thus be broadened and strengthened. Businessmen would be attracted to a party that was committed to developing business interests, which in turn would help the party and provincial development. His strat-egy was not new (the old Family Compact had done something similar to widen its base), but if followed under the responsible system, it was calcu-lated to keep the governor general on side and attract like-minded middle-class Conservatives, whose allegiance would be doubly secure: they would owe their position to the Reformers and criticism from the "aristocratic" Tories would push business even more strongly into the Reform fold.

The French-English Reform relationship was not without its trials, but by 1848 the Reformers succeeded in winning a majority in the House. However, the alliance between the followers of Baldwin and LaFontaine began to break up soon after responsible government had been won. The Clear Grits were the first to break off because of their admiration for American institutions and their opposition to state funding of religious organizations, including separate schools. George Brown, personally dis-appointed with the Reform Party leadership, led an increasingly vocal opposition to the ministry's ecclesiastical policy and French domination, although he supported the imperial connection and British institutions.

For Hincks, economic development was a corollary to political devel-opment. He believed in moderation rather than extremes and also that political and economic interest was a strong bond between members of Parliament, whether their background was French or English, Protestant or Roman Catholic. The encouragement of business and railways was at the heart of his economic program; so too was a free trade deal with the United States. These policies attracted businessmen-politicians to the Re-form Party. From the 1830s to the 1850s, Hincks was concerned with set-ting in place measures to improve the provincial credit rating. With this done, he reasoned, the climate in which business operated would also be improved and the resulting prosperity would bring together moderate Reformers and moderate Conservatives in various eco-nomic activities.

Thus, throughout his career Hincks promoted canals, and he worked diligently to improve the credit of the province and to ensure a steady revenue for provincial coffers. While negotiating trade deals with the Americans, he maintained a close relationship with Britain and the Empire. However, in order to facilitate trade, Hincks also had to keep Canada in step with transportation developments, and that meant that the province had to catch up quickly in the construction of railways; any tardiness would have given the Americans an advantage, and Hincks was determined that Canada should not be left behind.

Hincks played an important role in the promoting of railways from the time of his arrival in the new provincial capital of Montreal in 1844. He advocated lines within Canada and connections to the United States and the Maritime colonies, and he would have succeeded in getting agreement for the latter were it not for the fact that Joseph Howe, representing Nova Scotia, failed to show up in London in early 1852.[6] Instead, Hincks worked out an arrangement with Messrs. Peto, Brassey, Jackson, and Betts to underwrite a trunk line through the Canadas – the Grand Trunk Railway. He played important roles in the preliminary stages of that railway, buying out other charters and interests, as well as looking after his own speculative interests. These activities gave rise to a great deal of criticism and charges of scandal and corruption,[7] and ultimately weakened Hincks's standing in the Reform Party.

In addition, Hincks played a crucial role in orchestrating the Liberal-Conservative coalition of September 1854. He also helped to shift the political focus from the extremes to the progressive middle. His patronage and development policies had attracted businessmen to politics, and in attempting to broaden the Reform Party in this direction, he facilitated an alliance with moderate Conservatives. By 1854 the old Family Compact Tories were no longer in politics, and on the vote to secularize the reserves, few defended the vested rights of the Church of England. On the other extreme, George Brown had always been isolated, as he considered himself independent and unaligned, although he did support most of the Clear Grit opposition. Indeed, the basis of cooperation after 1854 was made necessary by Hincks's coalition. In Canada East, Hincks had made an effort to obtain the support of Reformers, particularly A.T. Galt and Luther Holton, but they were more concerned about his "corrupt" government and withheld support. So too did many Rouges, who were dissatisfied with the reforming efforts of the government and were isolated by Hincks and the MacNab-Morin coalition.

There does seem to have been an affinity between Hincks and some Conservatives. As early as 1840, Sir Allan MacNab and Hincks enjoyed a friendly relationship across the floor of the House. Their political differences were less important than their common interest in railway matters. By 1854 a more moderate MacNab advocated secularization of the clergy reserves, after years of opposition, and had no major difference with Hincks on other questions. Even if, as biographers of MacNab point out, MacNab had no real power and was little more than a figurehead in his later years,[8] he was someone Hincks did not mind trusting to maintain the Union in a business-minded way and to keep the tie with the mother country strong. Similarly, both Hincks and John A. Macdonald believed strongly in provincial development, and both had business experience that gave them an interest in the economic health of Canada. Macdonald, not yet "Old Tomorrow" but beginning to show the shrewdness he was sometimes credited with later, could be counted on not to alter Hincks's political strategy of avoiding divisive questions and concentrating on economic development.

Hincks undoubtedly guided the actual negotiations that led to the coalition of 1854, and though he denied influencing Lord Elgin's decision to ask MacNab to form a government, Elgin's choice did not worry Hincks, who at the same time was working to put together a Liberal-Conservative coalition, albeit one with John Wilson and the Hincksites as the dominant partners. Nevertheless, after MacNab approached French Canadian Reform leader A.N. Morin, the latter sought Hincks's advice and approval, as did MacNab. Hincks's stipulation that John Ross and Robert Spence, loyal Hincksites, be appointed cabinet members, ensured that the new government was dominated by his former colleagues, who, united with MacNab's Conservatives, pledged to carry out the policies of the Hincks administration as enunciated in the throne speech a few days before. Everyone involved was more or less satisfied with the outcome, and Hincks's coterie survived in better shape than expected. The Conservatives, however, were vulnerable and sought to distance themselves from Hincks in order to build up their own support. Still, Hincks's influence was useful in the House throughout the first session after coalition, and the young lawyer Alexander Cameron, who had helped Hincks during the campaign of 1854 and sat with him during the fall session in Quebec, claimed that Hincks's word was law.[9] Hincks thus deserves great credit for creating the Liberal-Conservative dynasty that dominated Canadian politics long after his temporary departure in the 1850s and 1860s, and indeed, long after his death in 1885. If Baldwin's legacy was responsible government, Hincks's was in implementing that principle through political and economic development.

Biography thus sheds new light on Hincks's role in economic development and political coalition. It can do more. The challenge of biography is to bring recent historical trends to help illuminate a particular character or period. Social history can be served by examining Hincks's relationship with his family and colleagues: wife Martha had property in Canada West, something rare for women at the time; Anna Hutton, daughter of Hincks's cousin William Hutton of Belleville, was governess of the four Hincks children; daughter Ellen married a British officer, Major Ready, stationed at Quebec City. Unfortunately, Hincks did not leave much family correspondence behind, although the political side of his life is found in over sixty manuscript collections.

Ethnicity is also important in studying Hincks, since questions of patronage and interest politics involved cultural links and nationalities. It was vital for a successful politician to balance the interests of national and ethnic groups as diverse as the French, Scots, Irish, Americans, and others. Robert Baldwin provided a clue to the importance of ethnicity when he said that the Reform leadership was like an Irish family. Hincks owed his introduction to Canadian society to his Irish heritage and the Baldwins' goodwill, and he provided the same welcome to the Hutton family of Belleville. Many friends and supporters were Irish, and the fact that five important members of the Hincks-Morin government had Irish origins led William McDougall, editor of the Toronto-based *North American*, to think that Hincks was trying to establish an Irish government in Canada.

Ethnic groups provided electoral support. Hincks rallied the Irish canallers to help win the 1844 Montreal by-election, and he was concerned with winning over the Orange Order, particularly in Toronto in the 1850s. His Irish origin also partly explains his fear of the Scottish voters of Zorra township in Oxford County: though they never posed an insuperable obstacle, Hincks campaigned there with influential Scots. The point about ethnicity should not be taken too far, since Hincks got along with Scots, Anglos, and native-born Upper Canadians, but his ethnicity should be kept in mind when looking at his appointments and policies.

Class must also have been involved, although status was a more valid way of looking at Hincks and the businessmen-politicians in mid-century. J.M.S. Careless points out the lack of clarity in class divisions. While the Canada West leaders, he argues, "might have formed an upper middle-class elite themselves ... there was no great social difference perceived or felt between them and the 'respectable' mass of the populace below."[10] To members of the elite at the time, class meant anything from "religious groupings" to "disctinctions of age or sex" or even "social or occupational status."[11] As yet, there has been little work on the interaction of the political leadership and businessmen in the mid-nineteenth century.

Religion also helps explain Hincks's character. He was born into a very religious family. His father was a Presbyterian minister and teacher, and his four older brothers were ministers (two of them also distinguished scientists – an orientalist and professor of natural history). Hincks himself was a Unitarian, though there is no explanation why he became one; in fact, he later became an Anglican. But between 1832 and 1855, he was also a dissenter, which, along with his Irish background, meant that he and others in the same position were not particularly worried by Roman Catholics; they came from a society in which Catholicism was the dominant religion and in which both Catholics and dissenters were denied "important civil rights under laws designed to favour the established church."[12]

There was nothing that could have been called an established Unitarian presence in Canada when Hincks arrived in the early 1830s. William Hutton, son of one of the leading Unitarian ministers in Ireland, went to a Presbyterian church in Belleville rather than not go anywhere, but the local minister refused him Communion because of his heretical opinions.[13] When Hincks went to Montreal in 1844, the first Unitarian church in Canada was just being built under John Cordner's guidance, and there was an important group of businesspeople in the Montreal congregation, including Theodore Hart, Luther Holton, John Young, Benjamin Holmes, and the Workman brothers, Thomas and William. And if Hincks encountered the same attitude as William Workman, his empathy with French Canadians might be better understood. Workman once said to a friend that, as a Unitarian, he was "accustomed to vituperation from opposing Protestant sects (never from Roman Catholics)."[14] These men provided Hincks entry into the Montreal business community, and he participated with all of them in one form of enterprise or another, from his newspaper to banking, telegraphs, and railway promotion. Thus, in his early years in Canada, the influence of religion can be seen in Hincks's career.

Finally, I think that interest – the use of patronage and government policies – is the most useful way of understanding mid-nineteenth-century Canadian history. Hincks sought to create a climate within which the province would advance and everyone would ultimately benefit. When founding the Montreal *Pilot* in 1844, Hincks outlined his political principles, saying that the "grand object" was "to advocate the interests of Canada." He added that "all classes of the population ought to combine together" to do so. And he stressed the need for harmony among all interests:

> The great interests of the Province – Agricultural, Manufacturing, and Commercial – will receive that share of attention to which their importance entitles them. Instead of fomenting jealousies between these different interests, every effort will be used to unite them and to teach them that the prosperity of the country depends on measures being adopted by the Legislature for the relief and advantage of all.[15]

Hincks carried this principle and, as he noted, "twenty years' experience in commercial affairs" into his editorship and his renewed political career four years later.

Hincks used development policies and patronage to build the Reform Party and extend it to include businessmen, with everyone committed to developing the province. This form of the politics of interest was a kind of boosterism, but it was more than that. If asked, most politicians were for progress. Hincks's achievement was that he managed to keep in check the varying interests within the Reform Party longer than anyone thought possible. At the same time, he made several positive advances for the province. Even when he left office in late 1854, few disagreed with his economic policies; however, there were just enough members who disliked his "railway morality," as well as his seigneurial and reserves policies, to make his continuing in politics impossible. He handed over power to a group of politicians more compatible than he, and supported the Liberal-Conservative alliance before his own departure from Canada in mid-1855 to take up his new office as governor of Barbados and the Windward Islands.

A biographical study of Francis Hincks is important, for it provides a framework for exploring of the roles of individuals, groups, and parties, the links between business and politics, the importance of class, religion, gender, and ethnicity. By focusing on Hincks, the biographer can re-examine the political, economic, and social development of the Union period, out of which sprang many forces that shaped Canada's post-Confederation period.

George Davison has specialized in pre-Confederation political and economic history, focusing on the early career of Francis Hincks in his doctoral dissertation, in several conference papers and articles, and in a forthcoming book. He has taught history at the University of Alberta, McGill University, Keyano College (Fort McMurray), and the University of Victoria. He is currently at the College of New Caledonia in Prince George, British Columbia, working on political commentary during the Union period.

Notes

1 D.G. Creighton, "Sir John Macdonald and Canadian Historians," in Carl Berger, ed., *Approaches to Canadian History* (Toronto: Macmillan, 1967), 53.

2 G.A. Davison, "Francis Hincks and the Politics of Interest, 1832–54" (Ph.D. diss., University of Alberta, 1989), 21.

3 J.K. Johnson, "John A. Macdonald, The Young Non-Politician," *Canadian Historical Association Historical Papers*, 1971, 150.

4 National Archives of Canada (NA), LaFontaine Papers, MG 24, B 14, reel M-860, Hincks to LaFontaine, 12 April 1839, 2.

5 Metropolitan Toronto Library, Baldwin Papers, vol. A 51, Hincks to Baldwin, 15 June 1843.

6 NA, Elgin Papers, MG 24, A 16, Hincks to Elgin, 7 May 1852, 6.

7 G.A. Davison, "The Hincks-Brown Rivalry and the Politics of Scandal," *Ontario History* 81, no. 2 (June 1989).

8 See Donald Beer, *Sir Allan Napier MacNab* (Hamilton: Dictionary of Hamilton Biography, 1986).

9 Archives of Ontario, F 62, A.N. Buell Papers, Cameron to Buell, 30 October 1854, 3.

10 J.M.S. Careless, ed., *The Pre-Confederation Premiers: Ontario Government Leaders, 1841–1867* (Toronto: University of Toronto Press, 1980), 24.

11 Alison Prentice, *The School Promoters: Education and Social Class in Mid-Nineteenth Century Upper Canada* (Toronto: McClelland and Stewart, 1977), 90–92.

12 R.J. Morris, *Class and Class Consciousness in the Industrial Revolution 1780–1850* (London: Macmillan, 1979), 38.

13 Gerald Boyce, *Hutton of Hastings: The Life and Letters of William Hutton, 1801–61* (Belleville: *Intelligencer*, 1972), 53.

14 Gerald Tulchinsky, "William Workman," *Dictionary of Canadian Biography*, vol. 10, *1871–1880*, edited by Francess G. Halpenny (Toronto: University of Toronto Press, 1972), 718.

15 Francis Hincks, *Reminiscences of His Public Life* (Montreal: Wm. Drysdale, 1884), 125–26.

Chapter 20

Michael Collins and
the Problem of Biography

Michael Hopkinson

A century after his birth, Michael Collins remains a fascinating subject for biographers, and thus far, there have been five major biographies. In 1990, the centenary of Collins's birth, Tim Pat Coogan's *Michael Collins, A Biography* was published, selling 400,000 copies within three weeks of publication. The outpouring of work on Collins has been justified by the frequent emergence of new Collins papers. Rex Taylor's and Margery Forester's biographies, published in 1958 and 1971 respectively, used major new private sources, and Coogan gained access to further Collins family papers, including material in a notorious black box.

The dramatic events of Collins's life have guaranteed interest. Two issues have been the source of intense debate ever since: Collins's alleged link with the assassination of Sir Henry Wilson, the former British chief of Imperial General Staff, in June 1922; and Collins's own death two months later. Three books have been written on the theme of "Who killed Collins?" and there are periodic waves of correspondence on that subject in the Irish press. Collins, moreover, is an attractive study because of his forthright, approachable personality, admired by the Catholic Irish, who find Charles Parnell and Eamon de Valera aloof and complex. Collins was a backslapper and a drinking companion, and no one doubted his "essential Irishness." Considerable interest in him has been shown outside Ireland: Mao Tse Tung and T.E. Lawrence are said to have studied Collins's guerrilla warfare tactics; and during the Israeli fight for independence, Yitzak Shamir used the codename "Micail."

Interest in Collins is bound up with consideration of the Irish past, present, and future, and particularly with the circumstances of the Irish

Free State's formation. Disappointment with the political and economic performance of the Southern Irish state has often been attributed in part to the loss of so much of its leadership, and particularly the leadership of Collins, during the civil war of 1922–23. Such a small country could ill afford to lose so much of its new leadership class so soon after rejecting the Irish Parliamentary Party's aged elite. Collins's sympathizers argue that Ireland would have been better governed if he had lived. Detractors suggest that he might have become an Irish Mussolini or that he represented a ruthlessness that inspires the Irish Republican Army (IRA) today.

Collins's significance in the revolutionary period may have been exaggerated by close colleagues and biographers. Colonel Charles F. Russell claimed that Collins "was everything." Many said that they were swayed in their decision to support the Anglo-Irish Treaty by loyalty to Collins. Liam de Roiste, the Cork TD (member of the Irish Parliament) and long-time critic of the military dominance of the Sinn Fein movement, noted in his diary entry for 8 January 1921 that Collins was alert, active, assertive, aggressive, and "possessed of business capacity," but lacking in intelligence and political leadership.

The traditional biographical and narrative approach to the revolutionary period stressed the contribution of "great men." The paperback edition of Dorothy Macardle's *The Irish Republic*, once a standard text, has a preface by de Valera and his photograph on the cover. Historians of the Anglo-Irish Treaty and civil war period have debated personal motivation and blame, principally relating to Collins and de Valera. The considerable achievement of Coogan's book is lessened by a preoccupation with de Valera's personal responsibility for the treaty and civil war divisions and his lack of respect for and jealousy of Collins.

Collins has been all too easily romanticized, and some of the perennial fascination with him has amounted to bad taste. Margery Forester's book concludes with shallow comparisons between Collins and John F. Kennedy. While sometimes critical in detail of Collins's actions, Coogan's book is generally positive, in thrall to his contribution to the winning of Irish independence.

With Collins, as with all historical figures, the problem for the biographer is how to place the subject in context without claiming too much for him. However entertaining it is to read historical biographies, it is wise to approach them sceptically.

An alternative approach is stimulated by Desmond Williams, who argues that "the seeds of civil war lay not only in the weaknesses and suspicions of personalities, but in the whole nature of the national struggle before 1922." I hold that attention should be paid to wider considerations of the failure of nationalist institutions, both political and military, to control reaction to the Anglo-Irish Treaty. Attention should also be paid to the difficulties faced in claiming on the one hand that the republic came into being at Easter 1916, or in January 1919, and on the other hand that compromise with the British on the future status of Ireland was necessary. Individuals should not be made to bear all the responsibility for the difficulties in moving from guerrilla warfare to centralized government and in bringing a dominant military force under political control.

I wish to consider two questions. First, did Collins's career demonstrate the consistent application of an overall philosophy? And secondly, would the course of Irish history have been significantly different if Collins had not lived? For all my reservations about the biographical approach, my answers to both questions are in the affirmative.[1]

To understand Collins's political philosophy, one must understand his West Cork origins. The Clonakilty/Skibbereen area had a strong Fenian tradition. Collins's father, who was seventy-five when Michael was born, supplied vivid memories of the famine era of the 1840s. When Collins moved to London at age fifteen, he joined the Irish Republican Brotherhood (IRB), the Gaelic Athletic Association, and the Volunteers. In London he made contacts crucial for future intelligence work and arms acquisition. In the British capital, he worked in banks and offices, which helped to make him a disciplined, clear-minded administrator and an efficient Irish revolutionary, a rare phenomenon. In later life, he was frequently unforgiving of his countrymen's sometime disorder and inefficiency.

An examination of Collins's youth is important because of the amazing speed with which political leaders of what became known as Sinn Fein and the IRA emerged. The rapid emergence of new organizations, loosely related to each other, made the role of individuals more important than is usually the case in more settled periods when people are restrained by institutional controls. No one could have predicted that a clerk in London (Collins) and an equally obscure mathematics teacher in Dublin (de Valera) would within four years become internationally known.

Collins participated in the Easter Rising in a junior role but was critical of Pearse's ideology of blood sacrifice and of his romantic, theatrical tactic of taking over prominent buildings in Dublin. Shortly after the rising, Collins wrote to a colleague that "the Rising was bungled terribly, costing many a good life. It seemed at first to be well-organised, but afterwards became subjected to panic decisions and a great lack of very essential organisation and co-operation." That "essential organisation," Collins trusted, would be supplied by a reorganized Irish Republican Brotherhood, in which he played a dominant role following his release from internment at the end of 1916. Because of his role in the IRB, Collins rose into the upper echelons of nationalist circles.

To understand Collins's character, one must be aware that he strongly believed in the use of physical force to win Irish independence. He also saw the need to become involved in public organizations. He played a significant role in getting the imprisoned Joe McGuiness to stand in the Longford by-election of May 1917. Collins's involvement in the by-elections of that year and the next, with the exception of de Valera's campaign in East Clare, suggests that Collins saw the importance of demonstrating public support for the emerging Sinn Fein coalition. He had become prominent enough by September 1917 to be chosen to deliver the funeral oration for Thomas Ashe, a fellow member of the IRB Supreme Council, who had died on a hunger strike. Following the firing of rifle volleys over the grave, Collins declared that nothing additional remained to be said. "That volley which we have just heard," he added, "is the only speech which it is proper to make above the grave of a dead Fenian."

By late 1917 Collins had become a key figure in the reorganized Irish Volunteers and a member of the Sinn Fein executive. He supported the Sinn Fein tactic of refusing to take up seats in Westminster following the massive victory in the December 1918 general election, and he became a member of the newly established Dail in 1919, having ensured the election of many IRB colleagues to the new assembly in Dublin. His emerging dominance was all the easier to achieve because others, including de Valera, Arthur Griffith, and the old Sinn Fein leader, were imprisoned following the "German Plot" arrests of May 1918.

Collins's achievements during the Anglo-Irish War have been extensively documented, particularly his building an intelligence network that reversed the nineteenth-century tradition of Irish secret societies being undermined by British spies and informers. Support for the British government in Ireland had largely disintegrated among the young Catholic middle class, whose members formed the majority of the civil service and local government, and Collins was the one man among the nationalist leadership who spotted the potential for Irish infiltration of government and police forces. He also had the necessary ruthlessness to deal with agents brought over from Britain to deal with the threat that he represented. His most remarkable achievement was to avoid capture, but that says as much for the ineffectiveness of British intelligence as it does for Collins's shrewdness and unflappability.

How effective, however, was Collins in directing from Dublin the IRA campaign in the provinces? The answer would appear to be much less than has often been supposed. Through his IRB contacts in the main British, European, and American ports, Collins was able to bring in arms for the use of the IRA, and he was regularly approached by IRA men in the provinces for arms and ammunition. He was, however, able to supply only small amounts and was dismissive of appeals from inactive areas. Plans to obtain arms from the Continent went unrealized. The majority of IRA arms were obtained by capture, thanks to local initiative. Collins did set up important intelligence contacts in some areas, gaining access, therefore, to the intelligence codes of the Royal Irish Constabulary, but the IRA intelligence system in most parts of the country was much less effective than has frequently been depicted. Only that can explain the regular failure of ambushes and the reduced effectiveness of the guerrilla warfare during 1921. The guerrilla tactics had never been centrally planned and were confined to limited areas of the Twenty-Six Counties. IRA success outside Dublin was largely dependent on local initiative.

The other main nationalist achievement during the Anglo-Irish War was in the publicity field, and Collins contributed little to that. He had little sympathy with hunger strikes and sacrificial suffering. He was anxious to keep men out of prison in order to continue the armed struggle. His contempt for the politicians within the movement, those he labelled "the bargaining kind," was increased by what he regarded as the poor performance of most of the republican government during the war. Collins himself was one of the few success stories of the government, his energy and administrative ability contrasting sharply with that of most of his colleagues, which led to much jealousy. De Valera and Collins had a strained relationship even before the treaty negotiations, made worse by de Valera's attempt to change the military tactics of the IRA upon his return in December 1920 after an eighteen-month visit to the United States.

Collins's pragmatism, together with his contempt for politicians, led to controversy during the treaty negotiations. In the war, the military side of the republican movement had dominated. The truce of early July 1921, however, returned the initiative to the politicians, particularly de Valera, during negotiations. Collins was miffed at not being chosen a member of the group who accompanied de Valera to London for preliminary talks with Lloyd George in July. Ironically Collins also protested about being a member of the negotiating team when the full-scale conference began the following October, perhaps because he suspected de Valera's motives when the latter refused to participate.

Collins's participation in the treaty negotiations not only gave him a new role, but also exposed him to public scrutiny. He was aware that the resumption of effective guerrilla warfare would be all but impossible if the talks failed, because his intelligence system was largely defunct and the British military effort would be greatly increased. Meanwhile he was faced with the difficult task of reconciling his republicanism with two facts: partition had already been established, and the British government would not grant more than dominion status to the South. The situation was complicated by divisions within the negotiating team, and between them and the Dail cabinet in Dublin. Because of Griffith's poor health, Collins frequently had to take over the leadership of the Irish delegation and became increasingly angry about what he saw as de Valera's interference.

Robert Barton, a member of the Irish negotiating team, noted that only on the melodramatic final evening of the negotiations did Collins declare his hand by promising to sign the treaty. The British government, especially Lloyd George, realized that his was the crucial signature, without which the document would probably not have won enough military and political acceptance at home. It is scarcely surprising, therefore, that considerable attention has been devoted to Collins's reasons for signing.

First of all, it appears that during the negotiations, Collins began to realize that nothing further could be won from the British government. Though he was always keen to stress that he had no aptitude for politics, Collins appreciated British political realities far better than did de Valera. He heeded advice given to him by C.P. Scott, proprietor of the *Manchester Guardian*. "You have got to think of our politics," Scott told Collins, "if you want to get anything done." When at de Valera's request, following the stormy cabinet meeting in Dublin the weekend before the treaty's signing, the Irish delegation in London reintroduced de Valera's "external association" compromise (which stipulated that recognition of the authority of the Crown be limited to external affairs), Collins was so infuriated that he refused to join further discussions.

Secondly, Collins frequent avowal that he did not see the treaty as an end in itself, but only as a means to the eventual republican end, should be accepted at face value. The vital point for him was that British troops would be quickly removed from the Twenty-Six Counties as a result of the treaty.

Collins's emphasis was on practicalities. He wrote in August 1922 that "true devotion lies not in melodramatic defiance or self-sacrifice for something falsely said to exist, or for mere words and formalities, which are empty." And he added that he and his colleagues had fought for "the greatest measure of freedom obtainable." Time after time during the Dail debates over the treaty, Collins expressed his impatience with those who based their opposition to the settlement on abstract, constitutional formulae.

Thirdly, Collins and Griffith signed the treaty in London without honouring their commitment to refer any document to the Dail cabinet at home for approval because they thought that referral would have led to more prevarication and delay. The treaty would have better prospects of being accepted in Ireland, the two men believed, if they signed it without delay. Almost certainly Collins knew that Lloyd George's threat to resume fighting was nothing more than a tactical device.

Fourthly, Collins saw no possibility during the negotiations of changing the constitutional status of Northern Ireland. He accepted Lloyd George's vague offer of a boundary commission to adjust the border with the Six Counties "in accordance with the wishes of the inhabitants, so far as may be compatible with economic and geographic conditions," only as a means of bringing the talks to an end by sidetracking the Northern question. In reality, he had little faith in a commission to solve the problem.

Unlike hostile republican commentators, I do not believe that Collins's republican attitudes altered while in London. His new-found appreciation of the virtues of dominion status, as expressed in an article under his name in the *Manchester Guardian* the day following the signing of the treaty, had no great significance, to judge by his appeasement of the republican opposition in the following six months.

Of course, Collins was well aware of the immense risks that he had taken in signing the treaty. He was unable to control nationalist reaction, even amongst the IRA and the IRB. During his last year of life, he tried to reconcile the contradiction between his public adherence to the carrying out of the treaty terms and his continuing commitment to separatist republicanism. In the first six months of 1922, Collins sought to avoid civil war by attempting to compromise on constitutional issues with the opposition by drawing up a republican constitution, by trying to use the IRB in peace initiatives, and by following a policy of prevarication and delay, notably in his notorious pact of 20 May with de Valera, which set up a joint Sinn Fein election panel to ensure that the June election did not appear like a referendum on the pact. The pact with de Valera also offered the prospect of a coalition government following the election. Collins's true instincts, however, remained with the republic – witness his role in planning a joint IRA Northern offensive from late January to June 1922. While reassuring the British government that he was doing his best to combat anti-treaty IRA activity on the border, and while publicly following a policy of accommodation with the Northern government, Collins supported the kidnapping of prominent loyalists as a retaliatory gesture for the arrest of the Northern IRA men, and he helped arrange an arms swap with Southern IRA divisions to avoid detection of their own arms by the British, who at that time were supplying military material to the provisional government.

The leopard, therefore, had not changed his spots. Collins frequently reassured old colleagues that the republic for him took precedence over the Anglo-Irish Treaty and that it was tactics not ends that divided them. Collins told the Sinn Fein Ard Fheis (convention) the day after his pact with de Valera was published that "unity at home was more important than any Treaty with the foreigner, and if unity could only be got at the expense of the Treaty – the Treaty would have to go."

In late May, however, Lloyd George summoned Griffith and Collins to London and read the riot act to them because of the draft Free State Constitution that he had just received. Collins had desperately resisted going to London then, and once there, he was determined to bring up grievances concerning the North rather than face up to questions on the constitution. At that time, Lionel Curtis, a civil servant in the Colonial Office, compared negotiating with Collins to writing on water; and Lloyd George described the water as "shallow and agitated." By that time, no one in the British government trusted Collins. He returned quickly to Ireland, while Griffith stayed in London and was forced to agree to British-dictated amendments to the Constitution. Two days before the election, when Collins urged Cork voters to make their choice irrespective of the Sinn Fein electoral pact, he was acknowledging the changed reality. British insistence on carrying out the treaty had ended any hope of political reconciliation between pro- and anti-treaty elements.

Even after the election gave a clear mandate for the establishment of the Free State, however, Collins showed great reluctance to deal with the republican challenge to the provisional government's authority in the form of an IRA occupation of the Four Courts and other major buildings in Dublin. Finally, his hand was forced by Westminster's hard-line, hysterical reaction to the assassination of Sir Henry Wilson in London on 22 June by two IRA men. Some evidence suggests that Collins gave the orders for the deed. He was certainly involved in abortive plans to help the assassins escape. It soon became clear that if Collins did not agree to removing the IRA from the Four Courts, the British would do it themselves. Politicians who were members of the provisional government had long been in favour of such an assertion of their authority. When faced with the final British ultimatum, Collins agreed reluctantly to begin the military conflict. He could no longer pursue his double game.

Collins may have hoped that the war would be short-lived and limited to Dublin. Prior to the attack on the Four Courts, he was aware that there was division within the IRA ranks and little enthusiasm for battle on the part of the key First Southern Division of the IRA, some of whom were allowed safe conduct back to Cork during the Dublin fighting. When the conflict did spread to the south and west and Collins had assumed the position of commander-in-chief, he showed a marked reluctance "to steam-roller the opposition," according to one of his senior officers. Collins also expressed opposition to the harsh censorship policy adopted by his colleagues. Demonstrating again that his attitudes had not changed, in early August Collins told members of the Northern units of the IRA, who had been stationed in the Curragh since evacuating the Six Counties, that at the earliest possible moment he would return to an aggressive policy against the Northern government.

Collins's doomed tour during August of army units in Munster was motivated by considerations other than those publicly stated. Through intermediaries, he was striving to achieve some form of accommodation with old colleagues. Notes made at the time suggest that he was thinking of allowing the republicans to return home without their arms, provided that they accept "the People's verdict." "We don't ask for any surrender of their principles," Collins wrote, and added, "We do not want to mitigate their weakness by resolute action beyond what is required."

The circumstances and the location of Collins's death – a confused ambush a few miles from the family home in West Cork, and the defection soon afterwards of the driver of the armoured car in his convoy to the republican side – have guaranteed controversy. Conspiracy theories based on circumstantial evidence point suspicion at British intelligence or at one of Collins's close colleagues, but the most plausible explanation is that the fatal shot came from a member of the ambushing party, who was unaware of the identity of his victim until the following day.

The debate over Collins's death is related to the debate over his decision to sign the Anglo-Irish Treaty. Republican sources, notably Sean

MacBride, have argued that Collins died the victim of pro-treaty and/or British political intrigue and that Collins remained true to his republican principles. On the other hand, Mary MacSwiney saw Collins as the most dangerous enemy. The Cork IRA's lacklustre contribution to the civil war may have been due to general dismay over Collins's death. Furthermore, long-term close military colleagues of Collins, such as Emmet Dalton and Liam Tobin, were soon to leave the pro-treaty forces in Cork.

Recently both J.J. Lee in his *Ireland 1912–1985* and Tim Pat Coogan in his Collins biography have debated Collins's possible contribution to Irish public life had he survived beyond age thirty-two. The loss of its one popular, charismatic figure was a major factor in the lack of popular support for the pro-treaty side after the civil war. Of the surviving leadership, Kevin O'Higgins had Collins's ability but little of his popularity, and Liam Cosgrave had a dour personality unlikely to win converts. The civil war became more bitter as a consequence of Collins's death, partly because Collins would most likely have opposed the execution of republican opponents. Of Collins's potential to lead the new state in directions different from those it took, there is cause for scepticism. Although he had shown considerable administrative ability and talent as a communicator, his economic views appear largely conservative. As minister of finance, he gave to his department a dominance reminiscent of the British Treasury. As a new nationalist, Collins gave priority to gaelicization. Where he did differ from leaders of the Free State who followed him was in the priority he gave to the Northern question.

The British government and civil service viewed Collins's death ambivalently. While concerned about the stability of the new Irish government in the midst of a civil war, some British commentators thought that he had paid his dues, and they contrasted the ease of dealing with William Cosgrave, the new president of the executive council, with Collins's "film-star attitudinising," a phrase used by the leading civil servant Sir Samuel Hoare.

Collins is the crucial figure in the final struggle for independence. Now that the centenary of his birth has passed, and after the success of Coogan's book, it should be some time before another biography is published. By that time, it may be easier to place Collins in a wider context than has so often been the case.

Dr. Michael Hopkinson was born in Farnham, Surrey, England, and educated at Plymouth College and Gonville and Caius College, Cambridge University, where he was awarded a Ph.D. for a thesis on the Irish Question in American politics between 1919 and 1923. From 1969 to 1971, he taught American history at the University of Kent at Canterbury, and from 1971 to 1974, Irish and American history at the Queen's University, Belfast. Since 1974, he has lectured in the same subjects at the University of Stirling, Scotland. In 1991 and 1992, he is visiting fellow at Murdoch University in Western Australia. His major publication is *Green against Green: A History of the Irish Civil War* (1988). He is contributing two sections for a forthcoming volume in *A New History of Ireland* and is researching a history of the Anglo-Irish War, a project financed by a Leverhulme Research Grant. He has published articles on the Craig-Collins Agreements of 1922 and on American reaction to the Anglo-Irish Treaty of December 1921. Michael Collins has been a constant feature of Dr. Hopkinson's work for many years. In addition, Michael Hopkinson is a keen armchair sports enthusiast and would like to write on sport and leisure.

Note

1 This paper develops various themes followed in the author's *Green Against Green: The Irish Civil War* (Dublin: Gill and Macmillan, 1988). T.P. Coogan's *Michael Collins, Biography* (London: Hutchison, 1990) contains much valuable new material. The major primary Irish sources are the Richard Mulcahy and Ernie O'Malley Papers in the University College, Dublin, Archives; the Michael Collins Papers in the Army Archives and the National Library; the Florence O'Donoghue Papers in the National Library; and Dail and Provisional Government Files in the State Paper Office. In Britain, much material relating to Collins is in the Cabinet and Colonial Office Papers in the Public Record Office.

Chapter 21

The Significance of Biography in Historical Study: T.W. Anglin and the Evolution of Canadian Nationalism

William M. Baker

> I think that an historian's chief interest is in character and in circumstance. His concern is to discover the hopes, fears, anticipations and intentions of the individuals and nations he is writing about. His task is to reproduce as best he can the circumstances, problems and situations faced by another person in another time. He seeks insight and understanding that cannot be gained through application of sociological rules and general explanations.
>
> – Donald Creighton[1]

There is much truth in Creighton's assertion. Indeed, how could history exist without individuals? That would be like geography without places. On the other hand, the physical and social sciences do not examine individuals, but rather the entire species, human or otherwise. Or so it is argued. Even if this is true, the reality of the sciences is that none of the "laws" are immutable and many are stated in terms of statistical probability. In fact, some important breakthroughs in the sciences are the result of focusing not on the typical but on the unusual and unique. In the spring 1991 semester, the sociology department of the University of Lethbridge offered a course entitled "Biography and Society." Perhaps we stodgy historians who have studied individuals and have been preparing biographies for 2,500 years[2] need not be embarrassed in the face of our academic colleagues; we may just be at the forefront on this one.

Nevertheless, over the past three decades, historical biography has been considered slightly passé, the resort of the academically marginal or intellectually indolent. The *Makers of Canada* series in twenty volumes (1903–1908), and W.J. Karr's mercifully short school text *The History of Canada through Biography* (1929) helped to discredit the genre. While the biographies of Creighton, Careless, and Eccles were admired and the establishment of the *Dictionary of Canadian Biography* was greeted with enthusiasm, historians hoped that Canadian historiography might move beyond its emphasis on biography and start to emulate the work of Fernand Braudel, E.P. Thompson, and Eugene Genovese. What now seems an appalling indictment of the backwardness of Canadian historiography appeared in S.R. Mealing's 1965 *Canadian Historical Review (CHR)* article that suggested that the concept of social class might be considered relevant, even useful, to the study of Canadian history.[3] Thus, while Alan Wilson's 1965 paper on "Forgotten Men of Canadian History" provided some sustenance to those like myself who persisted with a biographical approach,[4] the atmosphere was generally negative. Don Wilson's comment in a *CHR* review was not atypical, though written in 1975: "Biography is losing its appeal to professional historians [who] are shifting their interest to the study of the collective, of social groups in time, of 'history from the bottom up.'"[5] Even today, despite the fact that all historians devote time to biography, few confess to writing one. And yet biographies continue to win a large number of academic prizes; they appear as book club selections and on course reading lists; and they remain popular with readers.

Let me suggest an argument that may help to unseat the anti-biography cynic inhabiting Clio's mansion. The starting point, previously enunciated by this historian in a defence of local history,[6] is to postulate four propositions or concepts that may redefine and justify biography.

First of all, "anything is a sub-set of at least one other thing and anything has its own sub-set(s). The ear, for example, is one part of the body, and in turn has a variety of component parts." Any one thing is thus part of a continuum of greater and lesser things. As a category, biography is a sub-set of the history of various social, political, economic, and cultural groupings. My biography of Timothy Anglin,[7] for example, attempted to examine Anglin within a variety of contexts, including the mid-nineteenth-century Irish immigrant community in North America, the English-speaking Catholic community, New Brunswick society, and the Reform or Liberal political grouping. Articulating the sub-sets of historical biography is more difficult, but just as economic history has a series of component parts (entrepreneurial activity, industrial development, staple production), biography's sub-sets include political philosophy, religious convictions, social mobility, and family life.

The second proposition set forth in my defence of local history is that "there is no hierarchy of intrinsic importance along the continuum. In other words, bigger is not better and smaller is not more beautiful. In terms of one's study, what one focuses upon is not by definition more or less significant or important but simply a vantage point which, as is the case with any vantage point, has its advantages and disadvantages." This proposition implies that biography is not the servant of, for example, national history. It is simply a particular focus. The disadvantages of that perspective may include the difficulty of comprehending the nature of forces in the society that may not have been understood or acknowledged by the subject of the biography. The advantages may include the opportunity to understand real-life experience with all its confusions, contradictions, compromises, and convictions. If we agree with David Hackett Fischer that one of the fundamental values of historical study is "to help us to find out who we are," biography is a supremely useful way to "help people to learn about other selves."[8] But if this proposition provides a justification for biography, it also means that biography is not a vantage point that is necessarily superior to other approaches.

The third proposition is that "significance lies in the relationship of an item to other aspects of the continuum or the totality. Such significance exists by definition since every item is part of the continuum. Therefore, 'significance,' as one usually refers to it, really consists of demonstrating relationships up, down, and sideways; backwards and forwards; near and far along the continuum."

And the fourth concept is that "the totality of relationships (i.e., 'significance') can never be completely described or explained." The implications of these last two propositions are obvious: if a biography is to have "significance," it should explore relationships along the continuum. It might examine the influence upon the individual of several factors, including the climate of ideas, of economic trends, of political organization, of regional characteristics. Equally, it would investigate the impact of the individual on the several components of the society in which the individual was involved, whether these be voluntary organizations, economic groups, or political parties. In other words, biographical study is an examination of an individual in society, the individual created by and in turn creating that society.

In short, biography presents challenges and opportunities that differ little from those of other forms of historical study. Ged Martin has suggested that "by focusing on the individual, the biographical approach may unwittingly distort the overall picture."[9] True enough. But what approach to history does not pose the problem of distortion? Surely it takes little reflection to come up with examples of histories of social groups – whether political groups, religious organizations, gender divisions, or social classes – that distort the general picture. Even attempting to focus on the larger picture itself can be distorting because the lens is so far removed from its subject. Is not that our usual complaint about textbooks? Dr. Martin also posed the following question: "If history is a complex process of the interaction of forces and personalities, is it possible to distinguish the role of the individual?" Again, the dilemma is not unique to biographers; the issue of causational agency is a concern to all historians. Is it any easier for the historian of a social group to distinguish the role of the group in the evolution of a society? I think not. Our understanding of how things happen is never better than provisional and contingent. Thus, the task of the historian/biographer is similar to that of other historians. There will be more, and less, successful practitioners of biography, just as there will be uneven quality in any other approach to historical study.

One method of exploring the interaction between biography and history is to examine one nineteenth-century man and one facet of nineteenth-century society: on the one hand, Timothy Warren Anglin; on the other, the concept of nationalism. What were the relationships between the two? What effect did the communities in which Anglin resided have on his perceptions of a nation and his view of nationalism? Conversely, what impact did Anglin have on the shaping of the nation and the country's definition of itself?

A sketch of Anglin's life begins with his birth into a Catholic middle-class family at Clonakilty, County Cork, in 1822. He received a good classical education, but his plans for a legal career were disrupted by the Irish Famine. He turned to teaching in his home town. Then he emigrated to Saint John, New Brunswick, in 1849 and founded a newspaper, the *Freeman*, which remained under his editorship until 1883. The paper allowed Anglin to establish himself as a political personage and spokesperson for Irish Catholics in New Brunswick. Elected in 1861 to the New Brunswick assembly, he vigorously opposed the initiative for British North American union and, for a time, was a cabinet member in the short-lived anti-Confederate government. Nevertheless, and despite the fact that the 1866 electoral victory of pro-Confederate forces in New Brunswick was built on an anti-Anglin scare campaign,[10] Anglin acquiesced in the new political order after Confederation, and from 1867 to 1882 he was an elected member of Parliament in Ottawa and a prominent member of the Reform (Liberal) Party. During Alexander Mackenzie's administration of the mid-1870s, Anglin was Speaker of the House of Commons. Following his electoral defeat in 1882, he moved to Toronto, where he took over the *Tribune* and became an editorial contributor to the *Globe*. In the 1887 election he ran against D'Alton McCarthy and was defeated. Thereafter he lost status within the Liberal Party and as a journalist, in both of his newspaper positions. Indeed, while he remained active, Anglin was unable to secure permanent employment until shortly before his death in 1896. Yet he and his second wife raised an accomplished family, including Frank, who became chief justice of the Canadian Supreme Court, and Margaret, the internationally acclaimed actress. In the final analysis, perhaps the best index of Anglin's ultimate prominence is the list of pallbearers at his funeral, for they included the premier of Ontario (Oliver Mowat), a representative of the lieutenant-governor (Commander Law), and leading judicial, political, business, and intellectual personages, Catholic and Protestant (Justice Falconbridge, Sir Frank Smith, Eugene O'Keefe, B.B. Hughes, and Goldwin Smith).[11]

Nineteenth-century nationalism is not easily defined. At the most basic level it meant a sense of group consciousness, of belonging to a particular collectivity tied together by some or all of language, religion, culture, geography, and history, and different from other groups. In the heady days before the 1848 revolutions in Europe, nationalism was a politically radical movement aimed at transforming or overthrowing established governments. Thereafter, it became increasingly apparent that the political right could make good use of nationalism in order to consolidate the power of the state and the control over society by ruling elites. Bismarck is the most prominent example but hardly the only one. But whatever the political leaning of nationalism, the doctrine had a homogenizing tendency. Nationalism also gave rise to the belief that each nationality should have its own country, its own nation-state. Thus, the ideal of the nineteenth-century nationalist was to have a political entity made up of homogeneous people who governed themselves. Both Ireland and Canada presented rather interesting challenges to this concept.

Anglin was a man of three "countries": Ireland, New Brunswick, and Canada. Determining the precise influence of Ireland on Anglin is complicated by the fact that no evidence exists of his views during the first quarter-century of his life when he resided in Ireland. Nevertheless, the opinions he expressed in the following fifty years confirm the common-sense assumption that his Irish years were profoundly formative.[12] The Ireland of Anglin's youth was a society epitomized by struggles for political autonomy, religious freedom, and economic viability. Protestant and English domination meant severe religious and political restrictions for most Irish and contributed to economic retardation. As a consequence, there was much Irish hostility to the union of 1801 with Great Britain. Anglin shared this hostility and throughout his life urged that Ireland be freed from the British yoke.[13] He also gained a certain scepticism about political authorities in general, equating centralized governance with despotism, and devolution of power with freedom and progress.[14] Irish circumstances taught him that the crucial function of government was the mundane, everyday development of the people's standard of living rather than grandiose affairs of state[15] and that, for this purpose, local governments were more responsive and effective than distant rulers. The consequence of rule from afar, Anglin claimed in 1863, was that the government of Ireland was "one of the worst in Europe," with the Irish people having to support a church establishment, absentee landlords, and increasingly heavy taxation despite diminished population and poor harvests.[16] But he was not cynical about politics per se, because Daniel O'Connell's non-violent agitation for Catholic emancipation had demonstrated the efficacy of mass political action.[17] Moreover, O'Connell's campaign argued the necessity of the political involvement of all responsible citizens of a country and the importance of the cooperation of those citizens for the common welfare. Thus, for Anglin, the Great Famine[18] had brought about at least one good. Shortly after his emigration from Ireland, he wrote:

> The good, the wise, and the charitable of every religion, and of every class in Society, forgetting every thing that had so long divided them, united heart and soul to work for the relief of their suffering countrymen. The Catholic Priests and the Protestant Rectors struggled together, might and main, to succour and relieve their afflicted people, never stopping to ask if this man were a Catholic, or that a Protestant. Those insane and contemptible feuds that had so long divided and weakened the people, and delivered them as it were bound hand and foot, to be dealt with by their Alien Government as it pleased, were now looked back with regret by

men who had once engaged in them earnestly. Irishmen began at length
to see that if they wished to save their country, the union of all classes and
of all religion was necessary.[19]

The influence of Ireland on Anglin was lasting. Even in 1880 he described
himself as "one who, though a Canadian, still regards himself as an Irishman,"[20] and as late as 1892–93 he was writing and giving speeches in
support of Home Rule for Ireland.

What of the individual's impact on society? As far as we know, Anglin
had little influence on the history of Ireland or on its concept of nationalism in the second quarter of the nineteenth century. There is little doubt
that he sympathized with the Young Ireland movement, which led the
abortive Irish uprising of 1848; rumours later circulated that he had been
involved in the only so-called battle of that sorry revolt, but Anglin flatly
denied the assertion.[21] It is possible, however, that as a schoolteacher in
Clonakilty he played a role in the traumatic events of the 1840s. Thomas
Flanagan's historical novels, *The Year of the French* and *The Tenants of Time*,
note the importance of schoolmasters in preserving and promoting Irish
national identity prior to and throughout the nineteenth century.

Anglin's Irish experience shaped his thinking on nationalism and polity.
He opposed domination from outside; he was wary of grandiose rhetoric that
ignored real-life problems; and he eschewed doctrines that attempted to weld
people into a homogeneous mass. Unlike D'Alton McCarthy and John Macoun,
also Irish born, Anglin was a member of the dominated and repressed Catholic majority. Not surprisingly, he was concerned with establishing Irish autonomy and with achieving rights, freedoms, and prosperity for Catholics
within the country. In other words, for Anglin, the lessons of the Irish experience were different than they were for McCarthy and Macoun, both of whom
later stressed assimilation to an Anglo-Protestant norm and adherence to the
imperial connection.[22] By contrast, Anglin was more willing to compromise
on the matter of ethno-religious conformity in defining a Canadian, and he
remained lukewarm, though pragmatic, about the relationship with Britain.
Anglin's position on the nature of Canadian nationality was the one that
emerged victorious in 1867 and following decades.

Before he became a Canadian, Anglin was a New Brunswicker. In
general, the New Brunswick years (1849–67) reinforced Anglin's sense of
nationalism and its utility. In his view a society should be judged by its
works and deeds, not by its appeals to group loyalty, which frequently
served to camouflage corruption and class rule. Nor was constitutional

form the crucial factor, since any form of government was worthless, he pointed out, "if the spirit of freedom and order and good government did not pervade the people as a whole, if they did not know how to reconcile the largest measure of individual liberty and personal rights with a profound respect for 'authority' and 'laws.' "[23] Although he constantly fought against prejudice and inequality of rights for Irish Catholics and found much to criticize in the political practices and development of New Brunswick, he discovered that circumstances were so much better there than they had been in Ireland that he became a New Brunswick patriot. Even his attitude towards Britain shifted, as was evident in the *Freeman*'s comment made during the visit of the Prince of Wales in 1860:

> We have never been accused of any excess of what in New Brunswick is called loyalty; we have never professed an intensity of attachment to her Majesty's person, or to her crown and dignity. When the power exercised in her name is oppressive and tyrannical, we never hesitate to denounce it, and there was a time when, in another country, we heartily desired its utter overthrow; but in this Province, where the people now enjoy so full a share of civil and religious liberty, where the Crown is the symbol of liberty and order and justice, founded on law, and there is no longer any wrong, save of the people's own doing, or any tyranny but such as we ourselves create for one another, the head of the Government is surely entitled to more than empty professions, even from those who have been warmest in asserting the people's rights.[24]

During the *Trent* incident, Anglin made clear his loyalty to New Brunswick. He argued that, contrary to what Yankees thought, the provinces of British North America enjoyed the right of self-government and that the connection with England was "merely nominal," except "in time of danger." The provinces now made their own laws, levied their own taxes, and spent revenues as they pleased, and they would strongly resist any American invasion. As for the Irish of New Brunswick, Anglin proclaimed, "the same sense of justice and love of right which in Ireland would make them rebels makes them conservatives in these Provinces. They value the blessings of liberty, sustained and regulated by law, and ... they know their duty to the country in which they live and of whose people they are truly an integral part, and knowing it will perform it."[25]

In his warning to the Americans, he seems to have thought in terms of the British North American colonies as a whole. Yet his response to the

Confederation initiative demonstrated that his real identification was with New Brunswick. Anglin was not keen on union, although he believed it a fine dream for the future, particularly if Britain broke the imperial connection. But at the time union was proposed, Anglin considered it neither necessary nor beneficial. Union would bring neither military strength nor substantial economic advantages, at least not for the ordinary residents in most of New Brunswick. The main beneficiaries, Anglin asserted, would be the politicians and businessmen of the Canadas whose extravagance, extremism, and incompetence had created that colony's difficulties. Public men there, and in the other colonies, would be better to occupy themselves in promoting essential material development, such as the building of roads, assistance to settlers, and the removal of barriers to mercantile activity, rather than in indulging in "chimeras and fancies at the public expense."[26] A major barrier to union, as far as Anglin was concerned, was the lack of community between the disparate, detached colonies of British North America, a fact not easily overcome by union.[27]

It is not surprising, therefore, that he opposed the proposal for union that emerged from the Quebec Resolutions of 1864. He considered the financial arrangements unacceptable. And he feared that tariffs would be raised; that Saint John would lag behind in transportation development and manufacturing; that representation by population would leave New Brunswick's distinct interests vulnerable; and that the scheme really called for not a federal but a legislative union that would effectively destroy New Brunswick. He was especially outraged at the intent of the delegates to Quebec not to submit the resolutions to the electorate, but merely to the colonial legislatures. "This is clearly a conspiracy," he warned, "to defraud and cheat the people out of the right to determine for themselves whether this Union shall now take place."[28]

The story of the circuitous route taken by New Brunswick into Confederation – the necessity of the Tilley government to call an election; the rapid disintegration of the victorious anti-Confederate government, with Anglin as minister without portfolio; and its subsequent defeat in the 1866 election – is a tale that cannot be told here. Note, however, that Anglin's Irish Catholic roots and sympathies became the basis of a so-called loyalty campaign by the Confederates against the antis. One New Brunswick newspaper, revelling in the success of the Confederates in 1866, maintained that the results meant that "Fenianism and Annexation, or, in one word, Warren-Anglinism was 'taken in and done for,' and the disloyal Fenian sympathizing brood fairly squelched."[29]

An examination of Anglin's views of nationalism and associated concepts during the Confederation struggle reveals much continuity in his thinking. In the first place, the intention of the Confederates to let the legislatures decide about joining the proposed union offended Anglin's democratic sense that it was preferable to let the people determine their political destiny. Secondly, the energy and resources needed to forge a new nation would sap the ability of leaders to provide for the material development of New Brunswickers, a major priority of Anglin's. Thirdly, the Confederates' tactics prior to and during the 1866 election increased Anglin's concern about the deleterious effects that appeals to nationalism had on minorities such as Irish Catholics. Finally, his concern about union with a vastly more populous and powerful polity was informed by the experience of Ireland in the union of 1801. He believed that New Brunswick, the territory to which he had given his allegiance, would be obliterated as a meaningful entity after Confederation. In June 1867, the *Freeman* ran an obituary notice for the province.[30]

However, the effect of Anglin's own experience on his views of the nation at the time of Confederation is made evident by comparison with that of others. D'Arcy McGee was Irish Catholic, Archbishop Connolly of Halifax a Maritimer, and Bishop Rogers a New Brunswicker;[31] yet all were prominent supporters of Confederation. Thus, while Anglin's Irish Catholic and New Brunswick background provided one perspective for viewing the Confederation proposal, other crucial factors were involved, such as his political opposition to the Tilley government in New Brunswick. Indeed, one could even make the case that his loyalty was not really to New Brunswick as a whole, but rather to the city and region of Saint John.

The impact of "history" on Anglin is readily apparent. What of his influence on history? Even if Anglin's contributions to the evolution of New Brunswick prior to the 1860s are ignored, it is evident that he was an effective force in the history of the Confederation struggle. The test of the counter-factual hypothesis is useful, for had Anglin not been involved, it is conceivable that the union proposal might have carried in 1865. Had Anglin's trenchant and cogent critique not been available to the New Brunswick public, the basis of opposition would have been more restricted and less vigorous. Had he not been present as a practising politician, his ability to translate anti-Confederate sentiment into practical politics would have been severely hampered. Thus, Anglin is a key figure in the defeat of union in 1865. Equally, however, he is central to the defeat of the anti-Confederates in New Brunswick in 1866. He became the target for the

Confederate campaign. In his person the union forces were able to focus all of the apparent threats to the colony: the fears of disloyalty to the Empire, of Fenian invasion, of annexation to the United States, of a Catholic conspiracy. In the struggle for Confederation in the mid-1860s in New Brunswick, Anglin played a prominent part. Of course, one might argue that his impact on history was fleeting, since he "lost"!

But such a view would be excessively narrow in its conception of the nature of causation and of the complexity of historical development. Confederation was not the triumph of one side over the other, not at least in the sense of a victory of centralist nationalists over provincialists. From the very beginning, Canadian Confederation was a delicate and shifting balance between centralist and regional impulses. Anglin represented one extreme of that balance. In his articulation of opposition to the Quebec Resolutions, he gave voice to the sentiments that have been behind provincial rights from his day to ours. He revealed the "provincial loyalties" side of British North American attitudes at the very heart of the creation of the nation. And by participating in the establishment of a dialogue among Canadians on the subject of federal-provincial powers, he contributed to the history of the country in a far from transitory way. Moreover, in his adjustment to the new nation, Anglin demonstrated Canada's ability to make converts.

In spite of his vigorous opposition to Confederation, there were aspects of Anglin's earlier perceptions that made his post-1867 outlook on Canada less negative than might have been expected. If the new regime in Ottawa could avoid camouflaging corruption and incompetence with bombastic nationalism, if it could avoid repression of minorities, if it could concentrate on economic development, if, in other words, it could provide good and just government, then Anglin would not oppose the experiment in nation-building. After all, he had transferred his loyalties to New Brunswick in the 1850s. There was no reason to believe he could not become a Canadian patriot in the 1870s.

Anglin's adjustment to the new nation began in 1867 when he decided to be a candidate in the first federal election. After his opposition to Confederation and his defeat in 1866, this was a significant step. He could have participated in politics on the provincial rather than the national level, but he was trapped by the very nature of his opposition to union. He had proclaimed that real power would reside with the central government and that the New Brunswick legislature would be insignificant. Given this view, one would stand for the parliament in Ottawa, for only there could the interests of New Brunswickers be protected. As Anglin saw it, while the question of union had been fully settled by the electorate, former antis had a continuing responsibility "to do all we can to make it as beneficial or as little hurtful as possible."[32] His new view of Confederation was logical, however ludicrous it seems that he was anti-Confederation and then sought election to the great distant parliament. Anglin still looked for efficient government and for the well-being of New Brunswick. Thus, he urged electors to select candidates "who, while willing to work with any party (no matter what its appellation) that was disposed to do what was just and fair, would above all feel bound to guard the interests of this Province."[33] In short, at this point Anglin's view on nationalism seems to have been that of an advocate of provincial rights.

By 1872, the final year of Canada's first parliament, Anglin had become more centralist, or pan-Canadian, in outlook. Of course, he had a wonderful time twitting those who had predicted that Confederation would bring great advantages to New Brunswick, but he rejected the options of obstruction, repeal, or annexation.[34] The people may have made a bad choice, but in Anglin's view they had made an irrevocable decision. "It is no use to wriggle under the yoke which they must carry," he argued, "or to believe that any change in its adjustment can make it very much less burdensome or less galling."[35] Yet Anglin recognized that as bad as things were for New Brunswick, they might have been worse. Over and over he demonstrated his acceptance of the new system by his extensive involvement in it; he was in fact one of the most active New Brunswick members in the Commons. His activity, his complaints, and his criticisms all implied that he believed that something could be done to alleviate New Brunswick's situation through political means. He had little hope that improvement would come from the provincial government,[36] and therefore he placed emphasis on the federal system to secure provincial interests, as much as that was possible.

Anglin had worried about the treatment of religio-ethnic minorities, particularly Irish Catholics, in the new union. After Confederation, he became their defender, not an easy task during a period of Fenian scares and the assassination of Thomas D'Arcy McGee. Anglin urged Irish Catholics to prove that they were honourable citizens, but he also maintained that the rest of the community had to stop discriminating against them. In urging ethnic and religious tolerance, Anglin was voicing his vision for the new country. "If this Dominion is ever to be as great, and strong, and powerful as its founders anticipate," he preached in the *Freeman*, "all these old-world feuds must be forgotten, and all its people must work together harmoniously to promote its prosperity and consolidate its strength, no sect, or denomination, or association seeking to degrade, to pull down or keep down any other, but each working earnestly and zealously for the elevation and aggrandisement of all."

Anglin was sure that Irish Catholics did not receive this kind of justice in Canada, but he saw no need to undertake an aggressive campaign for Irish Catholic rights. Indeed, he believed that the destiny of Irish Catholics in Canada was to find a reasonably comfortable position in Canadian life, one in which, far from being isolated from the mainstream, they would be an integral part of the country. Once again, he based his assessment of a nation on practical realities. The condition of Irish Catholics in Canada was not perfect, but it was improving, and at least they were better off than the American Irish.[37]

There is much additional evidence to indicate that Anglin quickly adopted a Canadian perspective. In the late 1860s he objected to the acquisition of the Northwest and British Columbia because such financial and territorial overburden threatened the very existence of the country. He castigated the Treaty of Washington (1871) as a base betrayal of Canadian interests. And he urged the federal government to intervene in the New Brunswick schools question in order to secure Catholic rights that he claimed were being violated by the provincial government. Frequently he was critical of policies initiated by Sir John A. Macdonald's government. But it is only by assuming that Macdonald and company were the only true nationalists that Anglin's views can be termed anti-national. By 1872 Anglin had become a member of the loyal opposition, as he attached himself to the emerging Reform Party under Alexander Mackenzie.

The Canadianization of Anglin continued apace after 1872. Much to his chagrin, the outcome of the New Brunswick schools issue demonstrated that the provinces were not as impotent as he had predicted. However, the defeat of the Catholic case pushed Anglin away from a desire to protect and promote provincial powers, confirming his view that the real hope of securing justice lay with the national government. The outcome did much to make Ottawa rather than Fredericton the prime object of his loyalty. Thus, Anglin's disgust with the Pacific Scandal reflected not only his party loyalties and his long-standing views on the ethical responsibility of public persons but also his sense that the scandal disgraced the national government and undermined the confidence of citizens in Canada itself.

Perhaps the ultimate irony of Anglin's career was that this fierce opponent of union in the mid-1860s became the "First Commoner" of the Dominion of Canada in 1874. As Speaker of the House of Commons under the Mackenzie administration, he held a prominent social position in the dominion, a factor that no doubt increased his loyalty to the nation. It was, in a sense, a vindication of his hope that Irish Catholics would come to occupy a proper social position in Canada. "The cause must be weighty and important indeed, and the necessity great and manifest," he once said as Speaker, "which would justify the dividing up of the Canadian body politic, so that instead of the people with interests in common we should become a set of associations, Catholic and Protestant, Irish, English, French and Scotch."[38] In 1877 he went so far as to claim that Canada had created a national society "to which all Canadians do actually and really belong."[39]

So thoroughly had Anglin transferred his loyalties away from New Brunswick that within a year of his defeat in the 1882 election he moved to Toronto. In a way this merely verified his warnings two decades earlier that central Canada would be the locus of power in the union, but it also refuted his prophecy that Canada would not be able to create a sense of community among its people. Moreover, Anglin's transfer to Ontario was an example of how political accommodation on the leadership level could promote national loyalty, for it was a strategic plan of the Liberal Party that brought him there. Anglin believed that politics and patriotism were inseparable. He supported the Liberals, he once explained, because of their adherence to the fundamental principles of good government: "They believe that government should be for the good of the whole people; that justice, truth, and right ought to be the guiding motives in every public transaction, as in every act of private life; and that under no circumstances would the people be justified in swerving a hair's breadth from those principles." Devotion to such standards would result in banishing religious and ethnic prejudices, which in turn would promote genuine national unity. "It is absolutely necessary that we stand together," he argued, "upon the basis of equal rights, and perfect justice, and thorough fair-play between denomination and denomination, between race and race, between sect and sect, that we may be in reality as we are in name, one Canadian people."[40]

Anglin's career in Ontario did not blossom. He failed to wean Ontario's Catholics away from the federal Conservatives; he was defeated by D'Alton McCarthy in the 1887 election; he lost his Toronto newspaper, the Catholic *Tribune*, and his editorial position with the *Globe*; and during the decade prior to his death in 1896, he lurched from one temporary patronage position to another. Yet this did not seem to undermine his identification with Canada. In 1888, for instance, he was an Ontario commissioner to an exposition in Cincinnati. As frequently happens to Canadians, Anglin found his patriotic pride excited by contact with Americans. He bragged about the extensive agricultural and mineral potential of Canada and defended its climate against the stereotype of frigidity.[41]

His four months in Cincinnati confirmed the mild anti-Americanism that had become part of Anglin's Canadian patriotism. In the mid-1870s he had claimed that the American government was wasteful and inefficient and that its society was corrupt and immoral. Annexation was unthinkable. Maintaining the imperial connection was accepted, for it guaranteed independence and liberty for Canada at no cost to Canadians.[42] Anglin's Canadian experience had modified his attitudes towards Great Britain developed during his childhood in Ireland.

Indeed, by the 1880s Anglin's Canadian perspective was so entrenched that it was influencing his views on Ireland. He favoured Home Rule for Ireland not just because it would provide a substantial measure of autonomy but also because the Canadian experiment provided a successful prototype. Canada's positive attitude to Britain had increased after the establishment of responsible government, and the same would be true for Ireland. Anglin told Lord Lorne that if the imperial government really wanted to replace ill feelings, separatism, and agitation in Ireland with goodwill and harmony, then London "must strive to ascertain rather how much of self government and how much of legislative independence can be allowed to Ireland, with safety to the Empire than how little will serve to keep Ireland quiet for a time."

Moreover, the federal system of Canada, whatever its faults, was proving to be a flexible and effective compromise between central authority and local control, especially given Premier Mowat's defence of provincial rights during the decade following Confederation. It was thus a model for Ireland, though Anglin felt that even greater devolution would be necessary in the Irish case – perhaps more akin to the relationship of Canada to the Empire than the provinces to the national government. The Irish government, he argued, must have control of civil rights, property, education, municipal affairs, landlord-tenant relations, public works, and so on.[43]

Canada also provided a positive example of the ability of people of different religions to get along, and Anglin was sanguine that Home Rule would promote religious tolerance rather than animosity, since Protestants had always been treated justly by the majority in Ireland. This was a very

Canadian perspective on the Irish problem, but Anglin felt that Canadians, particularly those of Irish extraction, had every right to give advice based on their experience.

Anglin had come full circle. His initial views of patriotism and the nation in New Brunswick and Canada had been shaped by his Irish Catholic background. This perspective was far from eradicated but it was transformed to the point where his Canadian experience with nationalism and loyalty substantially informed his views even about Ireland. His perspective on Canada had altered radically. Once an opponent of Canadian union, he became a proponent of provincial rights, then finally a proud patriot of a country whose federal system had proved effective and beneficial. The received interpretation of the 1867–96 period is that it was a time of economic difficulties, dashed hopes, and social conflict. The country seemed to have failed, and "truly national sentiments had apparently declined in strength," or so Creighton claimed.[44] Anglin's views may not pass Creighton's litmus test of what was acceptably "national." However, Anglin's evolution from the anti-Confederate of 1865 to a spokesperson for the country in the 1870s and 1880s arguably demonstrates the surprising strength of the concept of the Canadian nation as it developed in the post-Confederation era.

History clearly had its influence on Anglin. In turn, Anglin's impact was not negligible, though it is more difficult to demonstrate. But again, the null hypothesis is revealing. Had Anglin remained hostile to the new country after 1867; had he promoted repeal or annexation or revolution; had he not preached moderation and accommodation to his fellow Irish Catholics in British North America; had he not cooperated with the political party system that emerged from central Canada; indeed, had his primary focus been turned to achieving independence for his native land rather than to seeking to make his adopted one a prosperous and humane country, one cannot doubt that Canada's course would have been different to some degree. Anglin was not alone in defining the nation, but his contribution was important. In his opposition to the union proposal, he served notice that provincial sensibilities and concerns would be a fact of Canadian life. In expressing the view that politicians ought to promote material development and socio-cultural diversity rather than homogeneous nationalism by means of flamboyant rhetoric, Anglin was voicing the opinion of many Canadians. More than that, it was the only formula for a Canadian national identity that stood much of a chance of survival, given the strong regional, religious, and ethnic loyalties in post-Confederation

Canada. In short, Anglin's contribution to Canadian history is not so much that of a leading New Brunswick anti-Confederate or a Speaker of the House of Commons, but more that of a representative of those whose opinions and activities developed the practical definition of a nation wherein regions, provinces, and a national centre constantly search for balance. Thus, the nation and Anglin were involved in a reciprocal relationship. And for both, it seems to have been a beneficial exchange. Equally, the study of Anglin and the study of the concept of nation provide numerous examples of the benefits of combining biography and history. Not only is each enriched by the association but, quite simply, neither could do without the other.

William M. Baker is a professor of history at the University of Lethbridge, where he has taught since 1970. He is the author of *Timothy Warren Anglin, 1822–1896: Irish Catholic Canadian*, and has written articles on the Irish in Canada and on the Confederation era. In addition, he has studied the history of southern Alberta, particularly the 1906 coalminers' strike in Lethbridge. His interest in biography has remained strong, and he is currently preparing a volume of reports and other writings of R. Burton Deane, a North-West Mounted Police superintendent in southern Alberta from 1888 to 1914, for the Alberta Historical Records Publication Board. Future projects include a biography of Deane and a stage play based on Deane's experiences. Professor Baker is enamoured of biography because of the way it enables the historian to comprehend history in its most fundamentally human dimension, that of the individual within society.

Notes

1 Quoted in frontispiece of J.S. Moir, ed., *Character and Circumstance: Essays in Honour of Donald Grant Creighton* (Toronto: Macmillan, 1970).

2 A. Momigliano, *The Development of Greek Biography* (Cambridge, Mass.: Harvard University Press, 1971), 101.

3 S.R. Mealing, "The Concept of Social Class and the Interpretation of Canadian History," *Canadian Historical Review (CHR)* 46, no. 3 (September 1965): 201–18.

4 A. Wilson, "Forgotten Men of Canadian History," *Canadian Historical Association Annual Report*, 1965, 71–86.

5 D. Wilson, review of R.S. Patterson, J.W. Chambers, and J.W. Friesen, eds., *Profiles of Canadian Educators* (Toronto: D.C. Heath, 1974), in *CHR* 56, no. 3 (September 1975): 335.

6 W.M. Baker, "'So What's the Importance of the Lethbridge Strike of 1906?': Local History and the Issue of Significance," *Prairie Forum* 12, no. 2 (Fall 1987): 295–300.

7 W.M. Baker, *Timothy Warren Anglin 1822–1896: Irish Catholic Canadian* (Toronto: University of Toronto Press, 1977).

8 D.H. Fischer, *Historians' Fallacies: Toward a Logic of Historical Thought* (New York: Harper & Row, 1970), 315–16.

9 In his call for papers for the conference on biography at the Centre for Canadian Studies, Edinburgh, May 1991.

10 W.M. Baker, "Squelching the Disloyal, Fenian-Sympathizing Brood: T.W. Anglin and Confederation in New Brunswick, 1865–6," *CHR* 55, no. 2 (June 1974): 141–58.

11 Saint John Regional Library, Raymond Scrapbooks, vol. 14, 28. For details of Anglin's activities and views, see author's biography.

12 Anglin was knowledgeable about the history of his native land. In 1872, for example, he published a series of lengthy and learned articles in which he challenged the interpretation of Irish and Catholic history expounded by the eminent historian James Anthony Froude while lecturing in the United States. See *Freeman*, second and third week of November 1872. On 7 January 1873, the newspaper refuted Goldwin Smith's arguments concerning Ireland and its history.

13 See, for example *Freeman*, n.d., quoted in *Morning News* (Saint John), 18 February 1850; *Freeman*, 21 November 1863; *Gazette* (Montreal), 18 March 1868; National Archives of Canada (NA), Lord Lorne Papers, MG 27 (I B 4), Anglin to Lorne, 12 June 1883; and T.W. Anglin, "What Does Home Rule for Ireland Mean?" *Lake Magazine* 1 (November 1892): 200–9.

14 *Freeman*, 9 October 1866.

15 Ibid., 15 August 1863.

16 Ibid., 21 November 1863.

17 Ibid., 5 August 1875; and *Globe*, 6 June 1883.

18 The recollection of that calamity once brought Anglin to tears when speaking in the New Brunswick assembly (see *Daily Evening Globe* [Saint John], quoted in *Freeman*, 12 April 1866).

19 'J. A.' [Anglin] to Editor, *Morning News* (Saint John), 18 July 1849.

20 Canada, House of Commons, *Debates, 1880,* 20 February, 126–27.

21 *Freeman*, 12 July 1864 and 19 May 1866; New Brunswick, House of Assembly, *Debates, 1866,* 7 April, 105; and NA, New Brunswick, Lieutenant Governor's Letter Book, RG 7, G 8 B, vol. 62, Arthur Gordon to Duke of Newcastle, 31 December 1862.

22 See, for example, J.R. Miller, "D'Alton McCarthy, Jr.: A Protestant Irishman Abroad," chap. 17; and W.A. Waiser, *The Field Naturalist: John Macoun, the Geological Survey, and Natural Science* (Toronto: University of Toronto Press, 1989).

23 *Freeman*, 8 August 1863.

24 Ibid., 22 March 1860.

25 Ibid., 31 December 1861.

26 Ibid., 15 August 1863.

27 Ibid., 13 August 1863.

28 Ibid., 3 November 1864.

29 *Morning Telegraph* (Saint John), 7 June 1866.

30 *Freeman*, 15 June 1867.

31 R.B. Burns, "Thomas D'Arcy McGee," *Dictionary of Canadian Biography*, vol. 9, *1861–1870*, edited by Francess G. Halpenny (Toronto: University of Toronto Press, 1976), 489–94; D.B. Flemming, "Thomas Louis Connolly," *DCB*, vol. 10, *1871–1880*, edited by Francess G. Halpenny (Toronto: University of Toronto, 1972), 191–93; and A.L. McFadden, "The Rt. Rev. James Rogers, D.D.: First Bishop of Chatham, N.B.," *Canadian Catholic Historical Association Report, 1947–1948*, 53–58. On the dispute between Anglin and Rogers over Confederation, see W.M. Baker, "Document: The 1866 Election in New Brunswick: The Anglin-Rogers Controversy," *Acadiensis* 17, no. 1 (Autumn 1987): 97–116.

32 *Freeman*, 29 June 1867.

33 Ibid., 11 April 1867.

34 Ibid., 7, 11 and 18 January 1868; 16 July 1868; 20 March 1869; 3 and 6 July 1869; 31 January 1871; 6 and 8 July 1871; 7 October 1871; and 7 November 1871.

35 Ibid., 11 January 1868.

36 Ibid., 2 November 1867.

37 Ibid., 15 and 18 July 1871.

38 Ibid., 19 June 1877.

39 Ibid., 20 November 1877.

40 *Globe* (Toronto), 6 and 8 June 1883.

41 *Ontario's Exhibit at the Centennial Exposition of the Ohio Valley and Central States: Report of Hon. Timothy W. Anglin, Ontario, Sessional Papers, 1889*, no. 30, 6.

42 *Freeman*, 25 April 1876; 4 December 1877; and 25 November 1875.

43 NA, Lorne Papers, Anglin to Lorne, 12 June 1883.

44 D.G. Creighton, *John A. Macdonald*, vol. 2, *The Old Chieftain* (Toronto: Macmillan, 1956), 484.

Chapter 22

The Two Solitudes of
History and Biography

R.B. Fleming

Biography is indeed a "comfortable way of gaining access to the complexity of history," as J.R. Miller argues in chapter 17. Biography focuses on one individual, and the world is seen through his or her eyes. At the same time, the good biographer sketches in the background, moves the supporting cast on and off stage, and once in a while adds a correction or commentary, perhaps in the manner of a Greek chorus. History becomes more accessible. Biography does indeed simplify and clarify history.

At the same time, however, biography makes history more complex. In fact, without biography, without the biographies of the people who surround any event or issue, that event may appear at best two-dimensional. Furthermore, by focusing almost exclusively on documents without examining the biographies of the creators of those documents, historians may be committing the very error that biographers are accused of committing, that of oversimplification and omission.

To demonstrate how biography can reveal a multi-dimensional past, let me examine Sir William Mackenzie's relationships with his friends, associates, and antagonists, who were united by profit and efficiency, regulation and paranoia during the age of industrial capitalism from 1890 to 1920. Michael Bliss has called them "All in the Family," for they acted like a family unit, sitting on each other's boards, raising capital for each other, inviting each other to weddings, banquets, and parties. They rejoiced together and they grieved together; they carefully guarded family and business secrets; and like all good families, from time to time they feuded with one another. The relationships of these men help to demonstrate a paradox of biography: at the same time that biography makes history more accessible, it shows the past in all its human complexities.

I have called biography and history two solitudes, that very Canadian of metaphors, because I suspect that there remains among historians a lingering suspicion of biography, not, admittedly, as great as that of the eighteenth-century historian who confessed that he had "several times deviated and descended from the dignity of an historian, and voluntarily fallen into the lower class of biographers,"[1] or as great as that of W.H. Auden, who sniffed that biographers were nothing but "gossip-writers and voyeurs calling themselves scholars."[2]

On the other hand, I am not suggesting that we should agree with Thomas Carlyle that history is but the "essence of innumerable biographies,"[3] or with Benjamin Disraeli, who once advised people to "read no history; nothing but biography, for that is life without theory,"[4] or with W.B. Yeats, who suggested that "all knowledge is biography."[5]

A good biographer is always aware of the craft's biases: biography tends to exaggerate the role of the protagonist, while diminishing the supporting cast. One has only to read Creighton's biography of Macdonald to realize that when Canada is viewed through Laurentian eyes, regions and Riels are diminished in stature. Furthermore, biography of necessity ignores 99 percent of humans, the ordinary mortals who live and die leaving few traces, although collective biography rectifies that bias to some extent and social historians are broadening biography's base by recalling figures who in their day were known to few people.

Having confessed some of biography's biases, I now focus on Sir William Mackenzie in order to show how an investigation of the interconnections of lives can enrich history. Mackenzie was a figure both fascinating and frustrating for a biographer: he was full of inventions, he left few personal papers, and he disliked biographers. According to Augustus Bridle, Mackenize would have thrown his biographer from the third-floor window of his office in Toronto – or he would have given him or her a job so useful that there would have been no time for writing a biography.[6]

Mackenzie was born in 1849, in Eldon Township, Victoria County, near Lindsay, Ontario. His parents, members of the great wave of post-Napoleonic migration to North America, came to the Canadas about 1832, settling in Eldon Township a year or so before the Rebellions of 1837. In his youth, Mackenzie was a storekeeper, teacher, and reeve of the township, thus combining politics, profits, and patronage. He was a contractor for Ontario railways in the 1870s, and in the 1880s he built snowsheds and bridges for the Canadian Pacific Railway (CPR) in British Columbia. By 1891 he was a millionaire. Had he died that year at age forty-one, he would have deserved no more than a brief article in the *Dictionary of Canadian Biography*.

The memorable part of Mackenzie's career began in 1891, when he and three partners bought the horse-drawn Toronto Railway Company. By 1894 they had converted it to electricity. Within the next decade Mackenzie and his colleagues in Toronto and Montreal modernized urban transportation systems in several continents. From 1895 to 1918, with his partner, Sir Donald Mann, Mackenzie built the Canadian Northern Railway, one of Canada's three transcontinentals. In 1918 this railway was nationalized because its owners could no longer pay the interest on its enormous bonded indebtedness. It is for this grand failure, as well as for connections with patronage in Toronto in the 1890s, that Mackenzie is known today. He died in 1923. Although he was a friend of and adviser to three prime ministers and several premiers, and was toasted on three continents prior to the First World War, he is almost forgotten today.

Two important topics connected with Mackenzie were railway competition and electrical power in Ontario, issues that have been examined by several historians who have used sources such as government documents, board minutes, newspapers, and scarce private correspondence.

Let us begin with railway competition. Historians of development generally credit railways for opening the West to Euro-Canadian settlement. The CPR played that role, but it ended up being disliked for its monopoly clause and its apparently unfair freight rates. It is also generally agreed that the two new transcontinentals, the Grand Trunk Pacific and the Canadian Northern Railway, were competitors of the CPR and thus became the friends of farmers and politicians who benefited, each in their own way, from competition and reduced rates. That seems to be the thrust of T.D. Regehr's scholarly study *The Canadian Northern Railway*, published in 1976. John Eagle's *The Canadian Pacific Railway and the Development of Western Canada*, published in 1989, follows a similar line of argument.

Granted, this interpretation of the history of railways and competition is sound. An examination of the official documents does indeed lead to the conclusion that there was competition, sometimes quite ruthless, among the several railways that opened the Canadian West. The biographer, however, casts the net a bit farther in order to catch the lives of the men who were intimately connected with development and competition.

Behind closed doors, Mackenzie was always friendly with Sir William

Van Horne, president of the CPR. Mackenzie was a trusted contractor of the CPR. Van Horne sat on the board of Mackenzie's Winnipeg Electric Railway. The two men travelled together to England during the 1890s in search of investment money, and the CPR lent support in the form of workers and equipment for the construction of the first section of the Canadian Northern. In 1896 Van Horne's son, Benny, helped to survey a Canadian Northern line. Thomas Shaughnessy, successor to Van Horne as president of the CPR, was not as friendly with Mackenzie; yet even he admitted privately in 1901, when the Canadian Northern was about to become a major western railway, that the new railway would only benefit the CPR.[7] In 1901, when Mackenzie and Mann signed a deal with the dominion government agreeing to lower freight rates, Shaughnessy and J.J. Hill, president of the Great Northern Railway, claimed publicly that the new rates would be ruinous. In private, however, Hill, Mann, and Clifford Sifton were willing to spend $5,000 to encourage the Senate to pass the bill.[8] Canadian Collieries, a Mackenzie company, supplied coal to the CPR and to the Grand Trunk Pacific. As well, these companies shared stockyards and "union" stations, their presidents ran their private cars over each other's tracks, and in 1909 they jointly founded the York Club in Toronto. As a member of the board of the Hudson's Bay Company, Mackenzie approved land deals between the HBC and railway companies that were supposedly his rivals.

Biography does not deny that competition existed, but it does add an extra dimension by suggesting that some competition was a part of the promoters' mythology that was created in large measure during the Arbitration Hearings in 1918, which determined the value of Mackenzie and Mann's shares in the nationalized Canadian Northern Railway. By 1918 railway promoters were experts at publicity. They were defending their railway and attempting to obtain the highest value possible for their shares. They were speaking to the three judges assessing the value of those shares, and they were also addressing posterity, including historians and biographers who might one day assess the role of the Canadian Northern Railway in the development of Canada. Railway men on the witness stand wanted to prove that the Canadian Northern did indeed play an important role, and they thus emphasized competition and the role of their railway in opening parts of the Canadian West. Biography deals with necessary lies; ruthless competition, I would suggest, was one of them. More than we realize, railways cooperated with each other, and we can glimpse the extent of that cooperaton by examining the interpersonal relationships of the men involved in the issue.

Let us take a look at a second issue, the creation of Ontario Hydro, from the point of view of the leading figures involved. Historians who examine the issue by focusing on documents such as Hydro Commission acts, the results of various referenda, and the minutes of directors' and shareholders' meetings, paint a picture of an Ontario Hydro that was created to protect energy users from the high rates charged by privately owned energy companies. More recently, H.V. Nelles, in his *Politics of Development,*[9] argues convincingly that Ontario Hydro was created because of pressure exerted on the Ontario government by businesses and municipalities, mainly in southwestern Ontario, that used government to assert their own otherwise limited role in Ontario development; the campaign was led by Adam Beck, with the uneasy backing of Premier Whitney. In either interpretation, it appears that there were two sides in the debate: private capital represented by Sir William Mackenzie and his colleagues, on the one side, and public capital represented by Adam Beck and southwestern Ontario businesses and municipalities, on the other, with an ambivalent Premier Whitney finally opting for government ownership.

An examination of interpersonal relationships creates a more variegated picture. Throughout most of the hydro debate, Whitney was playing two roles: in public, he claimed to support Beck; in private, and sometimes even in public, from his election in 1905 until his death in 1914, he supported the private owners of electrical power. His government gave two million acres of fertile land to Mackenzie's Canadian Northern Ontario Railway and guaranteed $2,500,000 of the company's bonds. During the hydro debate, Whitney and Mackenzie met privately, at social functions in Toronto, Quebec, and London, England. In December 1906, speaking at a banquet celebrating the inauguration of the Toronto–Parry Sound section of the Canadian Northern Ontario Railway, Whitney used the word "splendid" to describe the work of Mackenize and Mann in developing Ontario and Canada. Privately owned electrical power first reached Toronto two weeks before the banquet, on the same day that the first train reached Parry Sound from Toronto. And that hydro power was brought to Toronto by one of William Mackenzie's companies. Whitney and Mackenzie argued from similar points of view on Reciprocity in 1911; and in 1913 the Whitney government appointed Mackenzie to represent it on the board of Toronto's new General Hospital.[10]

Until Mackenzie's biography, *The Railway King of Canada*, was published in 1991, one character was overlooked, and it is perhaps only in

Sir William Mackenzie, circa 1910, during often heated debates regarding ownership of hydro power in Ontario. Dubbed the "Railway King of Canada," he reigned over a business empire on which the sun was never supposed to set. (Photograph taken at 55 Baker Street West, London, by Elliott and Fry. Private Collection.)

biography that Scott Griffin becomes important. When he married Mabel Mackenzie, William Mackenzie's eldest daughter, in October 1901, Griffin was J.P. Whitney's private secretary. In 1903 Griffin and his wife moved to Winnipeg, where he became head of his father-in-law's Canadian Northern Telegraph Company. Griffin and Whitney, who became premier of Ontario in 1905, continued a warm friendship by means of letters and, whenever Griffin was in Toronto, visits. When Whitney wrote letters to Griffin, he was communicating indirectly with Mackenzie. During the election campaign of 1905, Whitney publicly proclaimed that Niagara power should be as free as the air. But on 24 August 1905, shortly after the election, Whitney told Griffin that Beck, who was pushing for some kind of public hydro, was his "obstacle." When Griffin told Whitney in 1905 that municipal ownership of utilities was a product of disordered brains, he was reflecting the views of capitalism and of his father-in-law. In February 1906 Whitney told Griffin that the Hydro Commission was set up not to replace but to regulate private hydro and to save it from its own excesses and tarnished image. What emerges in this private correspondence between Griffin and Whitney is that Whitney preferred private ownership of power, regulated by the Hydro Commission, in the manner of the Public Utilities Commission of Manitoba or perhaps in the manner in which the Canadian Radio-television and Telecommunications Commission regulates Bell Canada today.

Whitney was caught between various forces, and in the end, after an agonizing struggle, he opted for public hydro. An examination of key players and their private friendships and feuds does not change the fact that Ontario ended up with public hydro and that Ontario Hydro is the prototype for hydro corporations across Canada. But when biography is married to history, the hydro question is seen in greater complexity. History alone has tended to simplify the issue.

No biographer would claim a pre-eminent role for biography in the interpretation of the past. And no biographer would deny the biases of the craft. But no historian should ignore biography. No historian should fail to recognize the essential paradox of biography: though it focuses on one person and views a time and place through that person's eyes, it affords the reader access to the complexity and multi-dimensionality of the past. Biography and history may be two solitudes, but the lines of Rilke quoted by Hugh MacLennan in his introduction to his novel *Two Solitudes* consist of more than those two words. And like love, biography and history can "protect, and touch, and greet each other," in order to enrich our past.

R.B. Fleming obtained his Ph.D. in 1988 from the University of Saskatchewan. He has taught for the University of Winnipeg on a Manitoba Indian reserve and at the University of Guelph. From 1988 to 1990, he collaborated with Dr. Harcourt Brown in Winnipeg on memoirs. In the 1970s he wrote a local history of his native Eldon Township, Victoria County, Ontario. His biography of Sir William Mackenzie, *The Railway King of Canada*, was published by the University of British Columbia Press, Vancouver, in 1991, and won Fleming the Ontario Historical Society's Fred Landon Award. He hopes to pursue both biography and local history.

Notes

1 Quoted by P.M. Kendall, "Walking the Boundaries," in S.B. Oates, ed., *Biography as High Adventure* (Amherst: University of Massachusetts Press, 1986), 32.

2 Quoted by Robert Skidelsky, "Only Connect: Biography and Truth," in Eric Homberger and John Charmley, eds., *The Troubled Face of Biography* (New York: St. Martin's Press, 1988), 1.

3 Quoted by Alan Shelston, *Biography* (London: Methuen, 1977), 7.

4 Benjamin Disraeli, *Contarini Fleming: A Psychological Romance* (London: Longmans, Green, 1945), 133.

5 Quoted by Leon Edel, "The Figure under the Carpet" in Oates, ed., *Biography as High Adventure*, 21.

6 Augustus Bridle, "Sir William Mackenzie, Railway Builder," *Saturday Night*, 14 January 1911, 11.

7 Quoted by John Eagle, *The Canadian Pacific Railway and the Development of Western Canada, 1896–1914* (Kingston: McGill-Queen's University Press, 1989), 80.

8 James Jerome Hill Records Library, James Jerome Hill Papers, General Correspondence, 1901, 13 April–16 May, telegram from Mann in Toronto to Hill in St. Paul, 21 April 1901.

9 H.V. Nelles, *The Politics of Development* (Toronto: Macmillan, 1975).

10 *Canadian Annual Review*, 1913, 348.

Participants at the Conference
"Biography and History: A Canadian/Irish Colloquium," Centre of Canadian Studies, University of Edinburgh, 2–4 May 1991

William A. Baker,
   University of Lethbridge
Ann Barry,
   Centre of Canadian Studies
Réal Bélanger,
   Université Laval
Henry Best,
   Laurentian University
Robin Burns,
   Bishop's University
Elspeth Cameron,
   University of Toronto
Jean Cameron,
   Centre of Canadian Studies
John Connor,
   Acadia University
Michael Cottrell,
   University of Saskatchewan
Terry Crowley,
   University of Guelph
Georges Henri Dagneau,
   Ste Foy, Quebec
George Davison,
   College of New Caledonia
Owen Dudley Edwards,
   University of Edinburgh
Claire England,
   University of Toronto
Robin Fisher,
   Simon Fraser University
R.B. Fleming,
   Argyle, Ontario
Chris Gittings,
   University of Edinburgh
John L. Gordon,
   University of Richmond
Francess G. Halpenny,
   University of Toronto

Michael Hopkinson,
   University of Stirling
Cecil J. Houston,
   University of Toronto
David Kales,
   Edmonton District Historical Society
Catherine Kerrigan,
   University of Guelph
William Lawton,
   University of Edinburgh
Leon Litvack,
   The Queen's University, Belfast
Heather MacDougall,
   University of Waterloo
Margaret Mackay,
   University of Edinburgh
Anna Makolkin,
   University of Toronto
Ged Martin,
   University of Edinburgh
Janice Dickin McGinnis,
   University of Calgary
J.R. Miller,
   University of Saskatchewan
Ken Mitchell,
   University of Regina
R.J. Morris,
   University of Edinburgh
Ken Munro,
   University of Alberta
Barbara Murison, King's College,
   University of Western Ontario
Colin Nicholson,
   University of Edinburgh
David Nock,
   Lakehead University
Gerald O'Brien, Magee University College,
   University of Ulster

Jan Penrose,
  University of Edinburgh
Chris Raible,
  Ontario Historical Society
Colin Read, Huron College,
  University of Western Ontario
T.D. Regehr,
  University of Saskatchewan
David Rollo,
  Ayr College
Donald Simpson,
  Royal Commonwealth Society
William J. Smyth,
  St. Patrick's College, Maynooth

Ron Stagg,
  Ryerson Polytechnical Institute
James Sturgis,
  Birbeck College, University of London
Pauric Travers,
  St. Patrick's College, Drumconda
William A. Waiser,
  University of Saskatchewan
Peter Way,
  University of Sussex
Michael Williams,
  University of Edinburgh
Catharine Wilson,
  University of Guelph